The English Jacobins

REFORMERS IN
LATE 18th CENTURY ENGLAND

———◆———

BY

CARL B. CONE

CHARLES SCRIBNER'S SONS

NEW YORK

ILLUSTRATION ACKNOWLEDGMENTS

British Museum: 10, 12, 13, 14, 17, 18, 19, 20, 21, 22, 23

National Portrait Gallery, London: 3, 7

The New York Public Library: 1 (Picture Collection), 2, 5 (Picture Collection), 6 (Prints Division, Boswell's *Life of Johnson*, Vol. IV, Part III), 8 (*State Trials for High Treason*. Edinburgh. J. Robertson. 1794), 11 (John Kay, *A Series of Original Portraits* . . . Edinburgh. Hugh Paton. 1837-1842), 15 (Rare Books Division), 16 (Prints Division), 24, 25 (Prints Division, Rowlandson and Pugin, *Microcosm of London*, Vol. I)

Radio Times Hulton Picture Library: 9

PREFACE

THE original Jacobins, organized and militant, seized control of the French Revolution in 1792 and held it into 1794. They took their name from the Jacobin monastery adjacent to the Place Vendôme in Paris where their leaders met.

But why the *English* Jacobins? One of them, John Thelwall, in his *Rights of Nature* (1796) gives us as much justification for the title as we need. Thelwall accepted the name because "it is fixed upon us, as a stigma, by our enemies." Thelwall's "us" were persons who disagreed with Edmund Burke, the "grey-headed procurator of proscription and blood," who believed, according to Thelwall, that nine-tenths of the population were "insensate instruments of physical force," devoid of power or reason, undeserving of a voice in public affairs or a vote. The English Jacobins believed in the power of human reason; they thought that the people were capable of enlightenment; they demanded freedom of expression so that "the opinions, not of a *tenth-part*, but of the whole nation, can be freely delivered, and distinctly heard." And so they desired "a large and comprehensive system of reform," based not "upon the authorities and principles of the Gothic customary" but upon reason and the rights of man.

The English Jacobins desired change, said Burke. "True," said Thelwall, "And they ought to have it; and they must, or the nation is undone for ever." The need was simply stated to the English people. "Compare what ye are with what ye have a right to

iii

be." When rights are denied, "the people . . . have a right . . . to renounce the broken compact, and dissolve the system." Thelwall was not advocating bloody revolution. He abhorred "the sanguinary ferocity of the late Jacobins in France." But he admired their political principles, especially their emphasis upon equality. He thought reform in England, through organization, agitation, and education of the people in knowledge of their rights was possible and that by these means it could be obtained without a September Massacre or a Reign of Terror. The people have the power to make government respect them. The force of an aroused and enlightened public opinion is effective under any form of government. The love of freedom exists naturally in the hearts of people; they only need to be awakened to achieve reform.

When reformed, government can properly get about its business of promoting "the welfare and happiness of the whole." It does not require social upheaval or the destruction of property to help the laboring man gain the decent living he has a right to. "Equality of rights consists not in equality of distribution; but in equal opportunities of benefiting by the things distributed." Regulation rather than confiscation of property, the abolition of special privilege, and the recognition of the true worth of labor would suffice. If Thelwall sounds pre-Marxian, it might be remembered that Adam Smith also talked about labor value.

Thelwall, like his Jacobin colleagues, was much clearer when talking about political rights than about social or economic change. Neither he nor they envisaged all of the implications that historians of a later time, with the advantage of perspective, might find in their remarks. There was a kind of millennialism in the Jacobins' thought rather than scientific determinism. The well-being of men must follow upon political reform simply because the people's voices and votes must give expression to their desires, and because government controlled by the people must give effect to their demands. How and in what manner the future would reveal. But that things would be better, the Jacobins never doubted. "The crime of the Jacobin is," said Thelwall, "that he looks forward to a state of society more extensive in its refinements—more perfect, and more general in its improvements, than any which has yet been known."

Jacobinism then was a state of mind, a cluster of indignant sensibilities, a faith in reason, a vision of the future. It was also individuals and groups among whom Thelwall admitted there were "many different opinions . . . as to the extent" of change that was needed. English Jacobinism was not monolithic. The forms it took, the desires it expressed, the demands it made, the internal agreements and disagreements it revealed will be discussed in this book. If it turns out that the emphasis is upon the efforts for parliamentary reform, one remembers Thelwall's assertion that "a large and comprehensive system of reform" was the first object of the English Jacobins.

CONTENTS

LIST OF ILLUSTRATIONS

THE
ENGLISH JACOBINS

CHAPTER I

ASSUMPTIONS

A NOBLEMAN, a gentleman, a yeoman—that is a good interest of the nation and a great." It was also the supreme interest in the ranked and ordered society of pre-industrial England because it was synonymous with land and the social status that land conferred. When a squire of Huntingdonshire, Oliver Cromwell, was Lord Protector of England, he opened the session of Parliament on September 4, 1654, with these words and went on to explain that he had preserved this good society from "that levelling principle" which tended "to the reducing all men to an equality."

Equality, political or social or economic, England neither knew nor desired. Seventeenth century revolutionaries who mythologized the history of the Anglo-Saxon period, as they did Magna Carta, and professed to see in pre-Norman England a golden age of peasant democracy did not express the substance of English social philosophy. Yet this Gothic myth lived on. It inspired the "friends of freedom" who gathered on June 2, 1773, at the Standard Tavern in Leicester-fields, London, to reaffirm their devotion to liberty and a free constitution, symbolized by the head of Alfred the Great engraved on the society's silver cup. Twenty years later when the "British Convention of the Delegates of the People associated to obtain Universal Suffrage and Annual Parliaments" met in Edinburgh, a delegate from London, Joseph Gerrald, demanded the restoration of Englishmen's ancient rights.

Before the Norman conquerors destroyed the "goodly fabrick" of the Anglo-Saxon constitution, every man had a voice in choosing his representatives. If Gerrald was vague about the folkmootes attended by these representatives, he was certain that the "concurrence of the people was necessary to the administration of government, and they obeyed the laws which they themselves had made."

According to this misreading of English history, Parliament in the eighteenth century no longer represented the people as its ancestor had done in Saxon times. It was a corrupted descendant of the Anglo-Saxon Witan, the national folkmoote which the Normans had perverted into the instrument of a conquering minority. If, in this oversimplified version, the popular element recovered some of the lost recognition under the Edwards and the Henrys of the thirteenth to fifteenth centuries, it was nevertheless true that neither the kings nor their barons, neither the bishops nor the shire knights and town oligarchs conceived of Parliament as a popular assembly in the sense either of the Gothic myth or of modern democratic thought. Rather they believed by 1430 that in the absence of clear criteria for voting, elections for knights of the shire had become too popular and tumultuous because propertyless men, pretending to voices equal to those of "les pluis valantz chivalers ou esquires," were voting in the county electoral meetings. And so Parliament enacted a statute limiting the county franchise to men who owned land to the clear and respectable annual value of forty shillings (8 Henry VI, c. 7). This statute and especially its preamble proclaimed one of the great assumptions of English society—that property, particularly in land, and political literacy were indissolubly joined. When the statute was replaced by the first great parliamentary reform, the Act of 1832, the forty shilling freeholder qualification was preserved, supplemented by other and newly defined property qualifications. The Act of 1832 was in the spirit of the Act of 1430, for both connected the franchise with the ownership or tenancy of real property.

This relationship was the political application of a broader consensus about the nature of society. An early Elizabethan, Sir

Thomas Smith, and a later Elizabethan, William Shakespeare, believed in it. According to Sir Thomas, "day labourers, poor husbandmen, yea merchants or retailers which have no free land, copyholders, and all artificers . . . have no voice nor authority in our commonwealth and no account is made of them, but only to be ruled." This statement described the harmony between the social structure and the constitution. It supported Shakespeare's assertion that without distinctions of rank, order and degree, society would collapse into chaos. Two hundred years later, with comparable assurance, Edmund Burke reaffirmed Smith's view of the nature of the political commonwealth.

> The occupation of a hair-dresser, or of a working tallow-chandler, cannot be a matter of honour to any person,—to say nothing of a number of other more servile employments. Such descriptions of men ought not to suffer oppression from the state: but the state suffers oppression, if such as they, either individually or collectively, are permitted to rule.

Closer to Smith's time than Burke's, but in language both would easily understand and with a spirit they would commend, Cromwell defended the ancient social structure. He summarized it as "the orders of men and the ranks of men" and he proudly took credit for having suppressed the "levelling principle" that had threatened social harmony just after the Civil War. His political and social preferences appeared in the Instrument of Government, the constitution of 1653. It provided for a redistribution of legislative seats that as compared with the pre-war House of Commons greatly increased county representation and reduced borough representation. Cromwell's ideal was a Parliament representative predominantly of the country gentry. By curtailing borough representation he emphasized his lack of sympathy for the commercial interest, ignoring the fact that borough seats were held often by members of county families. The contemporary philosopher James Harrington was at one with Cromwell in this preference for the landed interest. In his ideal commonwealth Harrington gave the legislative preponderance to it, for there was something "peculiar only to the Genius of a Gentleman" that fitted him for governing and for leading armies.

The Leveller party abhorred by Cromwell and Harrington was a radical element in London and in the army which emerged from the ferment of ideas and debate after the defeat of Charles I. When considering the terms of a settlement with the defeated king, men discussed first principles of government. From the Leveller premise of the sovereignty of the people arose corollaries about the powers and composition of Parliament, and more specifically about the franchise and representation in the House of Commons. The Levellers seemed to repudiate the belief, expressed by Sir Thomas Smith among others, that the traditional, restrictive electoral arrangements as well as the theory of the constitution provided for the presence of all Englishmen in the House of Commons, actually or virtually. When the Levellers talked about the inequities of the distribution of seats in the Commons, and when they raised the question of the franchise and used terms like manhood suffrage, they seemed to be questioning the validity of the idea of virtual representation and to be advocating something like a precise arithmetical principle. In consequence the Levellers have been thought to anticipate the reform movements of the late eighteenth and the nineteenth centuries and therefore to be forerunners of modern political democracy.

The appearances are deceiving. In their own times they were radicals, as Cromwell testified. But it is necessary to understand their proposals in the idiom of their times, not in that of the ages of John Bright or Lloyd George. The Levellers' language carried for their contemporaries a meaning more modest than that grasped by readers two centuries later. As the historian R. G. Collingwood has said, we do not of necessity understand the thoughts merely because we possess the words of earlier writers. The difference in context and in meanings of words is a difference in substance. When the Levellers asked for manhood suffrage they did not intend literally that every adult male should vote. The term was qualified by the assumptions of the seventeenth century; it did not then require definition because the Levellers could take for granted that it would be understood as they meant it. Eventually the Levellers' view was made more explicit in the Army Council's "Agreement of the People." This document provided for a ratepayers franchise. It withheld the suffrage from the poor and from the servant class.

The Levellers never disguised their meanings. They expected men to understand their language in terms of assumptions tacitly agreed upon. Wage earners, as everyone should know, were servants, that is they worked for wages, were dependent upon their employers for their livelihood, and therefore could not be considered men of independent wills and judgments. These were the same people to whom Montesquieu in the next century would deny the franchise because they were persons "in so mean a situation as to be deemed to have no will of their own." Their subordinate and subservient status incapacitated them from becoming conversant with public affairs. Blackstone, when writing his *Commentaries*, must have copied from Montesquieu. He defended the property qualification for voting because it effectively excluded "such persons as are in so mean a situation that they are esteemed to have no will of their own." Persons of "indigent fortunes" must be "under the immediate dominion of others" and so "are suspected to have no will of their own. . . ."

This doctrine might be expected from Blackstone. It is not much different from opinions held by "radicals" of his time. One Regulus, writing in 1768 in the radical John Almon's publication the *Political Register*, excluded from among the "People" the "illiterate rabble, who have neither capacity for judging of matters of government, nor property to be concerned for." Complaining about the maldistribution of seats in the House of Commons, Regulus would strengthen the political influence of the monied and commercial interests by giving two or even three votes to men "of large property." Opponents of landed predominance were often sympathetic to the claims of other forms of property to a voice in public affairs. Similarly a Commonwealthman of one generation earlier than Regulus, Thomas Gordon, proud of his love for liberty, opposed the Test and Corporation Acts which excluded non-Anglicans from public life. He thought that Protestant Dissenters, if qualified by property in money and goods, should be free to participate in political life.* He remained anti-Catholic, however, and would perpetuate the restrictions upon Romanists. "The idle and indigent rabble" had no place among "the people," regardless of religion. Their poverty and ignorance indisputably disqualified them.

James Burgh, a Protestant Dissenter who conducted a well-known school at Newington Green, three miles north of the City of London, and who associated with leading radicals like Dr. Richard Price and Joseph Priestley and other members of the "Honest Whigs," published in 1774–1775 one of the most important political treatises of the age. In this *Political Disquisitions* he mentioned "the commonly received doctrine, that servants, and those who receive alms, have no right to vote for members of parliament," and so "an immense multitude of the people are utterly deprived of all power in determining" who shall govern the nation. Burgh was stating a political truth rather than expressing indignation. He would enlarge the electorate but only by including taxpayers. In 1776, when speaking for parliamentary reform in the House of Commons, John Wilkes, usually considered a radical, favored broadening the franchise by giving the vote to all males who were "free agents." The doctrine of free agency was almost universally accepted. In 1782 a member of the reform Society for Constitutional Information wrote a short tract called *The Principles of Government: A Dialogue between a Scholar and a Peasant*. They talked about representative government. The scholar wanted to know who should vote. Said the peasant, "All, who were not *upon the parish*. In our club [a box club or benefit society], if a man asks relief of the overseers, he ceases to be one of us, because he must depend upon the overseer."

The "peasant," Wilkes, Burgh, Gordon, Blackstone and Montesquieu echoed the Levellers. They did not infer slavery when they said that some men were not free in the political sense. They were only admitting the incapacity of large numbers of men to

* Although the Quakers might be considered Dissenters in so far as the Act of Uniformity was in effect a definition of Dissent, contemporaries called the Quakers by that name and reserved the word Dissenters for members of the Three Denominations, Baptists, Independents or Congregationalists, and Presbyterians.

deserve the franchise. What the Levellers meant of servants was more obviously meant of the poor—the people in receipt of alms, those supported by the poor rates, and beggars. Yet if the Levellers connected the franchise with property they were ready like later reformers to relax the definitions of property requirements. In the army debates where these matters were discussed, Cromwell's able son-in-law, General Henry Ireton, stuck to the old freehold franchise, which in legal terminology also included life tenants. When Cromwell had a chance to define the county franchise in the constitution of 1653 it was set for county voters at £200 clear annual value of real or personal property. The Levellers desired the franchise for ratepayers, that is those who paid local property taxes. This was essentially a nonservant, nonpauper franchise, and in comparison with the number of eligible freeholders would have doubled the size of the electorate.

Under seventeenth century assumptions and circumstances, as under those of the eighteenth century, manhood suffrage did not mean universal suffrage. To the Levellers it could not have meant that until all men recovered their birthright of free agency and with it their right to a voice in elections. The Levellers were not prepared to advocate social revolution as a means to this end, though Cromwell tried to make them appear to, and they did not contemplate radical economic changes as an approach to free agency. When the Levellers skirted the edge of agrarian questions or lower class grievances, it was not because they were afraid to discuss the possibilities of change in the economic system. It was rather that they did not even think of such change. They were concerned with the oppressions evident in master-servant or employer-worker relationships which might be alleviated by legal reforms. Such reforms would not remove the economic dependence of the lower classes and so would not elevate their members to the status of free agents entitled to a voice in politics. In this pre-industrial society, free agency was a function of property. If a man sank into wage dependence, or never rose out of it, he did not command his own labor. If he alienated this commodity, he was no longer a fully free man and deprived himself of the political perquisites attached to property. The difference between Cromwell and the Levellers on the franchise question concerned the amount and kind of property that ensured the free agency of the individual, rather than the idea that political freedom was itself a form of proprietorship.

Even in more subtle ways, property justified liberties. The seventeenth century used the word liberties rather than liberty, and measured the number and variety of them against property. The man of property possessed a status denied to dependent persons; the gentleman enjoyed liberties appropriate to his property-based status. This theme of class privilege, even legal rights, forms part of the corpus of social assumptions expressed or implicit in the literature of the seventeenth and eighteenth centuries. Thus in 1793 Lord Justice Henderland, in sentencing Thomas Muir, Esq., convicted of sedition, decided upon transportation to New South Wales. Whipping, he said, was "too severe and disgraceful, the more especially to a man who had bore his character and rank in life." Just so, Londoners were shocked to see William Prynne whipped at the tail of a cart under sentence of the Court of Star Chamber of Charles I. If Prynne deserved physical punishment, it should be consonant with his status as a university educated man; he ought not be made to suffer humiliation along with bodily pain.

In a society whose ethos and social structure retained much of the medieval group emphasis, the household was important as a basic social unit. This unit was patriarchal, a favorite seventeenth and eighteenth century thought, and it was more comprehensive than the restricted idea of household held by the servantless society of the twentieth century. The household was an enlarged family, including not only the biological parents and children, but the domestic staff and in rural households servants who had duties even outside the home. In this household the master ruled. Ranks and degrees existed within it. The servants had their identities only as members of it and not of society at large. As dependents they had no separate or individual or even class political interests. Their needs and wants, if recognized as something more than household concerns, found expression and custody in the voices or votes and in the hands of their masters. This idea had diminished reflection in the so-called "pot walloper" franchise peculiar to certain boroughs in England wherein heads of households, by virtue of being such, had the vote in parliamentary elections, provided they were not on poor relief. But there were only a dozen of these constituencies in England. Lower class family units and those of agricultural laborers were not normally considered households in any meaningful political sense.

In the commonwealth as in the household the place of the servant was a subordinate one. James Harrington stressed generally the connection between property and political authority. He excluded "servants" from citizenship, treating them virtually as a class outside the commonwealth, that is outside the sphere of political literacy. It was a servant's duty to obey as it was his lot to be governed. The statute and common law which formed the corpus of the master-servant law of England described and regulated the servant's place in the household and his relationship with the master. Something of its spirit was suggested by the editor of the 1805 edition of Adam Smith's *Wealth of Nations*. After excluding reading and writing as unessential to the education of the lower orders, the editor said, "To follow industry and learn to live on their income and be attentive to their duty, constitute the principal part of education in all the inferior ranks." This was also the belief of Timothy Hollis, a cousin of Thomas Hollis and with him one of the circle who in the 1760's deposited themselves in the tradition of the late seventeenth century Commonwealthmen. Timothy's anti-monarchical sentiments and his devotion to liberty had nothing to do with the lower orders. They had best be kept illiterate, he believed, else they might try to move out of their place in the social order. The Enlightenment ideal of the career open to all talent was bourgeois; it did not demand that the door of opportunity be opened wide to the menial people.

In the pre-industrial age, as in that of Disraeli, there were two nations in England. The people who counted were distinguished by possession of property or formal education and sometimes both. The lower orders depended upon their masters, employers, the poor rates or charity. Even the so-called liberal political thinkers were not concerned with them. Like Harrington, John

Locke, when he thought of them at all, held the laboring class and the poor apart from civil society which was composed of the propertied people. There was nothing unnatural about wage labor. It was simply that the individual who hired out for a wage was subjecting to the control of another person the property he possessed in his labor, entering into a condition of dependence, and absorbing himself in the mere business of subsistence. He had neither opportunity nor, normally, inclination to interest himself in the larger affairs of civil society. For all of its potentialities, Locke's individualism did not imply political rights for the people in mean situations. In his *Reasonableness of Christianity* Locke asserted "Where the hand is used to the plough and the spade, the head is seldom elevated to sublime notions. . . ." This sentiment, Biblical in origin and expressed in reference to matters of religion, extended as appropriately to politics and public affairs. A century later, Edmund Burke quoted it literally from the Bible, and referred it specifically to participation in politics. In his *Reflections on the Revolution in France,* Burke cited Ecclesiasticus, Ch. 38, v. 26: "With what wisdom shall he be furnished that holdeth the plough, and glorieth in the goad, that driveth the oxen therewith, and is occupied in their labours, and his whole talk is about the offspring of bulls?" Burke might have continued, for the remainder of the chapter elaborates the idea. Verse twenty-seven says that the driver of oxen "shall give his mind to turn up furrows, and his care is to give the kine fodder." Succeeding verses speak of skilled workers, each

> wise in his own art. Without these a city is not built. And they shall not dwell, nor walk about therein, and they shall not go up into the assembly. Upon the judges' seat they shall not sit, and the ordinance of judgment they shall not understand, neither shall they declare discipline and judgment, and they shall not be found where parables are spoken . . . their prayer shall be in the work of their craft. . . .

Even among the Protestant Dissenters, usually considered to have been the group in the eighteenth century most susceptible to the reform spirit and congenial to reform ideas, these social and political assumptions prevailed. Descendants of the Presbyterians, the Independents and the Anabaptists of the Cromwellian period, the Dissenters suffered from statutory restrictions upon their political and religious activities and so, it has been said, were naturally inclined to favor reforms that would remove the discriminations against them. But their reforming zeal did not embrace ideas of social revolution, let alone religious toleration for all. Anti-Popery was strong among them. They believed in the sacredness of property rights, they accepted the traditions of a ranked and ordered society, and they did not object to making status and political activity dependent upon property qualifications—so long as opportunity to achieve these was not denied to them for religious reasons or merely because they were Dissenters.

Inconsistent as it might seem with concepts of the equality of all men in the sight of God, Dissenting social philosophy was in one sense even harsher than that already described. For, to the social and political inferiority attached to propertylessness, the Dissenter added moral obloquy. Poverty, even economic dependence, indicated moral deficiency as well as political incapacity. This was social and economic orthodoxy, and it lasted beyond the eighteenth century. In 1828, Lucy Aikin, whose ancestors were among the Restoration heroes of Protestant Dissent, wrote to the Unitarian divine Dr. Ellery Channing of Massachusetts about Dissent as she knew it from family lore. Before Dissenters broke loose about the middle of the eighteenth century from "the chains and darkness of Calvinism, and their manners softened with their system," Dissenting men "were usually lordly husbands, harsh parents, merciless censors of their neighbours; systematically hostile to all the amenities of life, but not less fond of money, or more scrupulous in the means of attaining it, than the worldlings whom they reprobated."

If this generalization needs more testing for accuracy than it has received, there is nevertheless evidence to support it. Miss Aikin included the Reverend Philip Doddridge (1702–1751) among the new, more amiable type of Dissenter. Yet in 1741 in a letter to the gentle Isaac Watts, Doddridge complained that the frequency of bankruptcies among them was disgracing Dissenters. Doddridge's congregation had just expelled three members for *"failing in the world."* (Doddridge's italics.) Besides the moral censure it contained, this harsh attitude helps explain why Dissenters not only accepted but supported a tradition that made possession of property the proof of political literacy. The readiness of Dissenters to promote certain kinds of reforms did not at all mean that those among them who advocated parliamentary reform necessarily desired universal manhood suffrage.

The government of a Dissenting meeting house may suggest how the Dissenters would have distributed political power if control had fallen to them.* The "Custom" of the rich Bury Street Meeting (1723), where the hymn writer Dr. Isaac Watts preached, provided for thorough inquiry into the lives and beliefs of persons who desired to take communion with this meeting. While the scrutiny and interrogation were meant primarily to ascertain the religious orthodoxy of candidates, the words "inquiry into their conversation" had a much more general and inclusive meaning. Biographical information as well as the chapel regulations reveal a community of believers, a company of elect among whom due regard for rank and order and for economic distinctions was very important. This conception was reflected in the allocation of pews; the more generous subscribers had the first choices.

The Newington Green Meeting to which the famous radical Dr. Richard Price ministered during the third quarter of the eighteenth century displayed the same character. A poor man could not afford the guinea a year subscription which qualified a member for a voice in the meeting's affairs. This congregation was managed by the wealthy members like Matthew Raper, Daniel Radford, and Thomas Rogers whose successive preeminences carried the meeting through the last three quarters of the eighteenth century. The subscription lists of Newington Green

---

* Their Massachusetts brothers in fact governed their commonwealth until the nineteenth century under some interesting and restrictive statutory conditions for participation in public affairs.

are extant; they name individuals, but "the poor" are not among them, as the wills of the members make clear. Like Bury Street, Newington Green had its menials and its poor. The members' domestic servants attended services and sat in the back pews. They were the governed; they had no voice in the business affairs of the meeting. It had always been true that the poor among Presbyterian and Independent Dissenters and earlier among Puritans did not share in church government. Only among the Baptists, said the Puritan divine William Gouge in 1621, were there no differences between masters and servants. The eighteenth century Baptists were generally considered to be the poorer sort of Dissenters.

The poor were in the meeting but not of it, completely outside the community of believers, objects of charity or wage dependents. At Bury Street, on the third Sunday of each month there was a public collection at the door "for the necessities of the poor of the church." At Newington Green certain periodic collections were distributed to the "poor beings" or "poor objects" in the vicinity of Newington Green according to lists made out for a time by Mrs. Elizabeth Raper and later by Dr. Price. The congregation felt a special collective responsibility towards the poor of the neighborhood. Their charity contributed to the physical needs of the poor. Where the poor obtained spiritual nourishment is not evident. They did not receive it within the walls of the Bury Street or Newington Green meeting houses. In truth it was not provided for them at all. Thomas Rogers in 1785, after seeing Sunday Schools at Stourbridge, wished for them at Newington Green and Islington. He knew of "no place where there are so many poor people with so little attendance upon public worship." He hoped that poor children of the Sunday Schools would learn the habit of attendance at chapel services. He might have added that little encouragement was given to their attendance, and he need not have confined his remarks to his own affluent suburb. A Sunday School was not established by the Newington Green Chapel until 1840. The religious neglect of the poor and their own religious indifference was not the result of the industrial revolution of the nineteenth century.

Individual members of the congregation also felt personal responsibilities. In 1775, as an example, the will of Mrs. Mary Calamy directed payment of five pounds to the poor of the Newington Green Meeting House. Just so in 1748 Isaac Watts left fifty pounds for the poor of the Bury Street Meeting and in 1756 Samuel Price, the uncle of Richard, did likewise. These were bequests to the outside poor who were attached to the congregation, its special charges, almost its property. It was as though a congregation was incomplete without its poor. Dissenters usually made bequests to the poor, often, one feels, as gestures, as things to be done, as though a will without such a provision was not properly drawn. But the bequests to the poor were usually very small in proportion to the totals of the monies and properties mentioned in the wills. The impression left by studying the records of Dissenting charities and Dissenting chapels is that the poor lived in the same relationship to the congregation as Locke's poor to the civil community, physically proximate, not active participants but the governed.

Any sense of theoretical equality of certain rights was accompanied by practical, substantive inequality that found its rationale in history, in economic status, and in Scripture. The concept of social orders, developed when England was a rural, agrarian community, continued in the age of commercial expansion in the seventeenth and eighteenth centuries and was accepted as quite compatible with a bourgeois society. The distinction between landed and landless continued to be a crucial one for political purposes because franchise qualifications had become fixed before the end of the Middle Ages. The distinction between rich and poor, the people with money—land and rents, goods and profits—and the people who had only their labor to sell, and often were unable or unwilling to sell it, became increasingly important with the expansion of commerce. The commercial classes were no readier to lift political disqualifications from the poor than were the old landed groups, but they came to resent the ancient restrictions which disadvantaged them even while they were rich in worldly goods. The rise of Puritanism did not fundamentally change the traditional beliefs in the political incapacity of the lower orders.

If dynamic qualities in men were released or stimulated by Calvinism, or if the expanding commercial life, or both, encouraged social and economic mobility, so that in the seventeenth and eighteenth centuries new men acquired wealth and influence, these new men inherited and accepted certain old social distinctions. Commercial profits were often invested in land, and then the new man, or his sons, acquired status, and added "Gent." to their names. As the Elizabethan William Harrison had said, "who can live idly, and without manual labour, and . . . will bear the port, charge, and countenance of a gentleman, . . . he shall be called master, . . . and reputed for a gentleman." So Samuel Rogers, the early nineteenth century poet who stuffed his house in St. James's Place with objects of art, was descended on his mother's side from Cheshire linen drapers. The maternal grandfather, Daniel Radford, had been raised by his uncle, the great Dissenting clergyman and scholar, Matthew Henry. From his father, the banker Thomas Rogers, Samuel inherited the means to live "without manual labour." Similarly the Towgoods, connected even more directly than Samuel Rogers with the Dissenting martyrs of the Restoration period. Micaijah Towgood, a grandson of the martyr the Reverend Matthew Towgood, was a Dissenting minister at Exeter. His son Matthew became a London banker and a liveryman of the Worshipful Company of Fishmongers. Matthew's son John married Samuel Rogers' sister. The company records contain the names of Matthew's descendants, some of whom were Prime Wardens of the company and several were described as "Gentlemen."

These people, and many like them, accepted the traditional connection between property and status, and property and political rights. They bore grievances against some of the restrictions imposed upon them as Dissenters, but they were not democrats in any modern sense. If Thomas Rogers deliberately avoided the company of the landed nobility, he had no sense of inferiority. He was a man of property, he held freehold land. He desired parliamentary reform because he thought the ancient qualifications discriminated against certain kinds of property and wealth. Like Rogers, John and William Towgood, sons of the banker Matthew, became members of the Society for Constitutional Information in 1784, a society devoted to parliamentary reform, but whose program was not democratic in the twentieth century sense. The ancient assumptions that the lower orders had no claim to a share in active political life because they could not meet the tangible and worldly qualifications prescribed by statute and custom remained acceptable to people like the Rogers and the Towgoods.

The apparently democratic expressions of certain seventeenth and eighteenth century writers must be understood, not in the context of nineteenth century American and English radicalism, but in the context of their own times, and in terms of the social assumptions that underlay them. Otherwise the proper limits of the political thought of the period will not be recognized. Jefferson's phrase "all men are created equal" is as easily susceptible of misunderstanding as the Levellers' phrase "manhood suffrage." Wide and loose constructions have been given to such phrases by later interpreters who have been too much influenced by their own times and too little cognizant of the things that the earlier writers took for granted. Words acquire different meaning and new references with the passage of time and changing circumstances. A writer, like a conversationalist, takes that for granted which he believes needs no explanation. His audience will supply the context, and he can then get on without having painfully to rehearse elementary matters. But later it becomes the business of the historian to identify these assumptions if he would understand the meaning of the historical texts.

If knowledge of the assumptions is crucial to the understanding of political literature, it is also necessary for the understanding of political institutions. Those of eighteenth century England can be made to appear absurd, and have been, by persons who have judged in the light of modern social assumptions. But the political institutions of the eighteenth century were beautifully in tune with the social assumptions of that period because these were essentially the assumptions of the preceding centuries when the constitution of England was formed.

CHAPTER II

THAT HAPPY CONSTITUTION

IT MAY be that eighteenth century Englishmen achieved a closer union of social aspirations and political system than any other people. English society of that period was predominantly agricultural. Land conferred status and political privilege. The landed "interest" was the nation's first interest. The common law was basically the law of real property, having been refined out of the custom of a rural society in which land stood first. That system of law was only being shaped and adapted to the needs of the growing commercial interest. Except for London, the towns and cities were small. Bristol, the second city, an entrepôt for overseas and regional trade, at mid-century had a population of perhaps fifty thousand. The great industrial cities of the midlands were in the future. Sheffield and Birmingham enjoyed prestige in the eighteenth century as centers of the metal trades, but these were organized as small-scale manufactories. Birmingham was a place-name for a collection of villages whose inhabitants were governed on the rural pattern of justices of the peace and parish vestries. The textile cities, as the locations of great satanic mills, arose with the advance of technology, and this revolution was only passing out of its infancy at the end of the eighteenth century. The towns and cities, or boroughs if the political terminology is preferred, preserved much of their medieval characters and of their rural connections as market towns. The inhabitants still had intimate ties with the countryside. Even in

19

the metropolis a person was never more than a few minutes walk from open fields. To the east of the Tottenham Court Road toward the British Museum, founded in mid-century, were grounds for sports and games; just beyond the northern limits of the City of London a stroller found himself among market gardens and cows all the way to Islington and Hackney; orchards and market gardens dominated the local scenes at Hammersmith and Chiswick; Kensington was separated from Mayfair by open country.

The agricultural emphasis in the economy and the rural flavor of the towns were reflected in the institutions of local government. The counties were the satrapies of the squires who served as sheriffs and justices of the peace; the parishes, rural and urban, were the basic units of administration for keeping the peace, relieving the poor, and maintaining roads and bridges.

Most glorious of all in its identity with the social aspirations of England was Parliament, consisting of King, Lords and Commons. It was of Parliament predominantly that men thought when they spoke rapturously of their "Happy Constitution," their "Matchless Constitution," their "Balanced Constitution." Some would include the Church, that is, the Church of England established by law, and properly, a constitution includes the judiciary and the institutions of local government. Parliament was sovereign: there was no constitutional restraint upon its powers except in the ultimate and unlikely sense that it might outrage the limited electorate. Sir Thomas Smith had said that Parliament could do anything but make a man a woman, and it could have done that too if enactment of a statute would accomplish it. If it chose, but it would not, Parliament could statutorily make new arrangements for the religious life of the nation, for local government, for land and property; under the pressure of extreme necessity it had indeed altered the succession to the throne in 1689 and then fixed it by law. Parliament in the eighteenth century did not even think of making the other changes because the men who sat in the two houses were happy in their unique constitution, aesthetically pleased with its classical, balanced harmonies, proud of their ancestors who had brought off the Glorious Revolution and, in the words of the Solicitor General of Scotland in 1793, "laid the foundation of that happy constitution under which we now live." The men of the eighteenth century were confident that their constitution served their needs. It also served their interests, and most immediately those of the governing class. The King was both a part of Parliament and apart from it.* Without his consent, the two houses could not enact a statute; unless he summoned them, the Lords and Commons could not meet; when he desired, he could prorogue Parliament or dissolve the House of Commons.** At the beginning of the seventeenth century there was a long list of powers that belonged to the area of prerogative, and the first two Stuart kings interpreted them in a manner that alienated some members of the two houses. During the first forty years of the seventeenth century, a constitutional conflict developed in England. The high prerogative position of the King was opposed by the revolutionary claims of some members of the two houses. Religious issues, themselves in part constitutional, exacerbated tensions. By 1642 England was on the verge of Civil War. A party in Parliament presented to the King "Nineteen Propositions" as a formula for ending the controversy, and when the King, who had already conceded much, rejected them, Civil War followed. Said Charles I, in his "Answer," the Propositions would "subvert . . . the ancient, equal, happy, well poised, and never-enough commended Constitution of the Government of this Kingdom. . . ." It was, he said, a balanced constitution, a "Mixture," in the right proportions, of "Monarchy, Aristocracy, and Democracy," with the House of Lords "an excellent Skreen and Bank between the Prince and People [House of Commons]." At the end of his "Answer," Charles quoted an ancient phrase—*Nolumus Leges Angliae mutari.*

But if the King did not wish to change the laws of England, a powerful party did, and in the end Charles lost, first the war and

* Commonly the word Parliament is used in a sense that limits it to the two houses. The context usually makes clear whether the word is intended to bear its full constitutional meaning or the meaning of ordinary usage.
** Circumstances such as financial exigency might force the King to exercise these particular prerogative powers against his own desires. In the eighteenth century circumstances and developing customs of the constitution were infringing upon the King's discretionary powers.

then his head. The war and the ensuing struggle for power threw Cromwell to the top. A glorious, tragic figure, he failed in his search for a constitution to replace the ancient one. When he died in 1658, Englishmen quickly formed a consensus. Two years later the Lords Temporal and Commons took their places in the ancient manner and forms, and they restored the monarchy in the person of Charles II.

The restoration of the ancient happy constitution was in substance a return to the system that the Nineteen Propositions would have amended drastically. Yet the Civil War and the Cromwellian Protectorate had their effects. Charles I had rejected Parliament's demand to determine the constitution of the church and religious matters generally; Charles II conceded the demand and though he disliked it, he accepted the legislation by which Parliament settled the religious problem. The terms of the Restoration reaffirmed what even Charles I had accepted, that Parliament should control the raising of revenue.* The two great provisions seriously altered the so-called balance of the constitution and, in retrospect, may be seen as long strides toward the sovereignty of Parliament.

The religious settlement at the Restoration had strong political overtones. Clearly reflecting the intention to purge the Church of England of Puritan unorthodoxies, it also delivered the political system into the control of Anglicans. The Act of Uniformity, by prescribing tests for ensuring in religious observances just what the title of the act said, was the means also of depriving of their livings those clergymen who were not good Anglicans. Other laws prescribed religious tests for holding borough offices, thereby ensuring Anglican control of the electoral machinery of the boroughs. This legislation was so effective in restricting election of Protestant Dissenters that it was never necessary specifically to bar them from the House of Commons. During the next century and a half relatively few of them were elected. The act

---

* As head of the government, the king still enjoyed discretionary authority to spend money which Parliament voted to him in a lump sum. Only step by step during the next two centuries were modern appropriation and budgeting arrangements worked out.

which excluded Roman Catholics from the two houses was aimed more at Catholic peers than commoners. Not until 1828 and 1829 were the so-called Test and Corporation Acts repealed and the Anglican legal monopoly surrendered. In the intervening period these acts constituted a lively grievance against which some reformers and especially the Protestant Dissenters complained.

When after the death of Cromwell, Parliament was revived, it was under the old forms. With the repeal of a twenty-year-old law excluding the bishops, the upper house was once more composed of the Lords Spiritual and Temporal, the first group sitting by virtue of their episcopal offices and the second by hereditary right or as men elevated to the peerage by prerogative act of the King. The House of Commons was elected under the ancient county and borough franchises. Various electoral reforms discussed during the revolutionary period were gladly forgotten. And while much property had changed hands during the preceding twenty years, and many new men had gained prominence in the public and commercial life of the nation, no social revolution had destroyed the bases of society.

Ancient assumptions about the predominance of land, about the connection between property and power and status, about the inferiority of the lower orders and their second-class citizenship—"less a part of society than one of its problems"—and about the nature of liberty, remained vigorous and enjoyed homage. The "accredited elements in society" were those who held land by freehold or enjoyed the formal freedoms which meant borough citizenship. The word liberty had not yet acquired the general meaning of freedom under the law, which was a holistic conception made up of freedom of movement, thought, speech and press. The word liberty was more often used in the plural. Liberties were particular privileges, and the number, extent and variety enjoyed by any one person were in direct proportion to social status, and social status was determined more often than not by a person's relationship to the land.

The traumatic experiences of the mid-century wars and revolutions had resulted in some curtailment of the King's prerogative powers and some weakening of his authority relative to Parliament's. The growth of the power of Parliament meant an increase in the political authority of the classes which qualified for public service under ancient franchises. Individuals in these classes who chose or were chosen to be active in public affairs naturally benefitted from the enhanced authority of Parliament. More and more the active members of Parliament were becoming politicians in a sense approaching the modern. The English nobility were recovering their pre-Tudor authority but as politicians rather than feudal lords and warriors. If they opposed the King or one another, it was as politicians, or groups of politicians. Generally it is accepted that the continuous, as opposed to the remote beginnings of parties, date from the Restoration period.

It happened that religious differences continued to disturb the national life. Charles II was pro-Catholic and James II (1685–1688) was a militant Catholic at a time when Catholic France was the great threat to the European balance of power. A determined effort failed to exclude James from the succession on religious grounds, but the effort divided Parliament and the country. The Catholic threat seemed all the more dangerous because Charles, and more openly his brother James, tried to subvert the Restoration Settlement. The fear of Catholicism joined with the fear of Stuart absolutism to produce national unity. Anglicans and Dissenters saw the Church and Protestantism in danger; Englishmen saw the nation's independence threatened by French hegemony in Europe; men in public life, political thinkers, and common lawyers feared for their happy constitution, the authority of Parliament, and the liberties of the subject; men of substance thought their properties insecure.

When in June 1688 the Queen bore a son whose infant body contained the prospect of a Catholic succession, many who formerly shrank from disturbing the hereditary principle accepted the necessity of the times. The possibility of civil war did not deter the nation's aristocratic leaders. Believing that "we shall be every day in a worse condition than we are" and searching for "a remedy before it be too late for us to contribute to our own deliverance," a group of them invited William of Holland to come to England and place himself at the head of their movement to preserve their "religion, liberties and properties. . . ." William accepted. His duty required him to contribute "all that lies in us for the maintaining, both of the Protestant Religion, and of the Laws and Liberties" of the kingdoms of England, Scotland, and Ireland. There was no civil war. The King's army melted away; James fled to France. In the absence of settled authority, and "for the Preservation of our Religion, Laws, and Liberties," former members of Parliament joined with the City fathers of London to entreat William to take upon himself "the Administration of public Affairs." This he did.

It was a Revolution, not because the nation was plunged into war and blood was shed but because "King James the Second having abdicated the government, and the throne being thereby vacant," it was necessary to re-establish authority by means that were extra-constitutional and outside the bounds of settled procedure. The men who made decisions knew this; they departed no farther from the constitution than the exigencies of the case required. Like Lincoln's company drilling for the Black Hawk War, not knowing how to maintain formation when they reached the fence they fell out and fell in on the other side and went on from there. The throne being vacant, there was no King to summon Parliament, so William summoned it. This unconstitutional Parliament, passing over the baby James as the rightful successor under the hereditary principle, offered the throne finally to William and Mary jointly. There now being a King and Queen, the unconstitutional Parliament "declared and enacted" that the two houses, "notwithstanding any want of writs of summons, or any other defect of form or default whatsoever," are "as if they had been summoned according to the usual form." A year later it was enacted "that all and singular the acts made and enacted in the said parliament were and are laws and statutes of this kingdom, and such as ought to be reputed, taken and obeyed by all the people of this kingdom." And so by their own declaration and enactment, the illegitimate legitimized themselves, and a revolutionary regime became a settled constitutional order.

The forms of the constitution were unchanged, but the relationships and authorities of the parts, at issue throughout the preceding century, were redefined. The redefinition, confirming and extending the Restoration Settlement, permanently altered the balance of the constitution which Charles I had described in 1642. This was done statutorily; the laws enacted between 1689 and 1701 are called collectively the Revolution Settlement. With time it became sacrosanct, a supreme example of collective political wisdom that would make another revolution forever unnecessary. These laws were drafted with recent conflicts in mind. In many instances they reasserted earlier claims, and as the event proved, successfully. The most comprehensive was the Bill of Rights— "An act for declaring the rights and liberties of the subject and settling the succession of the crown." This act abolished the prerogative power to suspend laws and limited the dispensing power, reasserted (for the last time) Parliament's unique authority to grant taxes, made the existence of a standing army dependent upon the consent of Parliament, guaranteed certain rights of the subjects and of members of Parliament, and settled the succession to the throne within the Protestant line. The Mutiny Act, which provided for legal methods of maintaining discipline in the army, confirmed the dependence of the armed forces upon Parliament. This was further tightened by the new practice of annual parliamentary appropriations, not only for the armed forces but for the civil side of the government. This practice made annual sessions of Parliament a necessity, something that earlier statutes had not accomplished. By "an Act for exempting their majesties protestant subjects, dissenting from the church of England, from the penalties of certain laws," all non-Anglicans except Catholics, Jews and Unitarians came to enjoy a practical toleration. If they observed certain small requirements, they could worship publicly, organize chapels, and maintain schools. The "act for the frequent meeting and calling of parliaments," which qualified the ancient prerogative power to summon Parliament at will, was rendered superfluous by the new financial practices, though the law limiting the life of Parliament to three years effectively prevented the King from indefinitely postponing elections. Finally the Act of Settlement in 1701, taking account of recent deaths in the royal family, redrew the line of succession, directing it into the House of Hanover and confining it to communicants of the Established Church. Among miscellaneous provisions, the statute made the tenure of judicial officers dependent upon good behavior rather than the pleasure of the King.

Prosaic as all of this sounds, there was much meaning between the lines of the statutes. The Revolution Settlement had a significance that is not immediately apparent in the texts of the statutes. A person has to know the history of the constitutional conflicts in the seventeenth century as well as the eighteenth century sequel in order to appreciate the knowledge, subtlety, acumen and foresight of the men who judged the needs of the times and drafted the statutes that met them. Beyond the texts is the spirit of the settlement, its finality, its embodiment of a consensus that eventually became the nation's creed.

As a great constitutional amendment, the Revolution Settlement ended one era and began a new one. There could no longer be any question of the location of effective sovereignty in the community. Parliament determined the raising of revenue, the maintenance of the armed forces, the forms of religion, local government, the nation's commercial policy, and the succession to the throne. In this then the great ideal of the seventeenth century Commonwealthmen, the supremacy of the legislature, became transformed into a constant of the constitution, glorified by Locke and confirmed in the traditions of Whiggism. Men continued to speak of a "balanced constitution" in which one element was monarchical, but the substance of power was in Parliament. This was all the clearer because England did not know the kind of distinction between constitutional power and legislative power which would later be established in the American system of written constitutions. Parliament by statute could amend and alter the constitution; parliamentary statutes, depending upon content, could be constituent in nature.

Because Parliament was sovereign after 1688, its political authority was greatly enhanced. Therefore the King's exercise of his remaining prerogative powers was limited much more severely than literal interpretation of the constitution suggested. If the King still directed foreign policy, made war and peace, was head of the armed forces, appointed judges, and named his own ministers who were supposed to be responsible to him, he had always to take account of political realities in doing these things. The consequence was often tension in the relationships between the King and his Lords and Commons. Eventually the problem of relationships was worked out empirically. By the middle of the nineteenth century a set of conventions or customs of the constitution was developed that in effect left the King with the shadow of the prerogative powers, the substance being located in ministers who were in fact responsible to the House of Commons for the advice they gave to the King. Convention required that the King act only upon the advice of his responsible ministers.

The Revolution Settlement, clearly, had profound political consequences. The prestige and the power of Parliament, already great, continued to increase. But the two houses were too large to function effectively without management. If the members agreed in accepting the Revolution Settlement, they were bound to disagree about specifics—foreign policy, ministers, or financial and commercial measures. The Revolution of 1688 may not have been the source or origin of parliamentary politics, but it is not a distortion of history to see politics taking recognizably modern forms in that period—politics described as an art. The political leaders now relied upon management and influence to get the nation's business done in Parliament. Coercion was used too, but no longer could this be the kind of coercion the Tudor sovereigns had employed. The penalty of political failure was no longer death, but simply loss of favor and office. Politics on the higher levels was therefore the art of building, improving and preserving parliamentary support, that is, of gaining and holding office. The politicians worked with the materials at hand, and these materials were neither new nor unfamiliar. They were the ancient forms and usages of locality, of family, of property and influence and status, managed and directed to the end of winning elections and political support, and of obtaining the favor of the King who still possessed the royal attributes of primacy, patronage, property, and prestige.

The ancient social and political assumptions still prevailed. The

Revolution of 1688 was in no sense a social revolution; it did not disturb the basis of political power or social status. No proletarian cast tinged the events of 1688. Property rights were more secure and if possible more sacred than before, and along with the sovereign Parliament, an independent judiciary, trained in the mysteries of the common law, protected them from prerogative threats. The venerable traditions that kept society in its ranks and orders had not been at issue during the Revolution. The connections between property and the franchise, property and political power, property and social status remained distinct and intact; no one called, as the Levellers had done forty years earlier, for reconsideration of the internal composition of the House of Commons. The Revolution had the support of the nation; the nation had not demanded a reconstruction of the social order; and the immediate beneficiaries of the Revolution, in terms of political authority, were the same classes that had always worked the system. But these classes now had much greater opportunities for political self-expression because the power of the King had been reduced, and their support and consent were necessary for the exercise of the crown's remaining powers.

The electoral system of the century and a half following the Revolution was in important respects the one that had been devised and which developed in an agrarian hierarchical society. Not even Sidney or Locke had raised the serious question whether Parliament, which represented the nation, was indeed representative. They assumed, as did their contemporaries, that it was representative. Parliament in the eighteenth century continued to serve England's needs for political representation, though under increasing strain, until the industrialization and urbanization of England in the nineteenth century forced its reconstruction. Until that time came, the propertied classes continued exclusively to manage the electoral system, to make it serve the nation's interest—and their own. And why not? The leaders of the eighteenth century made no distinction between theirs and the country's interest.

The most obvious beneficiaries of the Revolution were the landed nobility, secure in their property as never before, and enjoying unprecedented opportunity for political expression and national leadership. There were about two hundred peers of the realm. Although title was separable from land in a sense that feudal baronage had not been, the peerage was still a landed class, and normally men connected the two. The peers were often local potentates, as Lords Lieutenants of their counties, as owners of landed estates, as men who could influence votes and elections in a variety of ways. Their national service was rendered as office-holders, as the King's ministers, and as members of the House of Lords. There they served with the Lords Spiritual who as time passed, came to identify their interest with the maintenance of the Hanoverian Succession; the cause of the dispossessed Stuarts ceased to agitate politics. The Church of England was a great landed interest and the bishops were at one with the Lords Temporal in identifying their own security with the preservation of property rights.

The beauty of the balanced constitution, a euphemism for the political status quo, was that it preserved the "liberties" of the people, meaning prominently the privileges and interests of those who had a stake in the country. And one of the elements in the balance was the aristocratic. The House of Lords, composed of men high in prestige, at the top of the social pyramid, and wealthy in land and rents, possessed great constitutional authority. If money bills had to originate in the House of Commons, the House of Lords was otherwise co-equal in legislative power, it judged in impeachment cases, and it was the highest court in England. Its political power was impressive because many of the King's ministers were peers, much of the political leadership of the kingdom was drawn from the House of Lords, and because the workings and the structure of politics, so much a function of "connection" or family relationship, were the means whereby its members influenced the House of Commons.

Blackstone described the House of Commons as consisting of all men of property who were not peers. Every such man had a voice in Parliament, personally or through his representatives. In a free state, said Blackstone, every man who is a free agent, that is, a man of property, "ought to be in some measure his own governor," and so one branch of the legislative power ought to reside in the people, meaning propertied men or the politically literate. The House of Commons was the democratic element in the balance of the constitution, democratic in the classical rather than the twentieth century sense. A man who sat in the Commons served for the whole realm, and though for practical reasons he was elected from a defined and limited constituency by only the qualified voters therein, he was not bound by his constituents unless he might think it "proper and prudent" to take their advice. Often members did, and sometimes when they did not they learned the political errors of their ways. In 1780 Edmund Burke learned such a lesson in Bristol, gave up the electoral contest before the voters had the opportunity to record their disaffection, and for a while was so discouraged that he thought of retiring from politics.

The eighteenth century House of Commons functioned within limits most of which had been prescribed earlier. Its size was increased by the addition of forty-five Scottish members in 1707, and until the union with Ireland in 1801 it remained at 558. In 1710, ostensibly "for better preserving the constitution and freedom of parliament," actually for certain political reasons related to the growing potential of commercial and monetary wealth, but in any case quite harmoniously with ancient and prevailing social assumptions, a landed property qualification for membership was stipulated. Borough members must have an estate, "freehold or copyhold . . . in lands, tenements, or hereditaments" of three hundred pounds a year clear annual value; for knights of the shire, the value must be twice as large. Exceptions were made for the heirs apparent of peers and for the four members who represented Cambridge and Oxford Universities. Generally though not perfectly these requirements were observed until their repeal in 1858.

The Act of 1710, hardly necessary to preserve the landed references of county members, reflected apprehension over the possibilities in the boroughs. For of the 558 members of the House of Commons, only 122 sat for the counties, 80 for England, 12 for Wales, and 30 for Scotland. They were elected by voters who met the ancient forty shilling freeholder qualification.* The preponderance of the membership therefore sat for the boroughs where in most instances the landed references were negligible as local franchise requirements. Borough representation in the Commons, conceivably, could gradually lose connection with the land. The act of 1710 recognized and tried to anticipate the possibility that changing social relationships might alter the character and composition of the House of Commons. It was nothing new for men who made money in commerce to set themselves up as landed gentlemen; on the contrary it was feared that in the future such men might lose the desire for the status. The fear was exaggerated; nevertheless the statute was passed.

There was no uniform franchise requirement for the 215 English and Welsh boroughs or the fifteen borough constituencies in Scotland. Since the thirteenth century when the King through the sheriffs first ordered the boroughs to send up men to speak for them, the English boroughs had been left free to determine their own franchise requirements. The consequence of this freedom of choice was variety, and variety meant opportunity for clever managers. During the Puritan Revolution men talked about and even made some effort to establish uniformity. But the men who achieved the Restoration were pleased to return to prerevolutionary arrangements. These survived the Revolution of 1688; in fact they were never at issue, for it was not the intention of the men who made that Revolution to alter the political system which they were learning to manipulate. That system was too congenial to their social and political aspirations. The eighteenth century inherited a set of medieval electoral dispositions which were happily adaptable to the needs and uses of the new political managers of England.

For ease of description it is customary to group the English and Welsh boroughs into categories according to broad similarities of franchise qualifications. In the dozen "pot walloper" bor-

---

* The term freehold was not strictly limited to ownership. Certain legal definitions were accepted that broadened it somewhat but did not defeat the purpose of the Act of 1430. The Scottish county franchise had a different origin but also rested upon the 40s. qualification.

oughs, inhabitant householders not on poor relief could vote. This in effect was household suffrage and enfranchised persons who were not embraced within the social definitions of a gentleman's household. There were three times as many "scot and lot" boroughs in which the franchise belonged to householders who paid the poor rates. These would be men who probably fit Blackstone's definition of "free agents," though they need not be well-to-do. In the ninety-two freeman boroughs in England, the voters were men who enjoyed the freedom of the borough. This was a formal status, though the qualification for obtaining it differed from one borough to another. London, usually classed with this type of borough, granted the franchise to members of the liveried companies. In the twenty-seven corporation boroughs, voting was by the members of the governing body; in the twenty-nine burgage boroughs, the right to vote derived from ownership of certain properties in the borough. There were six freeholder boroughs. In Edinburgh the council chose the city's representatives to the Commons; in the other fourteen Scottish burghs, members were chosen by a complex method of indirect election in groups of burghs whose total basic electorate, composed of members of the burgh councils, numbered less than fifteen hundred.

These varied franchises not only connected voting with property, directly or indirectly, but also restricted the numbers of voters. With some 20,000 voters, Yorkshire had the largest electorate of any constituency. The remaining county electorates ranged downwards in size from about 8,000 to about 800. Westminster, with some 12,000 voters, had the largest borough electorate. In London, almost 7,000 men could vote; in Bristol, 5,000; neither the notorious Old Sarum with 7 voters nor Gatten with 2 had any residents. A small electorate did not always mean a safe constituency. Each borough had its own history and its unique character. Local circumstances, family relationships, personalities, political management, and the nature of the franchise requirements determined whether electoral contests took place at general elections or whether members or patrons succeeded in evading the trouble and expense of a contest. Eleven was the largest number of county contests in England in a general election during the last half of the century. In the election of 1754, only 57 of the boroughs of the United Kingdom were contested; in the election of 1761, only 43 boroughs enjoyed or endured contests; the election of 1774 saw the greatest number of contests, 71. Normally a general election was not the occasion for nationwide electoral turbulence. Only in a minority of the constituencies in any eighteenth century election was the problem of choosing members of the Commons taken to the voters for decision.

All of this bespeaks excellent management by the politicians, the county families, the borough authorities and the active peers. In some instances they were moved by the desire to maintain peace in the localities, in others to save the expenses of a contest, in still others to continue family traditions of service and local leadership. On occasion contests came about because friends had to be provided for, because votes were needed in the Commons, because a vacancy had to be filled, or because an ambitious aggressor challenged the local status quo. Whether the object was to prevent or to win a contest, much energy, great sums of money, remarkable ingenuity, and consummate political skill were employed by the politicians. An anecdotal history of eighteenth century electioneering would be filled with amazing, shocking, funny and sad stories.

In 1716 Parliament had given to itself a maximum life of seven years. By a convention that served the interests of the politicians by reducing the frequency of elections and the attendant effort and expenses, among other reasons, a Parliament was permitted to run out its legal life or nearly so. Accordingly it never happened until 1784 that elections were called earlier than about every six or seven years.

This system of forms and actions produced results which were generally harmonious with the assumptions and aspirations of the age. The original purpose of a representative House of Commons was to give appropriate recognition to medieval estates or orders and not even in the eighteenth century to people counted by the head but rather to the interests which embodied the nation's affairs. Edmund Burke in 1770 seems to have been the first to describe explicitly the underlying reality of the economic and social character of the House of Commons. In his *Thoughts on the Present Discontents* he spoke of "new interests" which "must be let into a share of representation" if domestic peace was to prevail. He identified these as the official, professional, and military and naval interests, assuming that his readers would already know of the landed and commercial interests. It is possible to give Burke too much credit for originality. He was not formulating the concept of parliamentary interests. Cromwell used the very word "interest" to speak of land, and he clearly preferred it to the commercial interest in the composition of the House. Burke was simply mentioning important ones of somewhat later prominence in the House, but he was not telling his parliamentary colleagues anything they did not already know. The Tudor councillors or the late medieval lawyers in the House were interests in all but name; the armed forces as a parliamentary interest could hardly have appeared before a permanently commissioned navy or a standing army came into existence in the seventeenth century. But Burke's discussion helped make the idea a part of political thinking and gave to defenders of the established parliamentary constitution a strong argument to use against those who later agitated for representation of people. If these great national interests were represented in Parliament, was there any need, it might be asked, that people as individuals be represented? What was good for these interests was good for the country.

The men who spoke for these interests identified them with the national well-being. Land was the first interest. Commerce was also an old one and important, and it was agreed that to be useful in the Commons a member should understand commercial policy. The nation's security required direct representation of naval and military interests. The legal profession should also hold some seats. The lower classes, both the industrious and the idle poor, need not be directly represented. Their superiors knew what was good for the lower classes. When John Wesley contemptuously dismissed American arguments, he said that nine-tenths of the population of the United Kingdom had as much reason as the Americans for complaints about being unrepresented. But, added

Wesley, there was in fact no reason for complaints because all of the King's subjects were virtually represented.

The men who sat in the House of Commons came into it from the upper ranks of society. This does not mean that their origins were never humble. In English society there was mobility, up and down, and it was possible for men from obscure backgrounds to attain wealth and status. These had to be attained, however, before the doors of St. Stephen's Chapel were opened to them. Throughout the century about 20 per cent of the members were identified with the peerage, as sons of peers or as Irish peers. Membership in the Irish peerage had one advantage over the British; it did not disqualify a man from membership in the Commons. There were sports from among the noble families in both the Commons and the Lords; perhaps their sense of security gave them the courage to appear idiosyncratic. In the latter part of the century, three peers, the Earl of Effingham, Earl Stanhope, and the Duke of Richmond, were among the leading advocates of parliamentary reform. These men differed from most of their noble friends and relatives in thinking that land was over-represented in the House of Commons and that people were indeed proper objects of representation. In every House of Commons there sat about two hundred members who were called country gentlemen. They were such in a literal sense. They also fulfilled the eighteenth century political meaning of the words because they were landowners who sat in the House in their own interests and acted independently of factions or patrons.

The military, naval, and legal professions were well represented numerically. These members often played a double role. The first two groups were frequently related with landed families by blood or marriage; just over a third of the army members and about a fourth of the naval members came from aristocratic families. When there are added to these the service members who were of gentry origin, the conclusion is that overwhelmingly these two professional interests spoke for the land as well as for their professions.

While all members were supposed to speak for commerce as well as the land, the commercial interest also had its own representation. The merchants who sat in the Commons were the big businessmen, not the little shopkeepers. They engaged in banking, overseas trade, mining, manufacturing or wholesaling. Some had humble origins, most sprang from the middle class, some had gentry or even aristocratic backgrounds. They were never an exclusive group nor did they act as a block of voters single-mindedly concerned with trade and finance. Along with their expert knowledge of commercial policy and tactics they, like the professional men, had deep involvement in the land by inheritance, marriage, or purchase. To scan the marriage lists of the *Gentleman's Magazine* month by month through a run of years is to be impressed with the frequency of the marriage alliances between land and mercantile wealth. If most of the merchant members of the House of Commons had their businesses in London, their lands, ancestral or newly purchased, were located throughout the country, though mostly in the home counties.

Whether grouped by vocations, by social status (which was very nearly the same thing), in terms of their political ambitions as active or passive, or even according to their factional alignments, the members of the House of Commons participated in a remarkable homogeneity. Even when they differed over tactical political allegiances or over specific public issues they shared in a great consensus about the social aspirations and assumptions of the age. They agreed that property was a sacred institution. They saw free agency as a function of property and political literacy as a derivative. The political system which they managed was a perfect reflection of their social philosophy and their social order. The so-called balanced constitution was an agency not for bringing about social change but for preserving the social status quo by preventing undue concentration of political authority in any one part of the constitutional system. It protected the "interests" of those who had a "stake in the country," or rather, it accorded to such persons the means of protecting their interests by vesting in them political control. There were two nations, the governors and the governed, in eighteenth century England.

These happy arrangements had not been created by any single generation of Englishmen. To say that they had evolved is hardly

correct, for they were not the results of the operation of imper-
sonal "forces." These arrangements had been made by men who
knew what they were doing when they made decisions in their
understanding of public needs. The origins of the eighteenth century constitution were in the Middle Ages, to go back no further.
Later generations improved upon them by enacting statutes and
by establishing practices that became custom and hardened into
rules. The challenge in the seventeenth century was repulsed.
And the Revolution of 1688 did not question or threaten the inherited social assumptions. Rather, by placing the sovereignty of
Parliament beyond dispute, the Revolution confirmed the political supremacy of property and the propertied classes. Burke was
more profoundly correct than he realized when he said in 1790
that the men of 1688 "did not so much make a revolution, as prevent one. . . ." What in fact they preserved was the social order.
They acted outside the limits of the established constitution to
effect a political revolution and thereby postponed social reconstruction for two centuries.

The Glorious Revolution therefore became an event of blessed
memory. Sacred, hallowed, it was evidence that Divine Provi-
dence guided the destinies of England. This veneration of the
Revolution enjoyed a curious career. To upholders of the established political, constitutional and social order, the Revolution
had a character of finality. But as the eighteenth century wore
on, dissatisfaction with the established order grew. Yet the discontented did not repudiate the Revolution. They said rather that
it was not final, its promises remained unfulfilled, and that further
changes were necessary to bring to completion the good work
begun in 1688. A renewed devotion to the principles of the Revolution required men to act. When on trial for sedition in 1793,
one of the parliamentary reformers, Joseph Gerrald, said that although the Revolution had established the right of the people to
alter the line of succession to the throne, and affirmed their right
to change the constitution, it had not recovered for the people
their ancient right to vote. Four years earlier the Reverend Dr.
Richard Price, preaching his *A Discourse on the Love of our
Country*, said that the Revolution established "The right to resist

power when abused." It also established "The right to chuse our own governors; to cashier them for misconduct; and to frame a government for ourselves." Not only because Price located a constituent power in the people but because he thought the Revolution had not sufficiently recognized such power, his interpretation of the meaning of the Revolution was quite different from that of the proponents of the established order.

Whether the Glorious Revolution was a final act or an event of unfulfilled promises, Englishmen found its significance in its relation to their liberties, or liberty. The nature and extent of political liberty and the practical means of giving effect to it was the great issue to the men who made the Revolution, and a century later it remained the great issue between those who would not and those who would reform the political system. In their own judgment the English radicals, or the Jacobins of the late eighteenth century, when pursuing reform found their inspiration in their national history and national needs. The French Revolution stimulated their ardor but the substance and the justification of their cause were as English as the common law.

CHAPTER III

TAKE YOUR CHOICE

FROM the struggles of the seventeenth century, Englishmen of the Georgian age inherited both their "matchless" constitution and the strain of radicalism that criticized it. Amidst the prevailing complacency with the established and "balanced" constitutional order, occasional recommendations for improvement or expressions of discontent made no impression. Before the reign of George III complaints were directed mainly against the Septennial Act of 1716. The demands were for "shorter parliaments," that is for reducing the legal life of Parliament by requiring more frequent general elections. Generally the argument ran that the House of Commons was becoming too independent because M. P.'s were too far separated from the voters when elections occurred at approximately six or seven year intervals. Bolingbroke gave this argument a curious twist in the interest of preserving the remaining powers of the crown. The growing independence of the Commons threatened to upset the balance of the constitution, that mystique of harmony among the parts formed by the Revolution of 1688.

During the election of 1761 William Beckford, a supporter of William Pitt the Elder, raised a more fundamental question. He addressed a complaint to the Liverymen of London who had just reelected him to the House of Commons. "Gentlemen, our constitution is deficient in only one point, and that is, that little pitiful boroughs send members to Parliament equal to great cities;

and it is contrary to the maxim that power should follow property." This echo of Harrington sounded against settled arrangements. Beckford was not complaining that the inhabitants of London, as people, were underrepresented, but that as the wealthiest city in the kingdom, London sent only four members to the House of Commons. This was also the sentiment of Malachy Postlethwayt, a highly regarded writer on commercial subjects, who in 1751 had complained of London's ill treatment. But no more than Beckford was he advocating representation strictly by population.

Similar Harringtonian complaints were heard during the election of 1768. It is difficult to determine how seriously to take them. They seemed to reflect only the discontents of their authors and not those of any group or organization. Yet they expressed the sentiments that owners of personal property who lived in London or other commercial centers might be expected to feel, if they thought about the matter. Rotten boroughs rather than land were the objects of attack; seats in the House of Commons should be redistributed so that the counties and the larger towns received proportionately more of them. Thus "Regulus" in the *Political Register* demanded redistribution of seats in the House of Commons in order to give a larger voice to the monied and commercial interests. Urban dwellers had too few seats in proportion to the value of their property or to the taxes they paid. To give even greater effect to a widened franchise, Regulus desired annual elections to Parliament, with the voters protected in their franchise by the secret ballot. While these demands anticipated parts of the radical program of the next century, the first was founded upon the tradition that property, not people, was the object of representation.

Occasional demands such as these did not express the leading issue of the political agitation of 1768–1771. Regulus aimed at the nobility who as beneficiaries of the Revolution of 1688 engrossed political power. His argument secondarily was a complaint that land as such was overrepresented. Primarily he protested against the political alliance of the crown and the aristocracy. Before the agitation died down, Obadiah Hulme in his *Essay on the*

English Constitution (1771) pleaded for restoration of the mythical Anglo-Saxon democracy. The Revolution of 1688, he argued, had given power to the aristocracy, and quickly they consolidated their control of Parliament. The Septennial Act, following so closely upon the Act of 1710 establishing a property qualification in land for membership in the Commons, moved Parliament farther distant from the people and the voters and strengthened the control of the landed interest. To purge politics and the constitution of these evils, Hulme advocated annual elections, secret ballot, an extension of the suffrage, and the elimination of rotten boroughs. With its hint of popular representation, Hulme's program departed further from tradition than that of Regulus. Hulme advanced another idea that was full of the future. He desired associations in every constituency to communicate with one another and to demand from candidates pledges to support reform.

Such ideas expressed apprehension against what seemed to be the tendencies of politics. The unrepresentative character of Parliament was only in part responsible for them. And the fears were not the monopoly of the self-appointed heirs of the seventeenth century Commonwealthmen who had loved liberty and occasionally died for it. New patriots like "Old Whigs" thought the constitution was in danger because power was accruing to the crown. Both groups cherished the independence of the House of Commons which they identified with the liberties of Englishmen. A House subservient to the crown was potentially an instrument of tyranny. To restore the independence of the Commons was a cause worthy of Milton or Algernon Sidney whose memories the eighteenth century Commonwealthmen invoked and whose writings they reread. Thomas Hollis made a career of disseminating the great works of the seventeenth century champions of "liberty" like Locke and Milton. At the same time the Rockingham Whig, Edmund Burke, advanced his reputation by attacking antiparliamentary "influence" around the crown and helped make this an issue in politics during the period of the American Revolution.

The occasion for the political furor was the attempt by the

government to dispose of John Wilkes, who as early as 1762–1763 had shown his ability to irritate ministers and provoke the King. Expelled by the House of Commons in 1764 for writing and publishing *The North Briton,* "No. 45," and then found guilty of libel by the Court of King's Bench for republishing it and the obscene *Essay on Woman,* Wilkes had not appeared in court to receive sentence. An outlaw, he spent the next four years in Paris. He remained in communication with political friends and received financial aid from them. Early in 1768 he boldly returned, too late to make an effective campaign for one of London's seats in the House of Commons. But as a beneficiary of the publicity aroused by his unsuccessful attempt in London, he won election for the county of Middlesex. Then he appeared in court to receive the long delayed sentence. His outlawry was reversed on a convenient technicality, but he went to prison for his libel.

While still serving out his sentence, a hero in the eyes of the London mobs, Wilkes attacked the government in December 1768 in the *St. James's Chronicle.* For this fresh libel he was again expelled from the House of Commons. The voters of Middlesex promptly reelected him; the Commons once again expelled him; and then followed two more reelections and two more expulsions. On the last occasion, in April 1769, the majority of the Commons resolved that Wilkes was incapable of membership. They seated his opponent who had received only one-fourth as many votes as Wilkes, but, said the Commons, "ought to have been returned."

The Middlesex election controversy was a landmark in English political history. One effect of it was to arouse the parliamentary opposition groups, particularly the followers of Lord Chatham and Lord Rockingham, to protest vehemently against the threat to the independence of the House of Commons and to warn against the influence of the crown. Edmund Burke was inspired to write his famous pamphlet, *Thoughts on the Causes of the Present Discontents,* in which, among other things, he condemned what he saw as a new political system of "influence." Opponents of the government, not all of them supporters of

Wilkes but nevertheless ready to capitalize upon the opportunity he provided for them, organized a movement of protest. In certain counties and in London and Westminster they framed petitions directed to the King in protest against the actions of the majority in the House of Commons. The freeholders of Middlesex wanted George III to dismiss the ministry; those of Surrey and Worcestershire upheld the right of free election; the citizens of London asked the King to dissolve Parliament. In the north, Rockingham's home, the "opulence" of the county, both landed and commercial, was among the ten thousand signers of the Yorkshire petition.

The petitioning movement experienced internal stresses. Radicals wanted to talk about parliamentary reform while the Rockingham politicians desired only to request dissolution of Parliament and to talk in generalities about the rights of electors. Between country gentlemen anxious both for the independence of the Commons and for the rights of property, and the radical element, especially the urban radicals, tension and distrust arose even in the face of their common enemy. When in January 1770 the Commons debated a motion to acquaint the King with the nation's grievances, Richard Rigby, a leading opponent of Wilkes, condemned petitions and petitioners, expressing indeed some of the thoughts of certain petitioners who for tactical reasons did not say everything they were thinking. Rigby asserted that petitions had been promoted by "factious" people, and that even among freeholders who had signed them there were people "no better than an ignorant multitude whom it is absurd in the highest degree to suppose capable of deciding" public questions. If, said Rigby, "popular clamour" controlled the proceedings of the House, then "we must bid adieu to all government by law. . . ."

The more dramatic and in the long run the more significant outgrowth of the Middlesex election controversy was organized urban radicalism. It brought something of incalculable consequence into English political life. There may be reason to doubt the single-mindedness of Wilkes' interest in reform; he certainly exploited public support to increase his own popularity, to strengthen his nuisance value, and to gain municipal office, a parliamentary seat, and a regular income. But the radicalism with which he was associated presented a program which became an inspiration of later reform movements, even though they differed from it on details. Generally, the demands were for shorter Parliaments, that is more frequent general elections, curtailment of pensions and offices for friends of the government, the abolition of rotten boroughs, and a broader suffrage. It was hoped that Members of Parliament could be coerced into pledges to support these demands in return for electoral support. The constituents of the urban agitation were for the most part middle and lower middle class professional men, small merchants, tradesmen, and shopkeepers. From among the lower class—laborers, servants, journeymen, small craftsmen—the popular agitations drew physical strength. Among Wilkes' supporters there was always a sprinkling from the higher social and economic and political orders. The freeholders of Middlesex, mainly of the lesser sort, voted for him with remarkable persistency.

If these persons could get excited, and if the lower classes of the metropolis could be incited partly because of economic hardship, the movement did not aim at political democracy, let alone social revolution or social equality. Demands for freeman suffrage in the boroughs merely supplemented the emphasis upon landed property that characterized the county petition movement in 1769–1770. When in 1776 Wilkes proposed reform to the House of Commons, he desired to widen the suffrage even while restricting it to "free agents." This Blackstonian language and emphasis involved no contradiction in terms. Because of historical vagaries, many "free agents" did not possess the franchise in the eighteenth century; their enjoyment of it would not require abandonment of traditional assumptions about the nature of representation. Urban radicalism only superficially suggested a class struggle. A pre-Marxist, proletarian taint should not be given to it. Indeed, there was in the movement something almost antiquarian. Its adherents thought of their reform program as an effort to restore the purity, liberty and popular character of the mythical Anglo-Saxon constitution.

The theoretical side of the Wilkite controversy was best represented by the persons who in July 1769 met at the London Tavern and formed the Society of the Supporters of the Bill of Rights. Initially they undertook to provide financial and political support for Wilkes. Among the original members were Alderman John Sawbridge, M. P., wealthy by inheritance of land and by marriage with mercantile affluence, the Reverend John Horne,* perhaps the leading spirit in the founding of the Society, Aldermen Richard Oliver and James Townsend, the lawyers John Glynn and James Adair, and Dr. Thomas Wilson, rector of St. Margaret's, Westminster, who so admired Sawbridge's beautiful sister Catherine, the "republican virago," that he left his fortune to her. Altogether, the Society had about fifty loyal members until it split in 1771.

Within a year of its founding the Society had paid off twenty thousand pounds of Wilkes' debts, and had also moved to promote its more ambitious object, the protection and enlargement of "the legal, constitutional liberty of the subject." The grievances connected with the Middlesex election controversy of 1769—the independence of Parliament and the rights of electors —were not forgotten, but as stimuli for political activism yielded to a fresh controversy in 1771. When the House of Commons tried to enforce the standing orders prohibiting the publication of debates, freedom of the press became the issue. A split in the Bill of Rights Society, with Sawbridge, Horne and Townsend opposing Wilkes, did not prevent the opponents of government from winning in the printers' case. At the end of the parliamentary session the government dropped all legal actions, and the combined forces of the people of London, the officials of the City, and the press could claim victory. Nor did the continued struggles among radicals and others in City politics prevent the remnant of the Bill of Rights Society from developing more precisely their program for specific constitutional and political reforms.

On June 11, 1771, the Society took a notable action. They resolved that henceforth, throughout England, candidates for the

---

* In 1782 he added the surname Tooke, after that of a friend, and is best known to history as John Horne Tooke.

House of Commons should be asked to pledge support to a bill for shorter Parliaments and "more fair and equal representation of the people." If the idea of pledges did not win universal acceptance, it caught on in the metropolis. In March 1773, the London Common Council passed a motion to require from candidates pledges to work for shorter Parliaments. In November 1773, the candidate for a London seat in a by-election took the pledge. He also won his contest. In June 1774, the Common Hall of London, consisting of the eight thousand liverymen of the eighty-nine London companies, resolved to exact from City M. P.'s the promise to follow the instructions of Common Hall or resign. This extra-parliamentary pressure, with the program for parliamentary reform, confirmed the estrangement between the radicals and some of their former parliamentary allies. The Rockingham party had been able to cooperate with the radicals in the Middlesex election controversy and in the printers' case, but could not work with them to undermine a foundation of the eighteenth century political structure.

The radicals had set their course. It was all very well for the *Gentleman's Magazine* in February 1774 to use language suggesting boredom when it reported that for the fourth time (but not the last) Sawbridge "made his annual motion for shortening the duration of parliaments, which was over-ruled." Sawbridge was not quite so much alone as this quotation suggests. In the preceding spring, after some squabbling between the friends and former friends of Wilkes, the Middlesex freeholders had resolved "That the most effectual means of obtaining redress for the violated right of election, and other national grievances, is by bills for shortening the duration of Parliaments, for excluding placemen and pensioners from the House of Commons, and for a more fair and equal representation of the people." Not only was the idea of parliamentary reform in the air. It was becoming the program of organized groups forming deliberately for the purpose of exacting pledges from Members of Parliament, or would-be members, and for propagandizing the cause. More than that, there was a developing consciousness that some kind of extra-parliamentary pressure would be necessary before the eighteenth century political system could be reformed. If precedents were needed, the Irish Association and certain American examples would serve.

Already the idea of association was receiving theoretical treatment and exposition. In January 1774, the first volume of a remarkable book by James Burgh was published in anticipation of the general election. Burgh was a Dissenting schoolmaster who until his retirement three years earlier had conducted a successful school at Newington Green. He was no poverty stricken scholar scratching out a bare living. A cousin of the historian, William Robertson, he had studied at St. Andrew's. After trying various occupations he had begun his school in the pleasant neighborhood where some wealthy and influential Dissenters had their suburban homes. Here he married a widow, Mrs. Hannah Harding. She was a niece of Mrs. Sarah Seabrooke, the sister-in-law of the wealthy Stoke Newington Dissenter George Streatfield, himself once Master of the Merchant Taylors Company. Burgh lived in a substantial dwelling, assessed at the large sum of twenty-six pounds for the land tax, and he paid ten guineas a year for himself and "his young gentlemen" at the Newington Green Meeting House. His was the largest single annual contribution, and he and his scholars occupied the largest pew, remodeled especially for them. Richard Price became the preacher at Newington Green in 1758 after the death of Streatfield whose chaplain he had been. Price and Burgh, with the banker Daniel Radford, his son-in-law Thomas Rogers, and among others the Anglican parson of St. Mary's, Stoke Newington, founded a weekly supper club which met in rotation in members' homes. Knowing the later views of Rogers and Price, it is not difficult to imagine the conversations taking radical turns.

Still more likely to be of a radical inclination were the conversations of the Honest Whigs to which Burgh and Price also belonged. Meeting for dinner every other Thursday at the London Coffeehouse, Ludgate Hill, the club was active during the Middlesex election controversy. Boswell recorded a visit to it on September 21, 1769. An American named Benjamin Franklin belonged to it, along with Dr. Joseph Jeffries, a "supporter of the

Bill of Rights [Society]," William Rose, a Chiswick schoolmaster who was co-editor of the *Monthly Review*, Joseph Priestley, Andrew Kippis, and Theophilus Lindsey, among others. In religion predominantly Dissenting, and in politics strongly radical, this group must have listened sympathetically to Burgh's ideas, and perhaps furnished him with some. Possibly from Franklin he heard of American experiments with political activism. Possibly Sawbridge's sister Catherine and Thomas Rogers, his Newington Green neighbor, strengthened the anti-aristocratic bias so evident in Burgh's complaints against the managers of the electoral system. Rogers once warned his children against having anything to do with the aristocracy and recommended his own determination to avoid social contacts with them.*

Retired from teaching since the end of 1771 but still contributing the substantial sum of three guineas a year to the Chapel on the Green, Burgh was working hard to complete a major work on politics. Only the first volume of *Political Disquisitions* appeared before the general election; the second came later in 1774; the third, in which the idea of association was developed after only being mentioned in the first volume, did not appear until 1775. If it did not influence events of 1769–1774, the book reflected them, drew upon them, and was available to influence the radical movement of the 1780's. Burgh said that political knowledge was to be extracted from the "inexhaustible mine" of history, and that could mean very recent history. In any case, the *Political Disquisitions* provides a means of understanding the tendencies of radical thought after five years of chronic excitement in the metropolis.

Burgh desired to purify the unrepresentative and corrupt electoral system. He recommended the franchise for all taxpayers, and this meant essentially all men not in receipt of poor relief or alms. Thereby the imbalance in favor of landed property would

---

* Ironically Rogers' son Samuel, the poet, in the next century courted the aristocracy diligently and somewhat successfully, and became famous for his literary breakfasts at his house in St. James's. He lived off inherited money and the income from his share in the family bank which his brother Henry obligingly managed so that Samuel was free to devote the last sixty years of his long life to scrambling up the social ladder.

be corrected and the commercial and manufacturing interests would have a louder voice in public affairs. Further, Burgh desired annual elections and secret ballot. He sought ultimately the independence of Parliament. If the persuasion of reason did not suffice, a national association organized on the parish level up through county committees should exert pressure upon Parliament. If the weight of public opinion was not enough, Burgh suggested the possibility of even forcible means to direct Members of Parliament to their duty.* Burgh's remedy indicated that he did not expect much from Parliament unless outside persuasion were exerted through extra-parliamentary political associations. Otherwise his reform program was that of the urban radicals with whom he associated. His most significant contribution to late eighteenth century political science was the idea of association.

The Bill of Rights Society in the meantime had put together a miscellany of old and recent ideas. Combining them with the plan of exacting pledges, the Society offered an eleven-point program to impose upon candidates. Wilkes and John Glynn, the successful candidates for the County of Middlesex and three of the four winners of the London seats, including Sawbridge, took the pledge. The program they promised to support included the following provisions: redress of grievances before granting supplies; a law requiring candidates to take an oath against bribery; "full and equal representation of the people in parliament"; annual elections; prohibition by law of pensions and places; impeachment of ministers who had advised the violation of the rights of Middlesex electors; an inquiry into the conduct of judges toward juries; an inquiry into the expenditure of public money; expungement of the Commons' resolution for imprisoning the London magistrates in the printers' case; attention to the grievances of Ireland; and restoration to America of the "essential right of taxation."

If five of the eight metropolitan seats were won in the election

* In 1785 Dr. Price expressed to the Society for Constitutional Information his conviction of the legality of a National Congress in Ireland for the purpose of promoting reform of the Irish Parliament.

of 1774 by men who pledged to support this program, in the House of Commons they were virtually alone. The cause of parliamentary reform receded. It was too radical for an age which accepted the ancient assumption that property rather than people was the appropriate object of representation. Sawbridge's panacea of annual Parliaments was not incompatible with this assumption, and could obtain a hearing. When he made his motion in 1775, about one hundred members supported it. But in the following year when Wilkes moved for leave to bring in a bill for parliamentary reform he was badly defeated. In Parliament there was no more talk of it for five years.

But men outside of Parliament kept the idea alive. None did more to this end than Major John Cartwright. His indefatigable advocacy of the cause of parliamentary reform for the last fifty years of his life (he died in 1824) encourages the opinion that he must have been an eccentric, but such an opinion does an injustice to a remarkable man. He came from a good county family, served with some distinction in the navy during and after the Seven Years War, and then as the quarrel with the American colonies developed he sided openly with them, refusing to fight against them though he was a major in his county militia. He was able to link the American controversy with the idea of parliamentary reform, and in his famous pamphlet of 1776, *Take Your Choice!*, he argued for a radical reform of Parliament as a cure for the nation's ills at home and abroad.

His reform program ranged far ahead of the thinking of most of his radical associates of the 1770's and 1780's. It was more comprehensive than that of even the working class reformers of the 1790's. It only found full expression in the Chartist program of the 1830's and 1840's and did not attain final statutory enactment until the Parliament Act of 1911 provided salaries for members of the House of Commons. It is not surprising, then, to hear Cartwright advocating the abolition of slavery, the emancipation of Greece from Turkish rule, and the destruction of absolutism in Spain when later those became public issues. Specifically, Cartwright desired annual elections, literal manhood suffrage, secret ballot, payment for members of the Commons, and a redistribution of seats, one to each of 558 equally populated electoral districts.

Cartwright never claimed complete originality. He thought that annual elections and universal suffrage would only restore what a democratic Anglo-Saxon England had known, and lost with the Norman Conquest. And he clearly borrowed from James Burgh the idea of a national association or convention which would act when a corrupt Parliament refused to restore to England her ancient constitution and the lost purity of her civic life. Naïve, perhaps, and to many of his contemporaries hopelessly impractical, Cartwright as much as ever any Englishman deserves credit for his assiduous advocacy of measures that after they were enacted became commonplaces of modern political democracy.

His pertinacity was shared by a few of his radical associates during the early years of the American War. Some of them were Protestant Dissenters who, sensitive to political and religious restrictions laid upon them by statute, could the more readily sympathize with American patriots aggrieved by injustices imposed by the imperial Parliament. They were noble and ardent spirits—Dr. John Jebb, Dr. Richard Price, Dr. Joseph Priestley, Dr. Theophilus Lindsey, Dr. John Disney, Dr. John Aikin, Thomas Day, Thomas Brand Hollis—who with their separate special interests like Priestley's in chemistry, Price's in mathematics, Day's in abhorrence of Negro slavery, or Jebb's in medicine, shared a great love for liberty. They thought it incomplete in England as long as the franchise remained so narrowly restricted and the electoral system could be managed by and in the interest of a few men.

If these men retained the idea of parliamentary reform in their own minds, and talked about it among themselves, they did not after the election of 1774 do much to broaden public support for it. During the first years of the American War, Lord North's government did not suffer from unpopularity, and for a while an upsurge of loyalty supported it. There was an absence of opportunity, of some cause or issue to which a program of reform could attach itself. If the war had gone well for England, even the expenses and burdens it entailed would have been tolerable, and public discontent would not have burgeoned. But the war went badly, and so the attendant burdens seemed heavier. By 1779 dissatisfactions with the management of the national interests by Lord North's government were producing increasingly widespread and bitter criticism. Lord North himself desired to resign but the King would not hear of a change.

In Ireland in 1778 discontents extracted from the English government concessions in the form of relaxations of restrictions upon Catholics and upon Irish trade. These only encouraged the Irish to hope for more. The revival of hope coincided with a remarkable revival of political activity in Ireland. The Volunteer movement, organized first as patriotic organizations for the military defense of Ireland against foreign enemies, quickly converted itself into an extra-parliamentary association seeking political reforms. Its first success was by its agitation to alarm the British government and its second to force at the end of 1779 another installment of commercial concessions from the imperial Parliament. Thenceforth, the Volunteer movement became even more avowedly political in its activities and purposes. This phase of the Irish revival culminated in April 1780. Henry Grattan, one of the most esteemed of all Irish statesmen, delivered a dramatic speech in the Irish Commons. He demanded the independence of the Irish Parliament from British control. Political autonomy implied the possibility of parliamentary reform in Ireland, and so Grattan's demand brought that question into the open.

Simultaneously with the Irish revival there occurred a renewal of the political agitation in England. Once again metropolitan radicalism furnished a lead. In the autumn of 1779 when a death created a vacancy in a Middlesex seat in the House of Commons, a contest between the radicals and the government took place. In the scuffle the Wilkite candidate had to acquiesce in disqualification on a technicality but the government candidate withdrew, pleading fear of mob violence. In the end the seat was filled by a choice of the radicals. Not content with their victory, they decided to publicize their cause, claiming that government had impinged upon freedom of election as it had a decade before. Another attempt was made to arouse the counties and the freeholders, and Middlesex took the lead by framing a petition to the House of Commons. When it was presented on December 10, Lord North managed the debate very skillfully; his affable manner disarmed his opponents; the business fell flat.

If the cry for freedom of election failed to create a storm, other discontents existed, other agitations were gathering, and other remedies were being advocated. When the Middlesex freeholders met on December 20, a date fixed a month before, they were presented with a remarkable document. Prepared by Dr. John Jebb, it combined in mature form the idea of association suggested earlier by James Burgh and by the examples of the county meetings of 1769 and by the Irish Volunteers. Jebb desired a national organization composed of delegates from standing committees in the counties. With its membership apportioned according to population, this body must be superior to the unrepresentative House of Commons. Therefore, if circumstances required, it could supersede the Commons, with its decisions becoming law when accepted by the House of Lords and the King. Literally revolutionary, Jebb's scheme, for all of its naïveté, attempted to give institutional form to the potent idea of the sovereignty of the people.

The sense of the times was better represented by another movement that took form even while the Middlesex radicals were failing in their search for an issue. While they talked about liberty and rights, other men worried about material things like the mounting public debt and the wastage of public money caused by war and extravagances in the public service. The word extravagances is a euphemism for excessive pensions and places or favoritism in the management of government loans and contracts. In a word, these men foresaw heavy taxes.

It was possible for social philosophers to relate these evils to an even more ominous one, the alleged decline of the population of England and Wales. Thus, Dr. Price in *An Essay on the Present State of Population.* . . . , published first in 1779, attributed the decline to the increase of the armed forces, to emigration, enclosures, high prices, the pursuit of luxuries, and to rising debts and taxes. In the next year, he collaborated with John Horne [Tooke] in writing *Facts: Addressed to the Landholders, Stockholders, Merchants* . . . [and others]. Generally they accused the North government of mismanaging the nation's finances. These pamphlets harmonized with a swelling volume of criticism against government voiced by people who had a stake in the country and votes in parliamentary elections. Some who desired what came to be called economical reform thought it could be achieved only by reform (and purification) of the representative system, but others thought that even the existing representative system could be made to enact economical reform. For a short time, however, the movement for economical reform won the support both of friends and opponents of parliamentary reform.

In the House of Commons on December 15, 1779, Edmund Burke opened the subject.* An enemy of parliamentary reform, he gave notice of his intention to introduce a bill for economical reform which would not only save money for the taxpayers but would reduce the political influence of the crown. This is not to say that the idea of economical reform originated with Burke. On this point, he said that he *"met it on the way"* while he was pursuing the interest of the people according to his own notions. In fact when he met the idea it was already well on its way to London from Yorkshire. There, during the preceding month, Christopher Wyvill, a remarkable Anglican clergyman, and three of his friends had begun to form what became a national movement. Independently of Jebb, though perhaps like him influenced by James Burgh and Major Cartwright, they planned to organize Yorkshire, first to protest the waste of public money, then to encourage similar associations in other counties, and eventually to bring a great national pressure to bear upon Parliament and the government. Wyvill, however, had no intention of stopping with economical reform; his ultimate goal was a reform of Parliament, though one compatible with representation of property.

With the ground work laid, a meeting was held in York on December 30, 1779. It adopted a petition praying for an end to the

* On the same day the House of Lords, as it had a week earlier, rejected resolutions on the subject of extravagances in the public service, but decided to inquire into the nation's finances at a later date.

waste of public money and for the reduction of the influence of the crown. The Marquis of Rockingham, the political magnate of Yorkshire and the head of the largest and best organized opposition group in Parliament, worried along with Burke and other members of the party about their proper relationship to the developing Yorkshire movement. Burke had in a sense already committed the party to parliamentary action. Rockingham, aware of anti-aristocratic sentiment in the Wyvill camp, feared to alienate the gentlemen and merchants of his county. He attended the meeting of December 30 and quietly indicated his support for economical reform. He was in no position to oppose the decision to form a committee of correspondence which would bring county associations into agreement to instruct Parliament in its duty.

However distasteful it was to many of the Rockingham politicians, the Yorkshire movement was far less radical or ambitious than Dr. Jebb's scheme for a body that might have to supersede Parliament. Yet for the time being the Yorkshire reformers and the metropolitan radicals tried to act as though they agreed. The Middlesex meeting of January 7, 1780, if it did not repudiate Jebb, at any rate passed by his ideas when it adopted a petition identical with that of Yorkshire. It also resolved to support the plan for an association to promote economical reform. The Yorkshire meeting, its Middlesex counterpart, and the meetings of the other counties in which the idea of the association was spreading, demonstrated their lack of confidence in mere petitions and therefore in the reasonableness of the Parliament to which petitions were directed.

This much agreement could not disguise the differences, personal and ideological, among the associators. When Charles James Fox became the chairman of the Westminster Committee, he emerged as the rival of Wyvill for the leadership of the movement. Wyvill arrived in London in February to promote and to unify the efforts of the county associations. One result was a convention in mid-March to which came nearly forty delegates from twelve counties and four boroughs. By this time the real intentions of Wyvill were clear, along with the fundamental difference between the Yorkshire movement and the parliamentary followers of Rockingham. The latter were committed to Burke's plan of economical reform which he had explained in the House of Commons on February 11. The bill itself was defeated in committee before the end of March. The Association movement which by its petition had demonstrated its support for economical reform went beyond that. The March convention advocated triennial elections and the addition of a hundred county members to the House of Commons, and it proposed to demand support for these reforms from candidates in the next general election.

The Association program contained only one novel feature. The desire for shorter Parliaments was by this time a standing order among reformers, though there was disagreement as to whether elections ought to be held annually or every three years. The proposal to add county members was new in its particularity. Because county members were thought likelier to remain free of party or crown influence, an addition to their numbers would strengthen the independence and purify the soul of the House of Commons. County voters were freeholders, and county members were country gentlemen. The proposal was also a reaffirmation of the old belief that property, especially landed property, deserved preeminence in the representative system. Though the Westminster and Middlesex committees went along with the addition of county members, this was hardly the redistribution of seats or extension of the franchise that the radicals among the reformers desired.

On April 6, in the House of Commons, there was another manifestation of discontent with the political system. It was directed not against the constitutional structure but against the practical workings of politics. The House had under consideration the forty petitions which the Yorkshire movement had inspired. In the course of the debate the eminent barrister John Dunning, a leading opponent of Lord North's ministry, proposed a resolution which caught the government off balance. By a vote of 233–215 the House resolved that the influence of the crown had increased, was increasing, and ought to be diminished. Momentarily stunning as was this victory, Dunning's and certain kindred resolutions remained mere words. The mood which supported them passed away. When the House reassembled after a brief recess occasioned by the Speaker's illness, the government recovered its authority, aided in part by a split among the opposition. It was one thing to express dislike of crown influence and quite another to reform the electoral system in order to reduce it. Rockingham party members disagreed among themselves; for example, Burke was uneasy about the intimacy between Fox and the Westminster radicals.

Not only as the chairman of the Westminster Committee but as its adopted candidate for the coming general election, Fox was pledged to support parliamentary reform. When he appointed a subcommittee of the Westminster Committee to frame a program, he virtually dictated the result by naming to it Jebb, Cartwright, and Thomas Brand Hollis. By this inexplicable action Fox identified himself with a program more extreme than his own preferences. The plan, published on July 12, fixed the object of the extreme radicals for a century to come, anticipating almost precisely the letter of the Chartist program of the 1830's. Restating the Cartwright position, it called for universal manhood suffrage, annual Parliaments, equal electoral districts, single member constituencies, secret ballot, salaries for M. P.'s and abolition of the property qualification for membership in Parliament.

It is easy to read more into this program than the subcommittee of 1780 intended to put into it. The middle-class, doctrinaire radicals of the 1780's, though inspired both by their misconceptions of the Anglo-Saxon constitution and by the clichés of the Rights of Man philosophy, still assumed that certain social and traditional limitations would continue to qualify their political language. The abolition of property qualifications for M. P.'s meant only the repeal of the Act of 1710; it was not expected that propertyless men, any more than before that Act, which was never, would win election to the House. Rather the repeal would make eligible men who owned other kinds of property than land. Nor was it expected that salaries for members would enable working men to take time off from manual employments to sit in St. Stephen's. The idea that members of the lower orders would ever be elected to the Commons was totally beyond eighteenth century comprehension. Salaries might contribute to the independence of the House by rendering members more nearly immune to the blandishments of governmental patronage. Finally, with Cartwright a notable exception, most of the radicals did not intend that the phrase "universal manhood suffrage" would embrace all of the lower orders. It was meant to refer to householders and thus ratepayers, or people who contributed something to the support of local government, and not to the members of the lower orders who received support under the poor laws or who occupied the menial stations in the households of the middle and upper classes. Universal manhood suffrage would have broadened the franchise down into the borderlands where the lower middle class began to merge into the lower orders, but it would not have given the vote to every adult male by virtue of his being a man. The concept of the individual as a "free agent" still controlled the radical interpretation of the Rights of Man.*

This limiting assumption did not eliminate the significant differences between the Westminster Committee and the Yorkshire Association. The latter accepted the traditional structure of politics with its emphasis upon representation of interests and property, especially identified with land, though it would broaden the basis of representation by extending a somewhat larger place to the mercantile element. The political aims of the Yorkshire Association reflected the social philosophy of country gentlemen, albeit gentlemen who admitted that the electoral system was too

* It is not amiss to refer to the French Revolutionaries in this connection. Their Declaration of the Rights of Man and Citizen in 1789 seemed to be conceived of universals and absolutes, but it was in fact, as George Rudé has said, "essentially a manifesto of the revolutionary bourgeoisie and its clerical and liberal-aristocratic allies." When implemented by the several laws that became the Constitution of 1791, the inconsistencies became clearer. To take one matter. The Constitution distinguished between active and passive citizens. Only the former could vote, and there were progressively higher property qualifications for voting in the two stages of the electoral process and for eligibility to the Legislative Assembly. It has been estimated that in the first stage of the electoral process perhaps 70 per cent of the adult (over twenty-five years of age) males could vote. Domestic servants could not be active citizens; as in England, they were considered as lacking free agency.

narrowly based. The urban radicals desired precise arithmetical representation of people and, allowing for the limitations upon the franchise, implied readiness to accept majoritarian government. The differences were fundamental. Temporary cooperation with the Yorkshire Association had not brought metropolitan radicalism into basic agreement with the country gentlemen.

This fact was reemphasized when the London radicals organized quite separately from either the Yorkshire or Westminster Committee. In April 1780 the same men who dominated the Westminster subcommittee were among the group who founded the Society for Constitutional Information. This was the realization of a proposal made two years earlier by Cartwright when he suggested a "Society of Political Enquiry." In 1794 when John Horne Tooke was on trial for high treason, Major Cartwright appeared as a witness for the defense. He was asked about the SCI because Tooke belonged to it and because the Society was active in the reform agitation of that later time. Its object, said Cartwright, was "to give Constitutional Information to the public, particularly, and expressly, for the purpose of promoting a parliamentary reform for the recovery of their lost rights." So far as Cartwright knew, this original object had never been changed. While most members preferred annual Parliaments and universal suffrage, he testified, they would accept less if that was all they could obtain.

The Minutes of the Society detail its origin and activities from April 1780 up to the last entry on May 9, 1794. Among the fourteen men who organized the society were such devoted and dogmatic Lockians as Hollis, Cartwright and Jebb. Along with them were the respectable physician and friend of Burke, Richard Brocklesby; the barrister and disciple of Jebb, Capell Lofft, who was a great admirer of the seventeenth century apostle of liberty, Algernon Sidney; the Rousseauean author of *History of Sandford and Merton* and the foe of slavery, Thomas Day; the playwright Richard Brinsley Sheridan who was just entering politics; and John Frost, a barrister, who for advocating reform would be convicted in 1793 for uttering seditious words and imprisoned for six months. Meeting first at number 403, the Strand, and later in their own rooms in Tavistock Street, Covent Garden, the Society early formalized its existence. The minimum annual subscription was one guinea a year; life membership was fifty guineas. Clearly this was no lower-class organization. New members were admitted upon nomination and formal balloting. Four times a year there was a general meeting, as much social as business, and in December at the annual audit dinner the members received an accounting of the year's activity and of the state of the Society's finances. The weekly meetings from October to May and the monthly meetings in the summer were those of the committee for printing and correspondence.

This committee was the heart of the Society and carried on its main function. The members dedicated themselves to the great work of educating England in the history, traditions, and doctrines of liberty. From the start they maintained an ambitious program of printing and distributing contemporary, recent, and older works or extracts relating to politics, political philosophy, and public affairs generally. The costs were borne by the membership fees and occasional *ad hoc* subscriptions by the members. If the Yorkshire movement was an immediate stimulus, the Society had its roots in the earlier Bill of Rights Society of the Wilkite agitations, and these were nourished by exciting events like the American Revolution and the Irish Volunteer Movement. The Society thought that Britain had made "unjustifiable attempts" on American rights, and it viewed with pleasure the desires of the Irish Volunteers to obtain parliamentary reform. The latter movement was considered a fruitful example of the theory and practice of political association for the purpose of agitating a good cause. While the SCI was not itself a national association, it encouraged the association idea. In 1780 and later it communicated with various kinds of societies. During the anti-Catholic Gordon Riots in June 1780 the SCI encouraged private citizens to organize for the purpose of protecting property.

Always eager to extend liberty, and watchful of potential infringements upon it, the SCI was able to find the cause of liberty at stake in many matters. It supported later efforts to repeal the Test and Corporation Acts which imposed religious tests for holding certain national and municipal offices, including seats in Parliament. This was not so much because members were Romanist in sympathy as that these laws effectively excluded Protestant Dissenters from English public life, and Dissenters were prominent in the SCI as they were generally in the struggle for liberty. When there was talk in 1784 of creating a London police force, the SCI protested. It formed a committee to watch the progress of Pitt's bill for this purpose and particularly to be alert for any regulations that might affect unfavorably the liberties of the people or tend to establish a military police system under control of the crown.

But steadfastly its leading interest was reform of Parliament. Never in agreement with all details of the plan drawn up by some of its members for the Westminster Committee in the spring of 1780, the SCI could agree that a reform of Parliament was in the tradition of English liberty. It is important to observe that all of this occurred a decade before the French Revolution. English Jacobinism was not French in its immediate inspirations nor of the eighteenth century in its remoter ones. Its origins were in the commonwealth tradition of the seventeenth century, and the members were fully conscious of the British ancestry of their radicalism. Their publishing program was intended to make Englishmen proudly aware of the island sources of their love of liberty. In the first nine months of its existence the SCI spent eighty-four pounds ten shillings and eight pence to this end. At the audit dinner of December 12, 1780, where this accounting was rendered, the SCI pledged anew its love of liberty. Members toasted:

The Majesty of the People

The Genuine British Constitution

Magna Carta

Annual Parliaments

Charles Fox and the Independent Electors of Westminster.

A month later, to be specific, the Society resolved to support the Duke of Richmond's plan for "annual, equal and universal Representation of the Commons."

To win reform by breaking through the existing electoral

structure to gain control of Parliament would be a hard struggle. The election of 1780 made that clear. It followed shortly upon the ominous Gordon Riots of June. With these was identified the Protestant Association, the most dangerous pressure group of the time. Its prominence encouraged many persons to believe that an extra-parliamentary association could threaten the existence of the constitution just as the Protestant Association had threatened the physical existence of London. "The total effect of the Gordon Riots, however, was to make the average Englishman a little more afraid of playing with fire."

For this and other reasons, it seemed shrewd politics for Lord North to dissolve Parliament and ask for a general election. To the extent that there was a contest between the government and the parliamentary opposition, Lord North retained control of the Commons even while suffering defeats in some open constituencies and larger ones. The radicals were humiliated. They lost outside the metropolitan area. Cartwright was defeated at Nottingham on the reform issue. Westminster returned Fox but it also returned Admiral Rodney, the government candidate who was in service in the West Indies. Sawbridge lost in London though he regained a seat three months later at a by-election. Altogether, radicals won nine of twelve seats in the metropolitan area, but that was the center and total of their strength. Sir George Savile, prominent both in the Yorkshire Association and in the Rockingham party, summed up by saying that the temper of the times was uncongenial to reform.

The Yorkshire Committee refused to be discouraged. On January 3 and 4, 1781, they met at York Tavern to choose and instruct delegates to a projected London convention. Anticipating the demands of London radicals, the meeting instructed the delegates to oppose universal suffrage, a "theoretical, but unattainable Perfection," and to advocate instead economical reform and a mild parliamentary reform—shorter Parliaments, not more than three years, and the addition of one hundred county members to the House of Commons. This would correct the imbalance caused by the representation of rotten boroughs and give appropriate weight to the landed and commercial interests, especially the former which the Committee, curiously enough, thought was underrepresented. Beyond that the Committee defended the idea of association as a necessary means of achieving the reform which had to be won if liberty was to be preserved. When the London convention met, only eight counties were represented; excepting Yorkshire's, most of the forty delegates were from London or the adjoining counties. The convention was not as extreme as Yorkshire had feared. In a mood of caution the convention repledged allegiance to the Yorkshire program and to economical reform. It agreed that the influence of the crown was evil. The House of Commons rejected the convention's petition and expressed its contempt for Sawbridge's annual motion more by the absenteeism of members than by the vote of 95–29 which defeated it.

It was now the turn of the metropolitan reform leaders to demonstrate tenacity. They optimistically thought of the twelve seats in Commons occupied by members for London, Westminster, Southwark, Middlesex and Surrey, nine of them by reformers, as a potential leaven of the whole house. It was important to act in unison. To that end and thinking of expanding their influence outwards, committees from these constituencies began to meet in plenary sessions to plan for the future. A "fair and equal representation in parliament" was their panacea for the ills of the times, such as the American War. The term Quintuple Alliance, apparently used first by Dr. John Jebb, described the group and further distinguished it from the Yorkshire Movement. As the voice and conscience of English radicalism the Quintuple Alliance remained alive during the next three years in contempt of the coolness of the House of Commons towards reform.

The tribulations of the reformers did not mean apathy in factional politics. The autumn of 1781 and the winter were exciting because Lord North's government was at bay. The organized parliamentary groups gained the support of the independent gentlemen against a government which now was accused of losing a war and sinking the nation into burdensome debt, humiliation, and decline. The government died a miserable death. At the end of March 1782 the Rockingham ministry replaced it, pledged to a program of reform. But not parliamentary reform, even though Fox and the Duke of Richmond as avowed radicals and Shelburne as a supporter of the Yorkshire program were members of it. The new ministry owed debts not to the radicals, but to the independent gentlemen who had shifted their support to the corps which had opposed the late government. The Rockingham ministry enacted Burke's program for economical reform, as well as certain other measures designed to purify parliamentary life; parliamentary reform got no more than an airing on young William Pitt's unsuccessful motion for a Committee of Inquiry into the subject.

Rockingham's death on July 1 and the accession of Shelburne, with Pitt in the cabinet, encouraged the reformers. Wyvill especially took heart. His efforts to revive the counties, however, where they did not meet apathy encountered the distaste of many persons for the metropolitan radicals or the hostility of the radicals themselves. Once again the reformers were in disagreement. The SCI, revived after its slump in the fall of 1781, was able to report on January 10, 1783, of its recent "augmentation"; fifty-three members attended the audit dinner. Momentarily affluent, the Society was actively circularizing the counties. It sent out, for example, two thousand copies of the Duke of Richmond's *Letter to the High Sheriff of Sussex.* In it Richmond urged universal suffrage and annual Parliaments. Certain members were appointed to circulate tracts in particular counties. These efforts quickly used up the accumulated surplus and in May, when the Society numbered 169 members, it had to take up a subscription for extraordinary expenses. Thomas Rogers subscribed five guineas, as did his pastor Dr. Richard Price. Concurrently the Society studied the state of representation, deriving information from correspondents who sent in "well authenticated facts respecting the Boroughs of this Kingdom." Agreement about the facts could not assuage disagreements about their meanings.

When reform came before the Commons under Pitt's auspices in May 1783 the political situation had changed. Shelburne's government no longer existed; Pitt was a private member in opposition to the ministry; the "monstrous" coalescence of Fox with Lord North had forced the metropolitan radicals to reconsider their relations with their former friend, the member for Westminster. Pitt's proposal, stated in general terms, only went part of the distance the radicals wanted to travel. While Fox supported it, his colleague Lord North led the opposition against it. The proposal was beaten by a vote of about 2 to 1. The 149 votes in favor of it suggest that the House of Commons' thinking ran ahead of the electorate's. Still the majority vote was decisive. Three days later Sawbridge's perennial motion for shorter Parliaments sustained its annual defeat. The radicals rationalized their failure in the moderation of Pitt's resolutions. Wyvill chastized the doctrinaire radicals for rushing off in all directions instead of joining in support of a clearly formulated and practical program. Wyvill was embarrassed by political problems in Yorkshire where some gentlemen who subscribed to the old Rockingham connection found it difficult to ride Roman style. And in the House of Commons where Pitt led the opposition to the Fox-North coalition, many of the Rockingham party were identified with this coalition. Bravely facing up to the facts, the normally optimistic SCI resigned themselves to a long campaign against the "two intolerable grievances—inadequate Representation and long Parliaments. . . ."

Hardly had the SCI uttered this gloomy sentiment when the skies brightened. In December 1783 the Fox-North coalition came to an unexpected though planned end, and the King at once invited Pitt to form a government. The reformers were overjoyed even though they realized that the accession of Pitt did not guarantee enactment of a reform bill. The general election of 1784 gave to them an opportunity to place him under obligation, for example to Wyvill, whose support in Yorkshire was important. The Quintuple Alliance came out openly for reform as an election issue. Sir Cecil Wray, outgoing President of the SCI, lost in the Westminster contest, being denounced by Fox as an associate of radicals whose program was subversive of the constitution. In the metropolitan area Pitt's supporters won ten of the twelve seats, the other two going to Fox and Sawbridge. A desire for moderation rather than radical reform could therefore be expected from M. P.'s for the metropolis when the question of reform was an issue. Elsewhere parliamentary reform was not the great issue and Pitt's victory in the election was not a mandate for reform.

Though he intended to pursue this aim, and assured Wyvill that he would, Pitt could not speak for all of his parliamentary following. They recognized no duty to support reform for the sake of parliamentary politics. Outside Parliament there was little excitement and no significant widespread support for the proposal that Pitt introduced in April 1785. Though the SCI paid for the printing of its text in the newspapers, and supported the bill, some individual members along with Jebb disliked it. Pitt's measure was essentially the Yorkshire program. It would disfranchise thirty-six of the smaller boroughs, distributing their seventy-two seats and twenty-eight others to more populous places and to the counties. This proposal acknowledged the principle that representation should bear some relation to the distribution of population; it also conceded a property interest in representation by providing for compensation to the disfranchised constituencies. In contemplating extension of the county franchise to copyholders, the measure would enlarge the electorate without violating the ancient principle of a property qualification for voting. There was no element of social revolution or proletarianism in Pitt's proposal. If it passed, it would not alter significantly the character of the House of Commons. But it would affect particular interests and groups. It would encourage change. And, said its opponents, it would lead into uncharted political territories. The prestige of Pitt as prime minister counted for little. He did not make the measure a party issue. Beaten 248–174, he narrowed the margin of defeat in comparison with that of 1783, but he gained only twenty-five more votes than he had won as a private member.

The issue of reform seemed dead. When a month later Wyvill at a meeting at Thatched House forced a vote on the desirability of the program Pitt had proposed, he was beaten 63–39. After this, the Yorkshire Movement withered away. Among Wyvill's opponents were radicals and Foxites. Their dissent was not merely factional. The radicals were reasserting disagreement with the Yorkshire program, moderate reform, and continued political domination of the electoral system by the classes who traditionally had controlled it.

The SCI continued even after the defeat of 1785 to carry on its work of public education. Its interests broadened out to embrace all good causes. The Society continued to hope for friendship with America and an enlarged commercial intercourse on "just and equal and liberal terms." * It commended the efforts of certain Irishmen to promote a parliamentary reform in their kingdom. It continued its inquiry into the state of the representation in England, soliciting and receiving descriptions of electoral structures and practices in various constituencies. Occasional lacks of quorums at their meetings did not daunt the members. They joined in the movement to suppress the slave trade; they favored a plan for lazarettos as providing more effective means of quarantine of diseased persons; they desired to abolish impressment for the navy; they viewed with alarm the building of military barracks in various parts of London; they considered the question of applying to the proper authorities to obtain regulations for preventing soldiers from insulting the public in the streets; they resolved that protection of persons and property rested in the civil authorities and in men's natural right of self-defense rather than in the "unnecessary and highly dangerous" use of the military for these purposes. Yet they opposed an effort to provide a police force for London as inimical to liberty. Apparently they had already forgotten the Gordon Riots of 1780. They resolved that extension of the excise laws threatened public liberty. Along the way they had to send letters of reminder to members who were in arrears in paying their subscriptions. They

* The Society for Constitutional Information in 1787 included among its publications an extract from John Adams' *A Defense of the Constitutions of Government of the United States of America.* A year earlier the Society voted thanks to Adams, then the American Minister to the Court of St. James, for the mark of respect he showed to the memory of Dr. Jebb by marching in the funeral procession to the Bunhill Fields burial ground.

also continued to recruit new members, among them in 1787 an honorary member "Mr. Payne (Author of *Common Sense*)," and earlier Thomas Erskine who was destined to win fame as the defense counsel of prosecuted reformers in the 1790's. And at their annual audit dinners they drank numerous, spirited toasts, as in December 1785 at the Shakespeare Tavern in Covent Garden they drank to:

Major Cartwright, the Father of the Society

Annual Parliaments and the people's rights restored

The United States of America

The right of the subject to the possession and use of arms as secured by the Revolution and as asserted by the Irish Volunteers

Fair and equal representation of the Commons

May all true Whigs unite to repeal the Septennial Act

The British Navy

Dr. Franklin, President of the Council of Pennsylvania

Dr. Price

There was a kind of incongruity between the radicals of the 1780's and their program. They thought in universals. Theoretically, every man had a property in his life, his liberty and his labor. He had a right to defend the first two and to dispose of the last as an individual. He also had a right to participate in public life, and if he did not enjoy it, then he had a right to seek enjoyment of it. Thus, the SCI in August 1782 had recommended meetings attended by people of *all classes* in support of their "Common Rights," and had urged these meetings to petition Parliament for reform. Sentiments and expressions like these gave an egalitarian but condescending character to the Society. The nature of its membership and the stories of the members' lives raise doubts about the literalness of their meanings when they talked about associating with people of *all classes*. Invariably the members of the SCI were men of some status. Though they had no objection to corresponding with societies of whatever composition, there was no direct contact between them and the lower orders. The radical movement of the 1780's was not proletarian in any sense of the word. A wide gulf separated its members from the interests of the lower orders. The radicals thought exclusively in political terms; they showed no awareness of social or economic problems or of any relationship between them and the political and constitutional grievances which alone seemed to interest them. Parliamentary reform was an end in itself, not a means of ensuring that Parliament would recognize the economic needs of the lower orders. The movement for economical reform involved the interests of the higher orders who were concerned about confiscatory taxes and waste of public money, not problems of unemployment or social welfare. The economic hardships of the working classes were not the springs of the reform movement of the 1780's, and any connection between them was coincidental, not purposeful. If in the long run a reformed Parliament might be obligated to heed the demands of the working classes, this was a result neither contemplated nor intended by the reformers of the 1780's.

This is not to say that the movement for parliamentary reform was selfish or cynical. In the late eighteenth century, economic thought was already beginning to question whether the national government could or should concern itself with remedies for the problems of poverty other than to encourage some methods of alleviating distress by placing the burden on local authorities. The reformers simply did not think twentieth century thoughts; they represented the views and the aspirations that were possible to men of their times. If they did not extend their views to the full economic implications of the political doctrines they espoused, they broke through the limitations of tradition in a way that was profoundly significant for the future, and this under native English inspirations, not under the stress of the French Revolution.

Without realizing either the long run or the short run potentialities of what they had done, the radicals of the 1780's had seriously challenged the ancient assumptions about representation and the franchise. In 1776 Wilkes was still attached to the doc-

trine of "free agency," though he broadened it considerably to
include mechanics, peasants and day laborers. But this definition
still referred to property. In that same year Major Cartwright
went all the way. When he advocated universal suffrage in his
pamphlet *Take Your Choice!* he took care to be explicit, and he
expanded his discussion the next year in his *The Legislative
Rights of the Commonalty Vindicated.* God has "made men
equal, as well as free; . . . There are, therefore, no distinctions to
be made among men, or just causes for the elevation of some
above the rest, prior to mutual agreement. However much soever
any individual may be qualified for, or deserve any elevation, he
hath no right to it till it be conferred on him by his fellows." "It
is liberty, and not dominion, which is held by divine right." "Personality is the sole foundation of being represented; . . . property has, in reality, nothing to do in the case. The property of
any one, be it more, or be it less, is totally involved in the man."
Property should have the attention of Members of Parliament
"but it contributes nothing to his right of having that representation." * In somewhat plainer language, Cartwright said that every
man should have a vote "for a legislative-guardian, which is the
birth-right of us all."

Passing over the confusion as to whether those "pilfered
rights" of annual Parliaments and equal representation were God-
given or inherited from the Anglo-Saxon (who may have received them from God), there is no doubt that universal manhood suffrage meant literally that to Cartwright. Two qualifications are still necessary, however. He did not expect that the
lower orders would take control of the House of Commons; he
said that their habits of deference and jealousy among themselves
would force them to vote for members of the upper classes rather
than raise any of their fellows into Parliament. Cartwright's support for equal rights did not quite make him an egalitarian. He
recognized differences in the qualifications of men for seats in
Parliament, but he also thought that men who were not qualified

* In his pamphlet *The People's Barrier Against Undue Influences and
Corruptions* (1780) Cartwright specifically advocated abolition of the
property qualification for membership in the House of Commons.

for seats were qualified to determine who ought to occupy them. And Cartwright abstracted politics from social and economic life.

From this time forward, reformers had to explain themselves. If they talked of universal suffrage and personal representation, as the Duke of Richmond or Dr. Jebb soon came to do, it was possible now to think that some of them meant to be understood literally. While none of the reform proposals that came before Parliament in the 1780's embodied these terms, the breach with tradition had nevertheless taken place. Even before the French Revolution gave new impetus to parliamentary reform, English radicalism out of its own resources had produced this extreme political demand. It is not necessary to read French Jacobin influence into the demand of the London Corresponding Society in 1792 "that every adult person, in possession of his reason, and not incapacitated by crimes, should have a vote for a Member of Parliament." This was radicalism of the home grown variety and it was defined during the decade preceding the French Revolution.

The Revolution had its effect, not upon the content of radical thought but upon the spirit and character of radicalism and upon the social composition of the movement. The Revolution also stimulated a reaction against reform that made the decade of the 1790's different from the 1780's. In the end it created an atmosphere within which reasoned discussion of political and constitutional reform became temporarily impossible.

CHAPTER IV

THE GLORIOUS HARVEST

OF LIBERTY

TRADITION attributes to the defeat of Pitt's bill the beginning of a period of apathy in English public life that suddenly ended with the exhilarating news of the fall of the Bastille in Paris on July 14, 1789. Wyvill in 1786 was able only to hope for better things while he saw "the Party for Political Reformation . . . weak and dispirited" and his Yorkshire Association dissolving around him. Retroactively the exaggerated expressions of joy over the news from France in 1789 make the preceding years seem duller of interest or more devoid of efforts at improving works than in fact they were. Parliamentary reform was not, after all, the only cause to engage men's virtues and energies. Various measures, proposed or accomplished, demonstrated that now one interest and then another thought change both necessary and possible.

Technical and prosaic in detail but significant in their ultimate meaning, the reforms in the management of public finance begun in 1780 by Lord North were carried forward by Pitt. Hoary clerks, comfortable in the recesses of their offices and superior in their knowledge of arcane, antique procedures, feared the administrative improvements which ushered the public services into the age of the industrial revolution. So too the old trade policy came under scrutiny. The acceptance in 1787 of a commercial treaty with France gave a foretaste of the spirit that in another fifty years would replace protectionism by free trade, justified by

England's achievement of industrial supremacy. Obviously these signs were not read so easily by contemporaries as they are by historians having the advantage of the perspective of time. They signify nevertheless that the new interests and pressures which forced these changes might not remain contented with the traditional structure of politics. Wyvill, hoping for "favourable events" to advance the cause of "political reformation," did not foresee that constitutional changes would not remain exclusively political decisions.

Neither was change entirely a matter of economic determinism. When the socially prominent religious writer Hannah More in 1788 said that "the moral and intellectual scene about us begins to brighten," she was thinking of the examples set for society by the "Great." These were people like William Wilberforce who, moved by love of humanity and aversion against brutality, tried to ameliorate the conditions of unfortunates. The humanitarian spirit was not new or unique to these years just before the French Revolution, but it was unusually active. Between 1785 and 1790, according to the list in Ford K. Brown's *Fathers of the Victorians*, besides a half-dozen medical charities including the National Truss Society for the Relief of the Ruptured Poor, there were founded:

> The Society for the Support and Encouragement of Sunday Schools
>
> The Benevolent or Strangers' Friend Society
>
> The Society of Universal Good Will
>
> The Lock Asylum for the Reception of Penitent Females
>
> The Society for the Abolition of the Slave Trade
>
> The Philanthropic Society founded for the Prevention of Crime
>
> The Society for the Relief of Poor, Pious Clergymen, of the Established Church, Residing in the Country
>
> The Society for Carrying into Effect his Majesty's Proclamation Against Vice and Immorality

And founded during the preceding decade, the Society for the Discharge and Relief of Persons Imprisoned for Small Debts remained very active, if one may trust the newspaper accounts of its meetings. Of these organizations, the most spectacular was the Society for the Abolition of the Slave Trade. In 1788 it made its initial parliamentary effort, the first in a series of defeats until 1807 when the three-hundred-year-old slave trade which involved so many vested interests was declared illegal.

In the same year as the founding of this society, the Test and Corporation Acts came under attack. These Acts, more than a century old, were to many persons the bastions of the Established Church, the means of protecting the nation against levellers and republicans, of preserving the endowments of the Church of England, and of securing the ancient constitution of King, Lords, Commons, and Church. It would be difficult to imagine less likely levellers than the substantial, propertied merchants, bankers and "Gentlemen" (beneficiaries or embodiments of bourgeois business success) who organized the campaign against the Test and Corporation Acts. Yet Lord North could, and as Chancellor of Oxford University he spoke for those who thought the Church in danger. So did Sir William Dolben, an ardent foe of the slave trade, a steady proponent of parliamentary reform, an advocate of relief for insolvent, imprisoned debtors, but M. P. for Oxford University. Faithful to his constituency, Dolben worked to preserve the Anglican political monopoly which the Test and Corporation Acts created. He opposed the ambitions of Protestant Dissenters who desired to take official places in local and national public life or to know at least that the law would not bar them if they wished to participate.

The quiet staff work that organized the campaign was supplied by a remarkable group, the Protestant Dissenting Deputies, unremarked in the history textbooks. This body, which still exists, was formed in 1732 expressly to work for repeal of the Test and Corporation Acts. It was composed of two members elected annually by each Presbyterian (or Unitarian), Independent and Baptist congregation in London and its environs; the Deputies chose from among themselves a committee of twenty-one which in turn named the officers. Indirectly the Deputies represented the interests of Dissenters throughout the British Isles, and until the American Revolution spoke also for their colonial brethren. Skillfully and calmly if not always immediately successfully, they worked to remove the numerous, vexatious restrictions which kept Dissenters in the order of second class citizens, notwithstanding qualifications of wealth, intelligence and education which so many of them as individuals possessed.

The task of molding opinion against the Test Acts, as on other public issues like parliamentary reform, was to a large extent assumed by the Dissenting clergy. Heirs of a tradition as old as Puritanism, these clergymen were loyal to it; as their ancestors had done to Hobbes' distaste, they also made their pulpits the platforms from which to expound political teachings. Their sermons and writings carried great force, coming as they did from men who were preaching the word of God, and their congregations were able to find in their political doctrines the sanction not only of education and intelligence but of divine authority. Even in a day when newspapers and periodicals were assuming a larger share of the work of political education, the contribution of the Dissenting pulpit remained important.

In 1787, thinking the times propitious for another attempt to repeal the Acts, the Deputies made their greatest effort. Their Committee of Correspondence maintained liaison with local committees throughout the country, and a specially formed United Committee conducted the campaign. Henry Beaufoy agreed to lead in the Commons. Born to Quaker parents, educated by Dissenters at Warrington Academy, but now a member of the Established Church, Beaufoy was in the words of the Reverend Dr. Andrew Kippis "a true friend to religious and civil liberty." His speech of March 28, 1787, impressed the memoirist Nathaniel Wraxall as one of the greatest he had ever heard in Parliament. Prejudice and fear were too strong; even Pitt thought that repeal of the Corporation Act would make it too easy for too many Dissenters to gain borough seats. If they became too numerous in

Parliament, they would disestablish the Church. By a majority of 78, the House of Commons agreed with Pitt.*

Two years later, the Dissenters tried again, convinced that their effort in 1787 had contained evidence to encourage perseverance. In a smaller house, they lost this time by only 20 votes. This defeat was even more encouraging than that of 1787. The optimistic saw it as one of many signs indicating that better, freer times were just ahead.

Something of this spirit had stimulated the unusually enthusiastic celebrations that marked the centenary of the Glorious Revolution. Because the Norman Conqueror had destroyed the free Anglo-Saxon constitution, according to some persons, and the Stuart kings had frustrated the promises of Magna Carta, it was the Revolution of 1688 that ended the threat of tyranny, made Parliament triumphant, and secured the liberties of Englishmen. It was as though 1688–1689 was year one of England's regenerated constitution; though imperfect it could be improved, and liberty enlarged. The centenary observances were occasions for Englishmen to congratulate themselves upon the wisdom and courage of their ancestors, and occasions also for rededication to the task of completing what their ancestors had left undone.

Especially in the metropolis in 1788 the friends of liberty made memorable days of November 4, the birthday of William III, and November 5, the one hundredth anniversary of his landing in England. Their careful planning went far beyond the usual gestures of the metropolitan Dissenters who seem traditionally on this date to have paid their respects to the memory of the King who helped them gain such liberties as they enjoyed. The Friends of the British Constitution, two hundred strong and largely Scottish Presbyterians, heard the Scottish divine, the Reverend Henry Hunter, D. D., preach at the Scots Church, London-Wall, on the glories of the Revolution. Full of enthusiasm, they dined at the

---

* Along with their passion for liberty, the Dissenters had a strong strain of anti-Popishness. This comes out steadily in their writings and speeches; their proposal in 1787 would not have lifted the burden of the Acts from Roman Catholics.

Paul's Head Tavern where they resolved to meet again a year hence. In Westminster, on November 5, in memory also of the defeat of the Spanish Armada two centuries earlier, one thousand persons attended divine services at St. Margaret's before crowding for dinner into Willis's Rooms, St. James's Square. On this occasion Church of England men expressed their gratitude for their political liberties and for deliverance by England's naval heroes and by William III from the threats of Romanism.

Much more flamboyant was the meeting of November 4 of the Society for the Commemoration of the Glorious Revolution, better known as the Revolution Society. Composed of "friends of civil and religious liberty," both Anglican and Dissenter, who were proud of their Revolution principles, the Society boasted of its descent from one which, they asserted, was founded soon after the Revolution and ever since had commemorated the fourth of November. Many of the members belonged to the SCI and others had been associated with reform efforts. Among them was a strong admixture of Dissenting clergymen and London businessmen. The Society saw this centenary as an opportunity not only for continuing the attack upon the Test and Corporation Acts but also for renewing efforts for parliamentary reform. Two of the leading Dissenting preachers of the metropolis were featured, Dr. Andrew Kippis as preacher at the noonday service at the Old Jewry meeting house, and the militant Dr. Joseph Towers as orator at the dinner at the London Tavern, Bishopsgate Street. Their theme was liberty, both civil and religious, the right of men to enjoy it, and the need to enlarge it. To call attention to this theme, they desired a statute designating December 16, the date of the signing of the Bill of Rights in 1689, as a day of thanksgiving to be observed annually.* And to make clear their meaning, the Revolution Society stated as their principles the sovereignty of the people, the right of revolution, and the rights of private judgment, liberty of conscience, trial by jury, freedom of the press, and freedom of election. They also made plans for a membership drive and a permanent organization.

* Henry Beaufoy introduced such a bill in March 1789. The Commons passed it without enthusiasm; the Lords defeated it on the first reading.

The London *Times* tried hard to disparage these celebrations. It had to report that they were well and enthusiastically attended. Some of the buoyancy, it insisted, was mere drunkenness. Much of the purpose was conspiratorial, the furtherance of republicanism, said the *Times*. The meeting of the Whig Club, it continued, was avowedly factious, for the Club was made up of the parliamentary opposition, the followers of the Duke of Portland and the cronies of Fox who were already wondering whether something political might be made of the illness of George III. The rumors were in fact true. The King was mad. A regency would give power to the Prince of Wales who would surely bring his Opposition friends into office. If the Whig Club thus looked forward to better times, its members looked far back beyond the Revolution of 1688 to Magna Carta. In passing they paid homage to the Revolution in their self-advertised role of temple priests who guarded the ark of the Whig covenant formed by the Revolution Settlement. The toasts at the Crown and Anchor loosened their tongues; they pledged 1500 pounds towards erecting a column in Runnymede where King John had accepted Magna Carta.*

The centenary celebration passed into memory as attention turned to the King. From mid-November until mid-February, the royal malady was the crucial matter to Englishmen. The politicians fought furiously, the metropolis seethed, and the nation waited anxiously upon rumors and news of the King's condition. If he recovered before a regency was defined, Pitt would remain in office; otherwise the Prince of Wales would surely use the influence of the crown in behalf of Fox. On February 19, 1789, the Lord Chancellor announced in the House of Lords that George III was recovering. This ended consideration of the regency bill. On March 10 the King was able to announce his recovery. On St. George's Day, April 23, the nation held thanksgiving services. And for weeks thereafter the politicians ruminated over the Regency Crisis, trying to calculate the magnitude and meaning of the humiliation suffered by what the *Times* called the bankrupt firm of Fox, Burke and Sheridan. In short, the early stages of the

---

* They must have regretted their bibulous generosity. For years their political opponents delighted in reminding them of their unfulfilled pledge.

Revolution in France could not compete for the attention of Englishmen with the excitements of their own politics.

When the Revolution began and for some months afterwards, most Englishmen were not remarkably concerned about it. Among those who chose to pay attention, most seemed willing to congratulate France upon the dawn of her liberty, but with qualifications. Some, like Burke's friend Sir Gilbert Elliot, were pleased to see France too busy with her own affairs to be troublesome to her neighbors; some thought a regenerated France might become strong and dangerous; others, identified by the *Annual Register* as republicans, expected a free France to be a peaceful nation. Edmund Burke, whose last years were so filled with hostility towards the French Revolution, was thinking seriously of retiring from politics as late as July 10, 1789, just four days before the storming of the Bastille. Except for the completion of the impeachment of Warren Hastings, the former Governor-General of India, there seemed to be no great cause that required his continuance in public life.

It was the attack upon the Bastille, with all of its symbolic importance, that at last drew the attention of the world to the French Revolution. Some Englishmen then became rapturous, but not Burke who on August 9 said he would suspend judgment until events in France revealed their meaning more clearly. Fox saw the Revolution as the happiest event the world had ever known; Wordsworth, writing ten years later, remembered that "Bliss was it in that dawn to be alive / But to be young was very Heaven!" Yet it was not until a month after the news of the Bastille reached England that Major Cartwright mentioned the Revolution for the first time in his correspondence. To be sure, he was enthusiastic, hoping that France would imitate while improving upon the British Constitution. The minutes of the SCI are silent about events in France until November 27. Then the Society resolved almost as though between yawns that it could not be indifferent to the "exertions of the Neighbouring Kingdom for regaining to the Community those Rights of Representation the exercise of which had been long lost." The Society also hoped that the French example would stimulate reforms in other countries.

The first attempt publicly to connect events in France with English reform was made by the Revolution Society. Its celebration of November 4, 1789, had a spectacular and new significance. In 1788 members of the Society had marked the centenary of the Glorious Revolution as patriotic, liberty-loving Englishmen. In 1789 they were challenged to become citizens of the world, to join their strivings for liberty with those of oppressed people everywhere and especially with the French whose examples were furthering the cause of freedom throughout the world. At the Old Jewry Meeting House the Society gathered to hear the eminent Unitarian divine, Dr. Richard Price. The small, earnest, quiet man was himself a distinguished citizen of the world— friend of America and of many Americans, holder of an honorary degree from Yale University, member of the philosophical societies of Philadelphia and Boston, recipient of an invitation from the American Congress to accept citizenship and come to the United States, a man whose name "was a passport to the best society of revolutionary Paris," and in the estimation of the French philosopher Condorcet, "one of the formative minds of the century." Price, like Franklin or Jefferson, belonged to that remarkable international community whose members' careers and interests emphasized the unity of the eighteenth century revolutions. For Price, the essentials of freedom were everywhere the same, regardless of political frontiers. He had made this clear in his famous pamphlet of 1776 which supported the American cause. Then he had said that civil liberty was the power of civil society to govern itself by laws of its own making; there could be no legislative authority in the state superior to that which gives it being; the ultimate power resides in the people—"theirs is the only real omnipotence." This was the familiar revolutionary doctrine of the sovereignty of the people, and from it all else flowed.

In his sermon of November 4, 1789, Price elaborated upon this premise, connecting it with the Glorious Revolution and with the Revolution in France. Entitled *A Discourse on the Love of Our Country*, the sermon was not chauvinistic but humane; it appealed not only to the Revolution Society but to lovers of freedom and mankind everywhere. Price repudiated international aggressions: "we ought to consider ourselves as citizens of the world, and take care to maintain a just regard to the rights of other countries." At the same time, people of different nations could assist each other in achieving the blessings of liberty by spreading "just ideas of civil government" and showing how it is "impossible" for people to "submit to governments which, like most of those now in the world, are usurpations on the rights of men, and little better than contrivances for enabling the few to oppress the many." Philosophers since Milton had planted the seeds of these ideas, and they were growing up to a "glorious harvest. To the information they conveyed by their writings we owe those revolutions in which every friend of man is now exulting."

Not only English philosophers but English deeds contributed to the spread of civic enlightenment. The Revolution of 1688 broke "the fetters which despotism had long been preparing for us" and reasserted political principles of universal application:

> The right to resist power when abused.
>
> The right to chuse our own governors; to cashier them for misconduct; and to frame a government for ourselves.

These principles were not fully recognized in English political practice, Price complained. As long as the Test and Corporation Acts remained unrepealed, religious freedom could not exist; as long as Parliament remained unreformed, civil freedom was incomplete.

Price was optimistic. The times were favorable "to all exertions in the cause of civil liberty." Despite advanced age and ill health, he was cheerful. "I have lived to see the rights of men better understood than ever; and nations panting for liberty, which seemed to have lost the idea of it." France was an inspiration— "thirty millions of people, indignant and resolute, spurning at slavery, and demanding liberty with an irresistible voice. . . ." Price was excited, and unnaturally eloquent. "I see the ardor for liberty catching and spreading. . . . Behold, the light you have struck out, after setting America free, reflected to France, and there kindled into a blaze that lays despotism in ashes, and warms and illuminates Europe!" And last, he warned the rulers of Europe—"restore to mankind their rights; and consent to the correction of abuses, before they and you are destroyed together."

The temper and the tone were new. Resoluteness and enthusiasm were in the earlier reform efforts, but now there was also challenge, stridency, even grimness and threat. The English reform effort, hitherto insular or at most British, was linked up with a foreign revolution which by November 1789 was displaying a character of extremism. If some reformers already saw a connection, Price made it his theme. His *Discourse*, more than any reforming expression up to that time, provided opponents of reform with an argument they would not cease to exploit. Henceforth they were defending the British Constitution and the established order of King, Lords, Commons and Church not only from domestic attacks but from foreign threats. It would no longer be a question of resisting improvements, but of preventing the destruction that Price encouraged. The good Dr. Price who helped create controversy died before the darkest period came.

The prevailing sentiment of November 4, 1789, was buoyant enthusiasm. The Revolution Society, still glowing with the warmth of Price's sermon, ("reeking" from the effects of it according to Edmund Burke), gathered at the London Tavern where, with the maverick nobleman Earl Stanhope in the chair, they drank toasts and passed resolutions. Appropriately, Dr. Price moved the congratulatory address to the French National Assembly. The Society, "disdaining national partialities," expressed its "particular satisfaction" over "the glorious example given in FRANCE to encourage other nations to assert the inalienable rights of mankind, and thereby to introduce a general reformation in the governments of EUROPE, and to make the world free and happy."

Price's *Discourse* was published at once and became a bestseller. It was reprinted in Boston, Dublin and Paris. To the original sermon was added an appendix proclaiming the "fundamental principles" of the Revolution Society. These were the sover-

eignty of the people, the right of revolution, and the sacredness of
several civil liberties. Price also added an interesting, ominous recommendation. He urged the establishment of societies "throughout the kingdom upon Revolution principles [meaning the Revolution of 1688], to maintain a correspondence with each other,
and to form that grand concentrated union of the true friends
of public liberty, which may be necessary to maintain its existence." The idea of societies or associations or correspondences
was not novel. But under the new conditions they took on
added meaning, for the communications extended to France—to
the numerous revolutionary societies in Paris and other French
cities, and to the National Assembly itself. Private, reforming
groups seemed to be assuming responsibility for representing
English opinion abroad. As Burke later complained, they tried to
blow up the fulminations of a vocal, radical minority into the au-
thentic voice of the British nation.

Of the kinds of societies Price recommended, one already existed. With the prestige of its ten-year history to support it, the
SCI began to reassert itself after an interval of relative quies-
cence. Individual members had been prominent in the activities
of the Revolution Society, for there was considerable duplication
of membership. But in its associative capacity the SCI had said little about parliamentary reform since the defeat of Pitt's bill in
1785, having chosen instead to notice other kinds of improving
projects. Now, parliamentary reform was once again a timely
topic, in part as we have seen because of the French Revolution.
On November 27 the Society, in addition to acknowledging this
fact, adopted with pleasure the resolutions moved by Dr. Price
on November 4, that is, reaffirmed what its members who belonged to the Revolution Society had already done. The SCI also
resolved to meet on December 16 at the London Tavern on the
anniversary of the enactment of the Bill of Rights of 1689.

This meeting was also a glorious witness to the cause of liberty.
Dr. Price read a letter from the liberal Duc de la Rochefoucauld
expressing his pleasure in introducing to the National Assembly
of France the congratulatory address of the Revolution Society.
The SCI took official notice of Price's sermon of November 4 by

reading an extract from its pamphlet form. The members toasted "Dr. Price, the friend of the Universe." With more than their usual enthusiasm they also toasted:

The Majesty of the People

Major Cartwright, "the Father of the Society"

The Friends of Parliamentary Reform

The abolition of the slave trade (not yet accomplished)

And in the spirit of cosmopolitanism:

The Liberties of Ireland

France, on the Destruction of the Bastille,
the Abolition of Enslaving Privileges,
the Cooperation of the Army, and National Representation

The President and the Vice-President of the United States

Dr. Franklin

Finally, the SCI pledged to renew its campaign for parliamentary reform, calling for the support of all friends of freedom and recommending to voters in the coming general election all candidates who would promise to support reform.

Though the two would require separate statutes, parliamentary reform was linked to repeal of the Test and Corporation Acts. If the repeal seemed immediately to promise religious liberty, its implications were mainly civil and constitutional, for Dissenters had long enjoyed virtual freedom of worship. Even were this not the case, the prominence of Dissenters in the two movements and the general tendency of non-Dissenting advocates of reform to support repeal enabled opponents to establish the connection. And so it would come about that union, instead of giving strength, increased reformers' vulnerability and weakened the prospects of both parliamentary reform and repeal.

Since their effort to obtain repeal in 1789, advocates had continued quietly to recruit their strength by widening the basis of support. The Application Committee formed in 1786 by the London Dissenting Deputies had, with the efficiency so characteristic of the Deputies, expanded their fruitful contacts with clergy and congregations in the provinces. Before the end of the year 1789, at least fifteen local Dissenting associations were in communication with the London Committee. In Birmingham about this time a committee proposed a national union based upon local organizations. Dr. Price was aware of these activities, and may have been thinking of them when he recommended corresponding societies as a means of uniting the friends of liberty. He was one of forty-four metropolitan Dissenters who on December 4 recommended a national meeting to be held in London. Expressions of similar sentiments came from other country meetings. The traditionally cautious London Deputies found the pressure irresistible. Their Application Committee received country delegates into its meetings. By early March 1790 national union was decided upon, and by mid-May the organization of a national committee had been worked out. Its object remained repeal of the Test and Corporation Acts, to be expressed as the demand not merely of the London denominations but of English Dissent.

"Remained repeal" because on March 2 the House of Commons had rejected a motion for repeal. Perhaps it had been better for the Dissenters' cause if the London Deputies had retained complete control of the movement because the associative activity of the preceding months in the provinces had aroused fears among Churchmen. They reacted vigorously. They formed counter-associations. They tried to offset the efforts of the Dissenters to exact pledges from M. P.'s and candidates in the forthcoming general elections by seeking pledges against repeal. If the debate in the Commons accurately reflected men's thoughts, the opponents of repeal also had broader reasons for their fears.

Charles James Fox, whom the Dissenters had been courting since Pitt had let them down in 1787, was himself courting Dissenting influence in advance of the 1790 election. He also favored repeal because he thought it was right. In introducing the motion of March 2 he pled powerfully for toleration and scornfully denied any danger to the Established Church. But he destroyed whatever these arguments may have accomplished when he dragged in the French Revolution and Dr. Price. It was no comfort to the majority of the Commons to learn that Fox was happy to see a "neighbouring nation" returning to "first principles" and restoring the rights of men. These same members did not share Fox's pleasure in contemplating how an "enlightened philosopher" in England rose above " local attachments" to demand freedom for the human race. In their view, the good Dr. Price was a dangerous man.

No one was more persuaded of this than Edmund Burke. A month earlier he and Fox had clashed on the subject of the French Revolution, and now it seemed Fox was challenging him again. Burke met Fox's arguments and in no instance more directly than when asserting that the Church was indeed in danger. This was not a thought called up in the heat of debate. Two weeks before Burke had told a Dissenting friend in Bristol that there was in England "a considerable party . . . proceeding systematically" to the destruction of the constitution and the Church. Now he identified some of its members, particularly Price, Dr. Priestley, and Robert Robinson, all Dissenting clergymen, all on record as disliking church establishment, and Robinson ready to destroy it at once. Burke's alarm was shared by 293 other members, and only 105 favored the motion. The movement for repeal of the Test Acts clearly had lost ground since May 1789. The reaction against the French Revolution was setting in, and it showed first in the area of religion where passions most easily became bitter. The indiscreet enthusiasms of the Dissenters and the political radicals, revealed against the background of events in France in words and deeds, in sermons, resolutions, addresses and assemblages had wiped out the gains of the 1780's. Almost all of those who struggled for repeal in the campaign of 1787–1790 were dead when finally it was won in 1828.

It should have been apparent that there was little chance of carrying a motion for parliamentary reform in a House of Commons where the echoes of the repeal debate of March 2 had hardly died away. Yet the attempt was made only two days later. Deluded like the repealers with the fancy that the times were favorable for reform, the political radicals hoped to ride in on the wave of cosmopolitan enthusiasm that had been rolling since the fall of the Bastille and the November celebrations in England. The SCI enjoyed a favored position because its then chairman, Henry Flood, was the man who intended to bring a motion before the House of Commons. At its meeting of February 19 the SCI resolved to support and publicize Flood's motion. It was quite short of the "annual, equal and universal Representation" which they had endorsed in 1781, but offered more than Pitt's bill of 1785 which they had also supported. Flood would give the vote to resident householders. In effect this was a taxpaying qualification which would still exclude great numbers of the lower orders. If the SCI could appear ideological in discussing reform in the abstract, it could also be practical in its consideration of parliamentary realities. The "coach to Hounslow" philosophy expressed its sense of tactics. If the reform coach was rolling to the West, passengers might ride as far as they comfortably could, and those who went all the way could be grateful for the company of moderates who dropped off early at Hounslow.

The Commons' debate was good tempered and decisive. The consensus seemed to be that the times were unpropitious. According to Fox, who begged the question, this was because Flood's motion did not seem to have widespread popular support; according to Pitt, who took pains to avow his continued friendship to parliamentary reform, because of a kind of uncertainty in the air; and according to Burke's friend, William Windham, because the French Revolution had unloosed so many wild ideas that the motion could not be lucidly considered. The temper of the House may be judged by the effectiveness of Windham's statement, emotionally appealing, that the hurricane season was no time to repair one's house. In view of the approval given to Windham, Flood withdrew his motion.

The reformers accepted this defeat only as a temporary setback. They did not grasp the significance of the reaction to Windham's hurricane metaphor. They failed to realize that as long as the French Revolution endured the defenders of the old order would be powerfully assisted by it. The SCI pressed ahead. On March 19, with Flood in the chair, they resolved to advertise for a meeting of all friends of parliamentary reform to consider a vigorous campaign. A committee was appointed to meet with one from the Revolution Society. With some difficulty the joint committee finally found April 23 to be a suitable date for a great meeting. Preparatory to it they identified their object as extension of the franchise to all householders "contributing to the Public support."

What exactly went wrong is not explained by the records. It turned out that the great room at the London Tavern was "engaged" on April 23. Whether another room could not be engaged, or whether dissensions divided the reformers, it does not appear that the meeting was held. The SCI went into a decline that lasted nearly a year. No business was transacted at the meetings of May 7, October 22, November 19 or December 10. The Society held no autumn celebrations. Not until February 4, 1791, did the Society conduct a business meeting. After receiving a report from its auditing committee to the effect that many members were in arrears, those present resolved that delinquents be dunned.

For other groups and in other respects the last nine months of 1790 saw a waning of radical activity. Reform was not an issue during the summer in the general election, though in a few constituencies voters' attitudes may have been influenced by the relationship of certain candidates to the radical interests. Neither the prominent Dissenter William Smith nor Flood was returned. In Westminster, Horne Tooke conducted an active contest, trying to appeal to voters who desired a "free representation." Unless this slogan appealed strongly, Tooke had no chance, for by an amicable arrangement made in March, Westminster's seats were already allocated, one to Admiral Hood for Pitt's side, and the other to Fox for the Opposition. All Tooke accomplished was to force a contest and the expenditure of money by the parties who had hoped their deal would enable them to avoid both.

If the election had come three weeks later it is doubtful that the Bastille anniversary celebration would have influenced the outcome, except, perhaps, adversely for Tooke. It might have been disturbing to some voters to notice that the English friends of liberty celebrated a day which had been "appointed by the National Assembly of France." Again, Dissenters were prominent, and curiously, about one-fourth of the stewards for the dinner had connections with the Newington Green congregation —Dr. Price, Samuel Boddington, Philip Mallet, Thomas Rogers, Thomas Rickards, and John Towgood. The dinner, attended by 653 persons, was a disorderly affair, revealing tensions and disagreements among men who found it difficult to unite except for liberty as an abstraction. After Lord Stanhope and Sheridan praised the French Revolution and disparaged the British Constitution, Horne Tooke boldly took exception to some of their remarks. The British Constitution, he said, was basically sound. Before he could explain wherein it needed alterations, the crowd booed and hissed him into temporary silence. This encouraged a question about Tooke's loyalty to the reforming line. Tooke insisted upon proving his loyalty to parliamentary reform by offering a resolution that England did not face so arduous a task as France in renovating her constitution. The crowd seemed willing to accept this. Then Dr. Price diverted attention from Tooke and restored harmony by proposing "an alliance between France and Great Britain, for perpetuating peace, and making the world happy."

When Price called this a "very animating" meeting, he surely referred to the lift it gave to his spirits and his tired old body rather than to the tumult and the noise. In fact men left the meeting puzzled and unhappy. The reformers were not in agreement, and some of them had shown a tendency towards monolithism. Observers remarked that self-styled advocates of freedom did not accord it to any among themselves who disagreed with the popular sense of their meeting, particularly about the complete goodness of the French Revolution and the badness of their own constitution. The radicals' preferences for France, and their continued belief in her steady progress toward freedom, seemed to reveal their intentions of connecting the Revolution with the movements for parliamentary reform.

When November came again, the Revolution Society put on its usual performance. Though all "friends of freedom" were in-

vited, those who attended were persons who had met in July.
The same stewards superintended the arrangements. Dr. Price, as
it turned out, was making his last appearance at a reform gathering. If his enthusiasm had not diminished, his audience had, remarkably. Not only was the crowd smaller than expected, but
there were some notable absentees, among them Lord Stanhope
who was said to have resigned from the Revolution Society.
Horne Tooke's presence did not help matters. Men approved
when he attacked Edmund Burke, but they were shocked by his
criticism of Stanhope. Dr. Price presided in Stanhope's absence.
Despite his infirmities, Price clambered upon a table to propose
an indiscreet toast. "The Parliament of Britain—May it become a
National Assembly."

This toast had an ominous meaning for any who had read a
certain book that had been published just three days earlier, and
it gave point to a theme of the book. The Society noticed the
book and its author when with sarcastic bravado members raised
their glasses in the toast—"If Mr. Burke be ever prosecuted for
such a libel on the constitution, may his impeachment last as long
as that of Mr. Hastings." * The Revolution Society vastly under-
rated Mr. Burke and his *Reflections on the Revolution in France*.

The book appeared at a time when the reform movement
seemed to be breaking up. The SCI was virtually inactive. Many
members were derelict in paying subscriptions. The dinners of
July 14 and November 4 left drab memories. Some persons
doubted whether the Revolution Society would ever meet again.
As for some of the leaders, Stanhope seemed to be getting bored;
Tooke was staying home in Wimbledon; Dr. Price was ill. The
defeats in the House of Commons and the renewal of Pitt's
strength in the general election seemed more than when they occurred in March and July to demonstrate the dominance of anti-
reform opinion. For all of their brave talk, the example of the
French Revolution was not the strong inspiration the reformers
had hoped for.

Because events ran a certain course, it is impossible to speak

* The impeachment, already in its third year, would not end until 1795.
Burke was the leader of the prosecution.

confidently of what might have been—if. The if refers to Burke. The effects of his book are recorded in history. But in the light of the circumstances of November, 1790, it may be asked whether his book was as necessary or the dangers as great as he thought when he began writing it nine months earlier. If he had not written it, the reform movement might have died for want of attention, both from its adherents and from opponents. The movement thrived on controversy; it could not survive indifference. The reformers, contentious by definition, if left alone could only disagree among themselves or lapse into boredom. If attacked, they would rally, unite, fight back with words as weapons. They loved to appear in print with resolutions, addresses, and pamphlets. In the autumn of 1790 they badly needed an argument, something to outrage their sense of justice, some opportunity again to demonstrate the anomalies of the established order and the absurdities of arguments for it, some defender of the constitution to attack. Burke's *Reflections* was Heaven sent.

Looking back from 1794, Francis Plowden, a novice in the Jesuit order at the time it was abolished by papal bull, and later a writer, a barrister, and a moderate reformer, blamed the pamphlet war upon Burke. His *Reflections*, said Plowden, provoked Paine into writing the *Rights of Man* and thus "kindled that political flame of controversy" which swept over England in the years 1791–1794. The reformers were never properly grateful to Burke for resuscitating their declining movement. For without Burke, no Tom Paine; without Paine's *Rights of Man,* no reform Bible. Plowden oversimplified. Paine was not a person to be silent in the exciting time of the French Revolution. But because of Burke's *Reflections*, Paine's book took the form we know, and the pamphlet war in which theirs were the key writings revived a waning reform movement.

When he began his *Reflections* in January 1790 Burke was deeply disturbed. He had not been so in August 1789 when he first mentioned the Revolution in his correspondence. By early November he was uneasy, but neither passionate nor alarmed. Thereafter, with events, his judgments hardened. When the French National Assembly took over the estates of the church,

that is, placed them "at the nation's disposal," Burke was able to
discern the beginnings of a redefinition of the religious life of
France. Soon afterward he read Price's *Discourse* and found it
shocking, full of "seditious principles." He knew that in certain
societies in London the Dissenters were very influential. His dislike and fear of the Dissenters increased enormously, and he developed a strong hostility towards the activists among them, Price
particularly. Things began to form a pattern—a campaign for
parliamentary reform linked with a subtle movement against the
Established Church, and both with French connections. A letter
from Tom Paine, dated January 17, 1790, containing an excerpt
from one of Jefferson's to Paine, was evidence to Burke that the
Revolution was not a sequence of spontaneous happenings but a
systematic plan to spread a false philosophy and to destroy the
established European order. Burke became passionate; he quar-
reled with his party associates like Sheridan and Fox; he was un-
pleasant company because of his intensifying obsession over the
dangers of the Revolution. In the House of Commons the subject
of the Revolution became involved in the debates. On February
9, speaking upon the army estimates, Burke said that in her
"present distemper" France was spreading contagion throughout
Europe. There was "a danger of [England's] being led through
an admiration of successful fraud and violence, to an imitation of
an irrational, unprincipled, proscribing, confiscating, plundering,
ferocious, bloody, and tyrannical democracy. On the side of religion, the danger of this example is no longer from intolerance,
but from atheism."

Burke believed that he must warn England. Having been asked
by a French friend to write "a few words" on the Revolution and
on the sentiments of Englishmen about it, he began a response
which he hoped to complete shortly. In mid-February newspaper
advertisements suggested the original modest proportions of it.
Soon would be published "Reflections on certain proceedings of
the Revolution Society of the Fourth of November, 1789, concerning the affairs of France, in a letter from the Right Honourable Edmund Burke, to a Gentleman in Paris."

Burke's ambitions and passions grew as he wrote, and he trans-

posed the order of priorities. When the book was published on
November 1, 1790, the title revealed the changes—it was now
"Reflections on the Revolution in France *and* on the Proceedings
in Certain Societies in London relative to that Event: in a Letter
intended to have been sent to a gentleman in Paris." The larger
matter was the Revolution, though the activities of the English reformers were not ignored; and the "letter" was addressed to all of
Europe. Burke retained the epistolary form. He used strong language but he chose carefully every word and he formed deliberately every judgment, even such an unfortunate (as it turned
out) reference to the mass of the people as a "swinish multitude."

Burke's theme was the threat to the established social order in
England and Europe offered by the false philosophy of man and
society held by the French Revolutionaries and their English
counterparts. Whether he was contesting Dr. Price's interpretation of the Revolution of 1688, which he did in the first part of
the *Reflections,* or discussing the "reforms" and constitutional
enactments of the French National Assembly, he was always certain that these errors, and the dangers that would accompany
them, grew inevitably out of the specious philosophy, the false
view of history, the relativistic morality, and the emphatic atom-
ism of the revolutionaries. Rousseau, Voltaire, Helvétius—mad-
men and atheists—surely Europe could not accept them as
preachers and lawgivers. But some in England did. Dr. Price's
Discourse made that clear. Said Burke, "I looked on that sermon
as the public declaration of a man much connected with literary
caballers and intriguing philosophers, with political theologians
and theological politicians both at home and abroad. I know they
set him as a sort of oracle; because, with the best intentions in the
world, he naturally *philippizes,* and chants his prophetic song in
exact unison with their designs."

Throughout the *Reflections,* cumulatively rather than systematically, Burke expounded his political and social philosophy.
Founded ultimately upon the premise of a natural moral order,
governed by universal natural law and controlled in its develop-
ment by a prudential human reason that paid due regard to his-

tory and the wisdom of the past, to prescription, to circumstances, and to the limitations of men, this philosophy emphasized order, the complexity of social relations, the difficulties of nurturing constitutional systems, and the dangers of discarding institutions which had grown along with human experience. Leaving room for change, Burke rejected parliamentary reform, and he strongly defended the established churches of England and France.

Contemporaries thought the *Reflections* was an apology for the established social order. It was that, of course. Reactions were conditioned by the presuppositions that readers brought to it. The book was a bestseller. It strongly influenced English opinion. It infuriated radicals who rushed into print with refutations and attacks upon Burke. Most of the people who governed England, whether in St. Stephens' or Whitehall, cathedrals or parish churches, country homes or quarter sessions, received the book as justification of their prejudices and inherited assumptions. No reader was unmoved. The book forced men to choose. Henceforth people who thought at all about public affairs were either for or against Burke, that is, against or for the radicals and the Revolution.

Just when the radical movement was disintegrating, the *Reflections* appeared. Controversy flared; a literary battle began; Tom Paine jumped into the war of words; the reform agitation renewed itself; political societies revived and spread. Meanwhile the French Revolution moved into extreme courses; war broke out in Europe; economic hardships—scarcity and high prices—created discontents among the lower classes who were also becoming conscious of their political grievances. Out of the interactions of all of these came intense manifestations in England of enduring problems of social man—how to admit freedom of expression and provide for change without losing all sense of restraint and stability, and how to maintain stability without curtailing freedom.

CHAPTER V

THE PAMPHLET WAR

FOR a year and a half after the appearance of Burke's *Reflections* the revived contention between reformers and their opponents was mainly a pamphlet war. It was hardly a straight out presentation of the cases for and against reform; the arguments involved personalities and emotions as well as issues. Burke was in the center of the storm. Many of the pamphlets were attacks upon him or upon the *Reflections* (if there is any distinction). Though the need for reform was usually implied in them, as the dangers of reform were presented in the lesser number of defenses of Burke, it is doubtful if these pamphlets, with one notable exception, won new friends or made new enemies for reform.

The exception was Tom Paine's *Rights of Man*, the first part of which appeared in March 1791 and the second part the following February. After that pamphleteering continued, but not as the focus of men's attention. For along with the publication of the *Rights of Man* and in large part because of it, activism and militancy revived. Societies and associations, some with new types of membership, sprang up in England and Scotland and gave to the reform movement a different character. The once-happy and peaceful constitution no longer recognized itself amid the bitter condemnations of its deficiencies or the exaggerated praises of its virtues. The radicals threatened to change it drastically; its stubbornest defenders thought any change an evil; and a middle group of reformers wished to preserve it by removing its grossest anomalies.

Between the publication of the *Reflections* and Part II of the *Rights of Man*, some forty-five anti-Burke publications appeared, five of them during November 1790. Most of them were quickly and deservedly forgotten, significant only for the moment. A pamphlet that a modern reader scorns may have been read because of timeliness or as the latest installment in the controversy that many persons followed. Taken together the pamphlets tell something about men's minds during that year, their attitudes towards the Revolution and the nature of their thinking on the reform question. Most of the replies to Burke came from middle-class backgrounds, and if they differed in details, represented the kinds of reformers who had made up the movement from its beginning.* Only Paine's book had significant popular appeal, and that is one reason why it was so influential. Of all the replies to Burke, it was the only one which radicals continued to read, and which is read today by persons who are not students of the history of the period.

It would be tedious and fruitless, for reasons already suggested, to attempt a summary or analysis of individual pamphlets, other than Paine's. There was among them enough similarity, particularly of sentiment and point of view, to permit treatment of them as a group. Generally they said something laudatory about the Revolution of 1688 and the political principle which justified it and which Price had stated—the theory of revolution derived from the concept of the sovereignty of the people. The pamphlets also defended the French Revolution and admired its accomplishments. For greater effect, the authors tried various literary devices, ridicule, irony, hyperbole. Many professed admiration for Burke, especially the earlier Burke, and regretted his defection from the cause of liberty. Some hinted at ulterior reasons for what was judged to be Burke's turncoat behavior.

---

* The number would be larger by a half if one included writings appearing after February 1792 and uncountably larger if newspaper and periodical attacks were included. Among the later pamphlets there was a tendency to emulate Paine's popular appeal.

Every opponent of Burke paid homage to the simple, transcendent principle of the sovereignty of the people, which Fox in Parliament described as "paramount to all other laws." The author of *Temperate Comments Upon Intemperate Reflections* said the government should originate in the people. George Dyer, a Unitarian, considered "every man's right to make laws, as his most sacred property, and the exercise of that right as essential to liberty." The Baptist pamphleteer, Robert Hall, believed that no man should have dominion over another without that person's consent. Capell Lofft, one of the founders of the SCI, insisted upon the power of the people to determine when a constitution should be changed or a government dissolved, for in entering into the original social contract, the people remained sovereign. The reformers needed no other premise than this. From it, all other political powers derived their sanction. The reasoning from this premise could be carried logically to extremes, as Mrs. Catherine Macaulay Graham, a leader among the reformers' "Amazonian allies," admitted. But the proponents of popular sovereignty had sufficient faith in human reason to think that the people would never wish a tyranny upon themselves.

This doctrine was amenable to both historical and philosophical demonstration. The Revolution of 1688 exemplified its application, and the failure then to provide for fair and free representation of the people was rather a matter of political failure than of the theoretical inadequacy of the principle of popular sovereignty. The accepted philosophical proof was the social contract theory. Government originated in a compact made by the sovereign people; it was their creature, existing at their sufferance, limited and defined by the decisions which they made, and responsible to the will of the majority. If Burke, with his emphasis upon tradition, prescription, and the gradual accretions of human experience, more accurately described the growth of the British Constitution, the social contract theorists, in a superficial sense, could point to what the Americans had done and the French were doing as examples of sovereign people discarding old constitutions and making new ones.

The disagreement among English radicals over the extent of

parliamentary reform in England was less about basic theory than about practical applications. Many of the pamphleteers insisted with Wyvill that a timely reform was a wise preventive measure. The French Revolution illustrated the truth of this belief, and should serve as a warning to England. The French had to be revolutionaries because of the blind inertia of their former rulers. The pamphleteers had much to say about the old regime—the "Military, Sacerdotal, and Judicial Aristocracies" as James Mackintosh, the author of *Vindiciae Gallicae*, one of the best replies to Burke, labeled it. Considering the nature of the pre-revolutionary government, the French people had acted with surprising moderation. And if there were some excesses in France, they were not the dangers Burke thought them. Mackintosh described the French experience since 1789 as "transient anarchy," the prelude to "established liberty."

It was characteristic of reformers' confidence in their own righteousness to think that their efforts had utterly defeated Burke. Of his opponents, said Wyvill,

> some . . . were completely victorious, and overthrew the positions of their Antagonist with a very superior force of reason and true masculine eloquence. Not one of them was wholly unsuccessful, and unable to prove him erroneous in any important instance; not one failed to produce some example of gross misinformation. . . . By these united efforts to support the Cause of Freedom, the authority of our modern Filmer has been reduced to its proper level.

The pamphlet replies to Burke collectively set forth a coherent message. From the achievements of the Revolution of 1688, and on the basis of natural rights doctrine, touched with millennialism and a suggestion of utilitarianism, they argued that any government which did not respect the national will as expressed through a truly representative legislature and was not established with the consent of the majority determined by a wide suffrage, was not to be endured. France was an example of a nation which had reacted against unrepresentative government. The pamphlets emphasized Burke's misconception of French history and of the French Revolution. They asserted that the Revolution was the inevitable consequence of accumulated abuses brought home to the people through the force of reason and philosophy. They warned England to expect a similar outburst if grievances continued to multiply without redress. And they pointed out the course England should take in order that abuses might be removed, equality restored, and the general happiness increased. The remedy for England's ills and the preventive of future troubles was parliamentary reform.

The most famous, influential and widely read of the replies to Burke, Paine's *Rights of Man*, was not strictly speaking an argument for parliamentary reform. The middle- and upper-class reformers firmly dissociated themselves from Paine's doctrine, even while acknowledging the great effect of the pamphlet. Horne Tooke said he might ride on the coach with Paine only as far as Hounslow, because he did not desire to accompany Paine all the way to republicanism. In this Major Cartwright agreed with Tooke. They could not accept Paine's republicanism; England had a sound constitution, basically, which only wanted some amendments to make it more adequately representative. On May 9, 1792, at the Society of the Friends of the People, Cartwright proposed a resolution reaffirming the established constitutional structure—King, Lords and Commons. Charles James Fox doubted if many people, after reading the *Rights of Man*, could persuade themselves to agree with the "general tendency of that book," for it was "a performance totally different from all ideas of reform." Obviously, Fox was talking about the kind of people he associated with, not about the lower orders.

In fact, it was the "general tendency" of the book that many of them disliked. When Jack Anvil found Tom Hod reading the *Rights of Man*, he shouted, "What! thou art a leveller and a republican, I warrant?" Tom had not thought of it in those words, but, said he, "I'm for a constitution—and organization—and equalization—and fraternization." * Christopher Wyvill, who wrote a pamphlet entitled *A Defense of Dr. Price, and the Re-*

* See below, p. 150.

formers of England, warned his readers against associating the reformers with Paine. They desired to amend the British Constitution; Paine would destroy it. Henry Yorke, a clever, conceited young man of twenty-three, when on trial in York in 1795 for conspiracy to excite sedition and break the peace of the realm, identified himself as an advocate of parliamentary reform and a defender of the British Constitution who had always opposed the doctrines of Paine.

The radical literature of the period and the reports of the state trials of 1793–1795 contain innumerable references to Paine. They testified to the ubiquity of his book, the immense size of its audience, the horror it aroused in the governing classes, the distaste for it among the middle-class reformers, but also the admiration of literally thousands of persons for it, and the persuasive effect its spirit had upon many of them. When the Secret Committee of the House of Commons in 1794 reported on subversive activities in England, it decided that "the period from which it appears . . . material to trace in this view the proceedings of the Society for Constitutional Information, is that of the publication of the pamphlet so well known under the title of 'Rights of Man, by Thomas Paine.' "

The appearance of this book, therefore, was taken to signify a change in tone and emphasis of the reform movement. The reasons are apparent on every page of it. Its inelegance of style and phraseology, its common grammar may have repelled educated readers, but Paine was not writing for them. As Professor James Boulton has remarked, the word "vulgar" is misapplied to Paine's style if used in any sense except to mean plain or of the people. Paine was writing for the lower orders and the lower middle class, bringing them the advice and wisdom which he believed as an expert on government and as a political thinker he was qualified to dispense. Philosophically Paine identified himself with the interest of the people, though socially he preferred and sought the company of such as Jefferson, Washington, Lafayette, Condorcet, Horne Tooke, or at one time Burke and the Portland Whigs. Plainly, even coarsely, but clearly and memorably he expressed his thoughts. There was enough emotion to win sympathy, apt images fixed the idea in the reader's mind, the concreteness of illustrations enhanced the reality of the idea, and the apparent common sense carried the conviction of self-evident truth. When Burke seemed to shed tears over French excesses while ignoring the sufferings of the French people, Paine remarked that he "pitied the plumage, but forgets the dying bird." Paine's arguments were stripped of refinements and qualifications. Everything was reduced to simplest terms. The oversimplification, which the scholar rejects, but which with an appearance of logical inevitability made the arguments seem incontrovertible, was in striking contrast to the complexity and the subtlety of Burke. Paine ridiculed his opponent by saying that for the benefit of their readers he would undertake to translate Burke into language that could be understood. The person with a trained and educated mind cannot debate with a Hyde Park orator.

Paine's political philosophy was a simple version of the social contract theory. In the beginning, of Divine Purpose, men were born equal and possessed of natural rights. The individual surrendered into the common stock of society those rights which he could not preserve or exercise, and the aggregate of deposited rights constitute civil power. The definition of civil power and the arrangements for giving effect to it make up the formal constitution. That is, society is antecedent to government, and the social compact is among people for the purpose of establishing a government, not a compact between governors and governed. The people do not surrender their ultimate sovereignty; they retain the power to change the constitution and the government. "Every age and generation must be as free to act for itself in all cases as the age and generations which preceded it." "It is the living and not the dead, that are to be accommodated."

Ideally there should be no need for government. Because the power of human reason did not persuade men always to act in accord with their individual and mutual interests, government was necessary to manage the affairs of society in the interest of the people and under their control. Therefore, government "from its nature cannot be, the property of any particular man or family. . . . Sovereignty, as a matter of right, appertains to the nation only, and not to any particular individual; and a nation has at all times an inherent indefeasible right to abolish any form of government it finds inconvenient, and to establish such as accords with its interest, disposition, and happiness." Hereditary monarchy was an absurdity, an insult to common sense, and in the enlightened state of mankind, an anomaly. Men would be wise to hasten the decline of hereditary government, to anticipate the approach of representative government, and to "produce revolutions by reason and accommodation, rather than commit them to the issue of convulsions." "It is an age of revolutions, in which everything may be looked for."

Paine found the origin of government in the natural rights, contract philosophy, but he derived its purpose from the principle of utility. Government could contribute to the happiness of men so long as it conducted the "public business" in their interest. A representative, republican form of government would do this. It was in the power of government to harmonize the interests of men when they were not naturally identical. Government could do many things to lessen misery and to improve the conditions in which men lived.

In the second part of the *Rights of Man,* Paine offered an ambitious, idealistic program of social and economic reform. First, he expected that when revolutions ended, with the representative form of government universal, international peace would prevail. Popular governments would not make war. Universal peace would permit the reductions of armies and navies, and European governments would get out of the business of colonial empires. International trade would become free. The privileges of the aristocracy and wasteful monarchies would be eliminated. Then, freed of these burdens, governments would devote themselves to their true responsibility, promoting the general welfare. The crushing load of taxes would be lifted from the wearied backs of the people. A progressive income tax would replace taxes weighing heaviest upon the poor. The Elizabethan poor law system based upon rates or local property taxes would be abolished. The revenues of government, even after tax reductions, would be sufficient to provide subsidies or pensions directly to children, to demobilized soldiers and sailors, and to the aged in such liberal fashion that poor relief in the traditional manner would not be necessary. Paine also proposed national support for education to the sum of ten shillings a year for each child. He would grant twenty shillings for the birth of each child and the same amount for each marriage. Public funds would provide dignified work for the poor. In his welfare state, Paine envisaged the elimination of the stigma attached to poverty and misfortune.

Writing to his brother John, a fictitious Thomas Bull alleged that Paine had been heard to say, "When he had made revolutions against the Kings upon Earth, he would try his hand at a *Revolution in Heaven!*" Considering the ambitious program that would follow upon these earthly revolutions, Paine would not soon have time to play the role of Lucifer. But Paine's social program eventually became reality; England adopted the permanent income tax in the 1840's, something approaching universal elementary education in 1870, and the scheme of social benefit payments in the early twentieth century.

It is easy to see that all of this would be strong medicine for the governing classes whose political predominance it threatened, for the socially prominent whose status it jeopardized, and for economic interests who feared for the security of their property. Two words were joined to describe the followers of Paine—levellers and republicans—words with an intended pejorative meaning. It is also easy to appreciate the appeal Paine's doctrines had for the discontented and the aggrieved, the poor and the lower orders. It was inevitable that some among these last extracted more from Paine than even he meant. But when to these disturbing ideas Paine added his praise of revolutions in general and the French Revolution in particular, and at a time when war began on the continent and the Revolution moved into an extreme course, it would be surprising if the *Rights of Man* did not excite panic and bitterness. In the most peaceful of times the book would have been disturbing, but in 1791 and even more during the next three years it created terror among many of the governing and the propertied classes. That devil Wilkes could not be compared with that devil Paine. The *Rights of Man* preached social revolution.

If sales indicated anything, it was that vast numbers of people were exposed to this dangerous book. It has been estimated that by the end of 1792 the two parts had sold about two hundred thousand copies, and another three hundred thousand by 1802. These figures include the six-penny condensation which was distributed largely among the lower classes. The production in large quantities made possible the cheap price. Paine profited from the book. On July 4, 1792, he offered one thousand pounds of his royalties to the SCI to be used to support their educational activities. The minutes of the SCI suggest some embarrassment while members were deciding to refuse Paine's generous offer on the grounds that he had never received adequate reward for his services to humanity and should therefore keep the money for his own use. The SCI used truth to extricate itself from an awkward situation, but it misunderstood Paine. He was not interested in money. He desired to serve mankind, and his reward was the satisfaction of having done so. As he told the SCI "I have now done by the people of England the same as I did by those of America, and I sincerely wish them the same happiness."

A judgment about the nature of Paine's services must be a mixed one. There is no doubt that he won for himself fame and notoriety, both of which pleased him, but it is not quite so clear whether his efforts advanced the cause he was promoting. Certainly in the short run they did not. He probably did much to discredit parliamentary reform as many reformers attested. It was easy, after the *Rights of Man*, for opponents of reform to confuse the issues by charging guilt by association. Paine's popularity exposed reformers to the accusations that they really would destroy rather than merely improve the constitution, for was not Paine an avowed republican, an enemy of kings, aristocracies, and established churches? Was he not a leveller, and would not reform bring destruction of the social order? Far from converting England to republicanism, Paine made reform seem dangerous. Undoubtedly he stirred up the lower orders, stimulating the revival of old and the formation of new political societies, but their activities in turn intensified the opposition of the governing class to reform.

A long run view, with the advantage of historical perspective, supports another judgment. If the reform movement in the 1790's was suppressed, that decade nevertheless saw the lower orders become politically conscious and active in a way England had never before known. Whatever Paine contributed to the awakening of the lower orders was important in the "making of the English working class." The history of the 1790's is linked directly to the great popular movements in nineteenth century England—chartism, trade unionism, and eventually the extension of the trade union movement into politics. As Father R. R. Fennessy has said in his study of the controversy between Burke and Paine, the *Rights of Man* played a part "in the political transformation of the modern world." Which is another way of saying that the story of the English Jacobins in the early 1790's is an installment in the history of the political transformation of modern Britain. The opponents of Paine and of reform were instinctively correct when they expressed fear of his influence upon the "lower orders."

The early effects of the *Rights of Man*, that is of Part I, which appeared a year before Part II, may be traced in the minutes of the SCI. After a year of lethargy, the meetings became more regular and vigorous. The Society underwent some change of membership, and certainly a change of spirit, and both changes were influenced by Paine's book, even the anticipation of it. In addition to new members whose presence indicated a less exclusive group than formerly, some of the older members, like Horne Tooke and Major Cartwright, showed renewed interest. Paine himself attended more often; he had been an "honorary member" since December 7, 1787. The dinner meeting of March 7, 1791, seems to have been a decisive one, held for the purpose of rallying the members. The language of the resolutions and toasts was considerably more intemperate than formerly. The Society complained about the mildness of libel laws which permitted with impunity the publication of "any Reflections however false." The Society warned Englishmen to be on guard against "wicked Systems of Resistance" to parliamentary reform by "usurping Aristocracies" who slandered the friends of freedom at home and abroad. Among the toasts were:

The National Assembly
and may the Parliament of Great Britain become such

The Marquis De La Fayette

May the example of one Revolution be the means
of preventing the necessity of another

The momentum was accelerated by the publication a week
later of the first part of the *Rights of Man.* At its meeting of
March 23 the Society voted its thanks to Paine "for his most mas-
terly book" which exposed the "Sophistries of hireling Scrib-
blers" and stated political truths so convincingly as to accelerate
the reform spirit. It pleased the Society to think that one of its
members could write such a worthy book, and they resolved to
promote it. The enthusiasm of this language concealed the mental
reservations that some members had about specific teachings of
Paine.

While the SCI derived some satisfaction from denouncing
Burke as an apostate and from praising Paine, it is difficult to esti-
mate their success in "educating" the public about parliamentary
reform. Because their own respectability seemed to be under suspicion owing to their association with Paine, the Society thought
it desirable to reaffirm their purposes. Newspaper advertisements
were used liberally to this end. Then, just when this revival
threatened to lapse, the Society was able to attach itself to another cause. This carried it through the always difficult summer
months and into the year 1792. The promise of success in this
effort gave members a much needed lift of spirits, and prepared
the Society for a significant resurgence.

In May, 1791, Charles James Fox brought before the House of
Commons a legal problem of the utmost importance to freedom
of the press and the reform movement.* This was the question of
the authority of juries and of judges in libel cases. The problem
was an old one. As the judge-made law then was, juries could decide only the fact of publication; the judge decided the matter of
law, whether the material in question was a libel. The preferences

---

* In the eighteenth century the word press meant all manner of publications, not just newspapers. The word publish referred to any part in the
process of bringing a piece of writing before the reader, whether by authorship, by printing, by selling, or even giving it to the reader.

of the judiciary were usually in favor of government and the established order; it was widely believed that so long as judges held the power they had assumed for the courts, criticism of government could be severely limited. This is not to say that the press in the eighteenth century was continually shackled, but rather that government had at hand a powerful legal weapon to be used against critics if it chose. In times of stress the weapon could be particularly handy. It is not likely that Fox was inspired to act in 1791 because he foresaw the likelihood of repression if the fears of the governing class turned into panic. But as long as the dictum of Chief Justice Holt in 1704 seemed to describe the attitudes of the judiciary, the danger of repression existed. Holt had said, "If people should not be called to account for possessing the people with an ill opinion of government, no government can subsist. For it is very necessary that the people should have a good opinion of it." Certainly to some people the attacks of the parliamentary reformers upon the representative system appeared as attempts to spread an ill opinion of government.

If there was any doubt about this, an event of 1783 should have removed it. In that year, William Shipley, the Dean of St. Asaph, republished Sir William Jones' pamphlet called *The Principles of Government*. The prosecution for libel was a private action, but in one sense this was as disturbing to freedom of the press as a governmental prosecution. The SCI became deeply involved in this case, not only because Jones was a member but because the larger issue involved the very substance of the Society's being, public education. The defense was conducted by Thomas Erskine, ably as usual, but it required Lord Chief Justice Mansfield's willingness to agree with Erskine upon a flaw in the indictment to save the Dean from conviction. During the proceedings, Mansfield reaffirmed the authority of the judge and the limitation upon the jury in libel cases. Not only was the unsatisfactory state of the law reaffirmed, but the SCI had spent slightly over 250 pounds, raised by subscription among its members, to support the case. One consequence was the election of Erskine to honorary membership.

As a matter of history and principle, Fox's motion in 1791 interested the Society deeply. The bill moved quickly and easily through the Commons; there was no opposition; Pitt himself supported it. Apparently neither the government nor its supporters saw any ulterior or dangerous connections among the bill, the French Revolution, the *Rights of Man*, or the reform agitation. If they saw such a connection, they were nevertheless willing to risk the consequences for the sake of the great principle involved. The bill ran into difficulties in the House of Lords, mainly from the opposition of Thurlow, the Lord Chancellor.

At this juncture, friends of freedom became active. On June 3 a group met at the Crown and Anchor "to take into consideration" the bill on the rights of juries. This new society, the Friends of the Liberty of the Press, included some members of the SCI. The meeting resolved that in libel cases the principles of jury trial be applied as they were in other criminal cases—that is, that all matters of fact be brought before the jury, and that in libel cases the nature of the material in question be considered as matter of fact. Despite the unanimity of the Commons, the outside support, and the favorable opinion of the newspapers for giving to juries "their constitutional right," the Lords postponed their decision until the next session. In the spring of 1792 the bill came in again. Lord Camden who thirty years earlier had opposed the old restrictions upon juries placed the issue in its larger context of the freedom to criticize government. The bill provided that "the jury sworn to try the issue may give a general verdict of Guilty or Not Guilty upon the whole matter."

The passage of the bill caused rejoicing among the friends of freedom, and particularly the Friends of the Liberty of the Press. On June 15, 1792, they dined at the Freemason's Tavern to celebrate the event. Among the stewards were young James Mackintosh, George Rous, who had also replied to Burke, James Martin, M. P., Sheridan, Samuel Whitbread, Jr., M. P., and Thomas Rogers the banker. All of them were members of the SCI.

There are some mysteries about the passage of Fox's Libel Law. When the judges were asked for advisory opinions they reported unanimously against the bill on May 11, 1792. Possibly they alienated Parliament because their opinions about the powers of the judges went alarmingly far beyond the matter at hand. In any case the law was a reversal of judicial decision by the High Court of Parliament. Yet this occurred when the second part of the *Rights of Man* was still fresh, when reform societies were springing up all over England, when the popular mind was becoming more agitated than at any time since the French Revolution began, and when public disorder seemed to be epidemic. In 1790 the state of the times had been a useful argument against parliamentary reform; in the spring of 1792 the state of the times, more turbulent still, was not an effective argument against a bill which was bound to encourage reform agitation. It almost seemed that Parliament had more confidence in the juries than in the judges; certainly a powerful mystique surrounded the ancient institution of jury trial. For the sake of the principle, in order to define an enlarged sense of the competence of juries, Parliament seemed willing to take the risks involved. But if so, considering the variant property qualifications for jury service, why not a modest parliamentary reform which would enable these same respectable and trusted gentlemen to vote and to sit in the House of Commons as well as in the jury box?

It was the difficulty, and it even seemed the futility of persuading Parliament that sometimes discouraged the reformers, optimists by definition. In 1791 it took a sequence of small uplifts to carry them through the year, and they sagged between. Thus the publication of the first part of the *Rights of Man* was followed quickly enough by the first attempt to pass Fox's Libel Bill to sustain them into the summer. And then there was Bastille Day to bring them together again. About nine hundred persons assembled at the Crown and Anchor, ostensibly sponsored by the Revolution Society. Tom Paine, just back from France, did not attend. His physicians told him he was too fatigued from his journey. Horace Walpole said Paine stayed away because he was piqued by the general lack of enthusiasm. Walpole was not the only one who noticed this. Lord Stanhope and Sheridan were also among the missing, the latter, it was said maliciously, because the Prince of Wales had given him orders to stay away. There was in fact concern among the parliamentary Opposition about flirtations of their members with the London radicals, and some party leaders discouraged members from attending the celebration. Tension was increasing between the wing influenced by Burke and that led by Fox. Burke and Fox had publicly terminated their old friendship over the issues of reform and the French Revolution, and the Duke of Portland was trying pathetically to prevent this personal breach from disrupting the party. It happened that on July 14 Burke was at the Crown and Anchor in a separate room for a meeting concerning the Royal Academy. The newspapers reported this coincidence and commented impishly upon the irony of it.

If there was any exuberance among reformers at the Crown and Anchor, the afterglow was stifled by the news from Birmingham. The details were confused then as they are today, but the larger import of the news was clear. In the name of Church and King, mobs had attacked and destroyed property belonging to Dissenters and reformers during the evening of July 14. The riots were not quelled until Sunday, the 17th. One authority calls this "the last great action of an 18th century mob," but evidence exists for qualifying the word mob, if normally it is supposed to mean something spontaneous and undisciplined. Both Dissent and the reform spirit were strong in Birmingham, and the two were linked together. The recent attempt to repeal the Test and Corporation Acts had damaged the normal good relations between Churchmen and Dissenters, and the injection of the reform issue heightened the tension. Whether the bad feeling was the cause of failure, efforts to organize a Warwickshire Constitutional Society had not been successful. As late as June 27, 1791, Joseph Priestley, one of the best known Dissenters in England, had failed to persuade James Watt, the improver of the steam engine, to join the projected society.

There was a reform organization of sorts and on July 14 about ninety persons gathered at the Birmingham Hotel. Priestley was not among them, possibly, it has been suggested, because he read correctly the signs of trouble that were alleged to be evident earlier in the day. Besides gatherings of small, muttering groups, it is not clear what these signs were. Priestley himself later denied having seen certain inflammatory radical handbills, and he also denied that the celebrants had toasted "Destruction to the present government—and the king's head upon a charger!" As soon as the dinner broke up, about 8 P.M., a crowd attacked the hotel and then destroyed a Unitarian meeting house. Its leaders dissuaded it from attacking a Quaker meeting house, directing it instead against another Unitarian chapel and against Priestley's house which was destroyed. During this time the magistrates made no effort to disperse the rioters, and did not until noon of the next day when the mob began to get out of control and turn against public buildings. These belated efforts of the local authorities had little effect. The rioting went on until the military arrived on the 17th.

The general conclusions of the latest study of this affair make it appear both less and more ominous than a description of it as a mob action. The government acted with vigor and dispatch when it received the request for military aid and does not seem to have been implicated in any plot against the Dissenters. The local magistrates were culpable both for seeming to have encouraged the initial attacks upon Dissenting property and throughout for negligence in performing their duties. The mobs were never larger than about 250 persons, and there was a nucleus of well-disciplined and well-informed "rioters" made up of "foreigners," that is, imported from London. Priestley said that religion rather than parliamentary reform was the important provocation. With what truth it may be said bluntly that local Churchmen organized attacks upon local business competitors who were also Dissenters, or whether it should be stated as an attack upon Dissenters who were also successful businessmen, may be a matter of uncertainty. What is clear is that the Birmingham riot does not justify a quick conclusion that the lower orders of England were militantly pro-Church and pro-King. Many of them were, but during the next three years it became just as clear that many of them were not. In any case, the riot had little effect in dampening the larger movement for reform.

The reform spirit remained alive but not steadily vigorous. Thus, the November 4 celebration of the Revolution Society turned out to be its last. The new group of stewards were not well chosen. Samuel Boddington, Samuel Rogers, and William Towgood who had married into the Yerbury mercantile money, were of the younger generation of Dissenters who preferred to be gentlemen rather than activists. Though members of the SCI, they had not the taste for controversy. Captain Ralph Broome, a supporter of Warren Hastings, loved controversy, but preferred to carry it on independently by his mordant literary attacks on Burke. They were simply not good material for the work at hand. They did their duty once and invited the friends of freedom to dine at the London Tavern. Paine was there along with his friend from Manchester, the merchant Thomas Walker who presided. The usual toasts were drunk, along with one to Paine and to his response, "The Revolution of the World." Even allowing for the *Times's* bias, its judgment that the meeting was a miserable one is not far off the mark. Though the Revolution Society dissolved, its members continued their activities. There had been something artificial about the Revolution Society anyway; it was superfluous. As the centenary year of the Revolution of 1688 receded, the Society lost its reason for being. The members could seek parliamentary reform within other organizations like the SCI.

Just a week before this meeting, a forty-year-old shoemaker of No. 9 Piccadilly wrote a letter applying for a job. He expected to be released by his master, and was thinking of changing his trade. He applied for assistance to Francis Place, a journeyman breeches-maker half his age; he was willing to take a job in the counting house or as a country rider. The breeches-maker was unable to help him, and the shoemaker stuck to his last. However, he had other interests. Thomas Brand Hollis had given him some of the publications of the Society for Constitutional Information and he was busy reading the works of Dr. Price, Dr. Jebb, and Major Cartwright. This was one of the most fruitful of the educational efforts of the Society. Their pamphlets had come into the hands of Thomas Hardy who in 1792–1794 was one of the most important of the English Jacobins.

CHAPTER VI

THE FELLOWSHIP OF
THE PEOPLE

FIVE days after the Birmingham riot, a Lancaster justice of the peace reported on local conditions to the Home Secretary, Henry Dundas. He discerned a "very general spirit of combination amongst all sorts of labourers and artisans, who are in a state of disaffection to all legal control." The word combination had a specific legal meaning when referring to restraint of trade, for under the common law such a combination was indictable as a conspiracy. The existence of combinations suggests economic grievances so burdensome as to force workers to combine in spite of the risk of heavy punishments. Yet Dundas' informant found the country "wonderfully prosperous," with wages high and jobs plentiful. A year later the Secretary at War received a report from Sheffield which spoke of wages so generous that journeymen could live on the earnings of three days' labor, leaving them the rest of the week for "seditious machinations." Both informants found these activities stimulated in part by politics. In Lancashire in late 1791 "an unhappy party spirit about the Revolution in France . . . has added to the general ill-humour and may be a pretext for mischief and outrage. . . ." In Sheffield in 1792 the "lowest mechanics" were holding meetings where they read "the most violent publications," discussed them, and conducted correspondences with similar societies in other parts of England.

The correspondence of William Wilberforce in this period refers often to the disturbed state of the times. Christopher Wyvill told him of the uneasiness and sense of impending danger felt by propertied people in Durham. From the city of Leeds, Wilberforce heard of the "immense pains" being taken to stimulate discontent and rebellion among the lower orders. Tom Paine's "mischievous" work was being distributed as a six-penny pamphlet, "sold and given away in profusion." Copies could be seen in the homes of working men. "The soldiers are everywhere tampered with; no pains are spared to render this island a scene of confusion." The quantity of evidence convinced Wilberforce "that there is more cause for alarm than I had apprehended." Irony is in all of this. Neither Wilberforce nor Wyvill had been averse to agitating their own causes among their own kind, the upper middle class and the gentry. But the lower orders had no business doing this and certainly not the right to imitate their betters in pursuit of a radical reform of Parliament.

Throughout 1792 the Home Office received many reports like these. Near Bristol and Liverpool, combinations of coalminers were making wage demands, threatening strikes, and generally evincing discontent. Shoemakers at Liverpool and sailors at various ports along the North Sea coast were meeting, organizing, threatening, stopping work. The reports of these activities, like those from Sheffield, discovered political discontents mixed in with economic grievances. The manifestations of discontent seemed to be encouraged by some kind of troubled spirit of the times. The weakness of civil authority and the inability of the magistrates to control the discontented were remarked upon by reporters who thought at times that only the presence of the military could insure peace. As proof, an incident that occurred in the metropolis in November 1792 could be cited by persons who feared disorder. When it was learned that two "Levelling Societies" proposed to plant a Tree of Liberty on Kennington Common, troops of the Fifteenth Dragoons were marched from Maidenhead to camp on the Common. The "Levellers" abandoned their plans.

Early in 1793 William Pitt explained to the Commons the government policy during a debate over the use of armed forces as a police measure. Although the armed forces had been reduced because England was secure from her European rivals in spite of the war on the continent, the government was building barracks at various places in the interior. "A spirit had appeared in some of the manufacturing towns which made it necessary that troops should be kept near them." Corroborating Pitt, Rowland Burdon said that as a magistrate he had "felt the want of barracks last summer" in Durham County. The Secretary at War, Sir George Yonge, admitted frankly that this new provision for the troops "was necessary to the security of the kingdom."

The spirit so often mentioned in these letters and documents was to the governing class ominous in itself and doubly dangerous because it had embodiment. The story of the combinations of workers belongs more properly to the history of trade unionism, but their existence should at least be recognized. British trade unionism in its beginning related closely to the stirrings of the political consciousness of the working class. In the 1790's members of this class enjoyed neither political rights as individuals nor legal status of their combinations as workers. The efforts to obtain them went on simultaneously. Workers seeking economic betterment were painfully aware that they had not votes for Members of Parliament or a place in local government. While it is possible for purposes of discussion to keep the movement for political rights separate from the movement for trade union recognition, the interactions must be admitted. The two movements make up much of the history of the working class. Both manifested the spirit of the early period of the industrial revolution in England. The novelty of the working class self-consciousness alarmed the higher orders. Such a statement as that of a shipowner, Thomas Powditch, to Pitt on November 3, 1792, grapples the two movements together—"when I look around and see this country [Tynemouth] covered with thousands of pitmen, keelmen, waggonners and other labouring men, hardy fellows strongly impressed with the new doctrine of equality"—votes and higher wages. Tom Paine's message was getting through.

Obviously, it was not the SCI or the kinds of people who made it up or the old Yorkshire Movement that worried the magistrates

and the King's ministers. Passing over the Manchester Constitutional Society, formed in the autumn of 1790 by moderate reformers able to pay the half-guinea subscription, it still is true
that provincials pointed out the new direction, and probably first
a group of men of humble station in Sheffield in November 1791.
An extract from their correspondence, January 15, 1792, says
that the Sheffield Society for Constitutional Information

> originated in an assembly of five or six mechanics,
> who, by their meeting at some one of their Houses,
> and conversing about the enormous high price of pro-
> visions, &c.—the gross abuses this nation labours under
> from the unbounded authority of the monopolizers of
> all ranks, from the king to the peasant; the waste and
> lavish of the public property by placemen, pensioners,
> luxury, and debauchery, sources of the grievous bur-
> then under which this nation groans; together with
> the mock representation of the people—these being
> the subjects of their conversation, they concluded that
> nothing but darkness and ignorance in the people
> could suffer the natural rights of every freeman to be
> thus violated; and this excited them to invite and visit
> their neighbours, whence a small society of twenty or
> thirty soon commenced, and kept increasing, so that
> they were obliged to divide into separate bodies; and
> at this time, they have formed eight of these smaller
> societies, which meet each at their different Houses,
> all on the same evenings; this preserves good order,
> and none are admitted without his ticket, that they are
> perfectly safe from being intruded upon, and perfect
> regular good order kept up; these meet every two
> weeks. Their general meeting at which some hundreds
> attend, is held once a month. . . . We have now in
> the press a re-publication of Paine's Rights of Man, for
> 1,600 copies, by 1,400 subscribers, at the low price of
> sixpence each copy. . . .

It is all here—small masters and journeymen of the cutlery trade
while it was still organized in numerous, petty establishments, lit-

erate, greedy for knowledge, made indignant by what they knew of public affairs, pathetically eager to associate with friends and neighbors to exchange grievances and panaceas, simplistic in their formulations of them, able in the absence of any diversions after their work to give single-minded attention to their new found cause, showing intuitive good sense as organizers, and inspired by the latest in that great trilogy of English common readers, the King James Bible, *Pilgrim's Progress*, and Paine's *Rights of Man*.

The Sheffield Society prospered and grew. By mid-March it claimed two thousand members, organized in the first instance into two hundred tythings. Each of these named a delegate; the two hundred delegates met in tythings; each of the twenty tythings chose a delegate, and the twenty delegates formed the grand council. "By this method order and regularity will be maintained." If other societies, then forming, followed Sheffield's example, "a regular communication throughout the whole nation might be kept up with the most perfect harmony."

The Sheffield Society was an inspiration to the neighborhood. With "an attentive eye" upon it, societies were forming upon the Sheffield model in nearby towns and villages. As early as January 1792 people in Belpar, Derbyshire, thirty miles away, sought Sheffield's advice in organizing a society. Sheffield in turn, with the usual provincial deference and the natural sense of isolation from the metropolis, desired the encouragement and advice of the veteran London reformers. Going beyond the request for an epistolary communication, the Sheffield Society asked that twelve of its members be accepted as associate members by the London SCI. By this "close connexion," said Sheffield, it could better "render assistance to their fellow-citizens in this neighbourhood," and they in their turn "may extend useful knowledge still further, from town to village, . . . until the whole nation be sufficiently enlightened, and united in the same cause, which cannot fail of being the case wherever the excellent works of Mr. Thomas Paine find residence." This interesting suggestion for associate memberships was approved by the SCI and set a precedent soon followed by other provincial societies.

By this time another reformist organization had come into existence. It was destined to achieve such prominence as to overshadow the provincial societies and to win general recognition as the society which introduced the working class into direct political activity. The founding genius was the shoemaker, Thomas Hardy, of fair appearance though slightly pockmarked, tall and slender, plain in dress, hard working, an unrivaled example of probity, filled with the fire of indignant resolution that the people should recover their political rights. He had migrated from Scotland when in his early twenties about the time when the American Revolutionary War began. Dr. Price's famous pro-American pamphlet *Observations on the Nature of Civil Liberty* convinced him of the justice of the American cause and more important, aroused a permanent interest in public affairs. Hardy's affiliation with a Dissenting congregation in Covent Garden strengthened his reformist tendencies. Probably as a believer in the rights of man rather than in Anglo-Saxon democracy, Hardy spoke of "restoring" the right to vote, or "reestablishing" the rights of man. He meant all men "black or white, high or low, rich or poor." Thus, anyone opposed to the slave trade was in Hardy's mistaken judgment a friend of freedom and the rights of man. The paramount right, for Englishmen, was the right to vote.

On January 25, 1792, Hardy and eight friends, over pipes after supper at the Bell Tavern off the Strand, talked about hard times, high prices, heavy taxes, and parliamentary reform. Without an elaborate dialectic, they blamed their economic troubles upon the politicians. "Could not the nation, by a proper use of its moral powers, set itself free?" The answer to this rhetorical question was yes. They knew at once that if Parliament were reformed, the votes of the people would set things straight. They never framed a program of economic reform; their immediate object, beyond which they never got, was the radical reform of Parliament—universal suffrage and annual elections. They resolved to work for these "by all justifiable means," that is, by "informing the people of the violence that had been committed on their most sacred rights, and of uniting them in an endeavour to recover these rights." Before the group left the Bell Tavern they sketched out a plan of organization designed to bring working men—mechanics, shopkeepers, and small tradesmen—into political activity, and to promote political education among them. Hardy was chosen Secretary (surely by acclamation) and Treasurer. Returning home that night, he carried eight pennies in dues with which to begin the work of reforming Parliament and recovering the rights of Englishmen.

The first volume of the original letter book kept by Hardy begins with the resolutions of organization, prefaced by some examples of the deplorable inequality of representation and by a statement of intention to mobilize the opinions of the unrepresented. The organization was called the Corresponding Society of the Unrepresented Part of the People of Great Britain. Every man age twenty or over was eligible to join, at a one shilling entrance fee and one penny a week dues, if he believed in universal manhood suffrage, was willing to work to achieve it, and was recommended by a member. The Society grew slowly at first, both in membership and self-confidence. Hardy never hesitated to initiate contacts and ask for advice. From Sheffield in early April he obtained the idea of subdividing when the original society grew to unwieldy size. By that time the membership of the London Corresponding Society approached one hundred and the problem of organization and management was important. The solution was to throw off divisions of thirty members each when the original and subsequent ones reached sixty. Each division had its local officers, and each sent a delegate to the permanent committee which met every Thursday. On every Friday the delegates reported back to their divisional meetings. The most important committee was the Committee of Correspondence, but Hardy seems to have acted often upon his own initiative, and certainly carried the burden of the correspondence.

The first internal tension developed in March when the LCS decided to address the nation. Members could not agree upon the wording. Hardy told Horne Tooke, then a dominant influence in the SCI, of their difficulties, and even expressed impatience with his refractory colleagues. One draft of the resolutions was de-

1. Major John Cartwright, in an engraving published in 1823. One of the most radical reformers, Cartwright championed the cause of American independence and fathered the Society for Constitutional Information.

TAKE YOUR CHOICE!

Reprefentation and Refpect:	Impofition and Contempt.
Annual Parliaments and Liberty:	Long Parliaments and Slavery.

Where annual election ends, flavery begins.
Hift. Eff. on Brit. Conft.

A free government, in order to maintain itfelf free, hath need every day of fome new provifion in favour of Liberty. Machiavel.

I wifh the maxim of Machiavel was followed, that of examining a conftitution, at certain periods, according to its firft principles: this would correct abufes and fupply defects. Lord Camden.

And now—in the name of all that is holy—let us confider whether a fcheme may not be laid down for obtaining the neceffary reformation of parliament. Burgh.

LONDON:
Printed for J. ALMON, oppofite Burlington-Houfe, in Piccadilly.
M.DCC.LXXVI.

2. "Take Your Choice!" The alternatives, reform and stagnation, were boldly stated in the pamphlet published by Major John Cartwright in 1776.

3. Dr. Joseph Priestley, Nonconformist minister, distinguished chemist, and a leading English reformer. A portrait by Ellen Sharples.

4. Dr. Richard Price, the Unitarian minister at Newington Green; philosopher, mathematician, and author of radical texts. A portrait by Benjamin West. COPYRIGHT THE ROYAL SOCIETY, LONDON AND REPRODUCED WITH THEIR PERMISSION.

5. " View in the Strand," an engraving of 1815. The Bell Tavern and the Crown and Anchor, favorite meeting places of reforming groups, stood nearby.

6. Ludgate Hill and St. Paul's Cathedral in 1804. Nearby the Honest Whigs and the S.C.I. met in the London Coffee House.

7. John Thelwall, a portrait attributed to William Hazlitt. The author of "The Rights of Nature" (1796) was acquitted in the treason trials of 1794.

8. *(Opposite page, upper left)* Thomas Hardy, Secretary to the London Corresponding Society of the Unrepresented Part of the People of Great Britain. Hardy embodied the best qualities of the working class reformers, and his acquittal in the 1794 treason trials called forth wide-spread rejoicing.

9. *(Opposite page, upper right)* John Horne Tooke, a 1791 engraving by Annibal Scratch, entitled "Protheus on Privileges." A gentleman philologist, a founder of the Bill of Rights Society, Tooke was acquitted of a treason charge in 1794.

Published as the Act directs by Bentley & Co Feb 1 1791.

TREASON

COOL ARGUMENTS

10. Thomas Erskine, M.P., the eloquent counsel whose skillful defense secured acquittals for Hardy, Tooke and Thelwall. This 1794 engraving by J. Cruikshank is entitled "Cool Arguments!!!".

11. Thomas Muir, "Illustrious Martyr in the glorious cause/ Of truth, of freedom, and of equal laws" in this 1793 engraving. This prominent Scottish reformer was convicted of sedition in 1793 and transported to Australia.

12. Joseph Gerrald, sent from London to the Edinburgh Convention of Delegates of the People, 1793. He was convicted of sedition and transported to Australia in 1794, after this engraving was made by I. Kay.

13. "Citizen" Maurice Margarot, another delegate from the London Corresponding Society to the British Convention at Edinburgh, and also convicted in the Scottish sedition trials.

14. "The Rights of Man; or Tommy Paine, the little American Taylor, taking the Measure of the Crown, for a new Pair of Revolution-Breeches," 1791, by Gillray.

RIGHTS OF MAN:

BEING AN

ANSWER TO MR. BURKE's ATTACK

ON THE

FRENCH REVOLUTION.

BY

THOMAS PAINE,

SECRETARY FOR FOREIGN AFFAIRS TO CONGRESS IN THE
AMERICAN WAR, AND
AUTHOR OF THE WORK INTITLED "*COMMON SENSE.*"

LONDON:
PRINTED FOR J. S. JORDAN, No. 166. FLEET-STREET.
MDCCXCI.

15. Tom Paine's "Rights of Man" in the first edition, 1791.

16. Thomas Paine, an engraving dated 1793 from a Romney portrait. The peripatetic author of "Common Sense" and the "Rights of Man" was the most famous and controversial of the English Jacobins.

17. "Promenade in the State Side of Newgate." This caricature of prominent reformers and sympathizers was engraved by Newton in 1793. On the print is written "Choice Jail Birds," and among them are shown #7, John Frost talking with Joseph Gerrald reading a newspaper; behind them Thomas Lloyd faces Horne Tooke; and the second man from the right is the author and printer Daniel Isaac Eaton.

18. A Gillray caricature from 1790 of Dr. Price. Burke's hands bear the symbols of Church and King, and his spectacles support the "Reflections on the Revolutions in France." The title: "Smelling out a Rat; . . . or . . . The Atheistical-Revolutionist disturbed in his Midnight 'Calculations.'"

19. "The Friends of the People." Dr. Priestley and Tom Paine conspire under diabolical influence in this caricature by Cruikshank of 1792.

20. "Revolution Anniversary or, Patriotic Incantations," July 12, 1791, by Dent. The figures dancing around the cauldron of "French Spirits" represent Priestley, Fox, Dr. Joseph Towers, and Sheridan.

21. (Above) "Copenhagen House," a 1795 caricature by Gillray of the meeting held in Copenhagen Fields on November 12 to protest the "Two Acts." On the platform, right foreground, the speaker is John Thelwall. John Gale Jones speaks on the platform to left, while the tiny figure speaking with both arms raised in center background is William Hodgson.

23. "Fashion before Ease; or, A good Constitution sacrificed, for a Fantastick Form." Tom Paine laces Britannia's stays in this Gillray caricature of 1793.

22. *(Left)* "A Picture of Great Britain in the Year 1793." In this 1794 caricature by Cruikshank, the diabolical forces of reform attack Britannia and her defenders. Fox, leading the attack, is repulsed by Pitt, next to whom stands John Reeves.

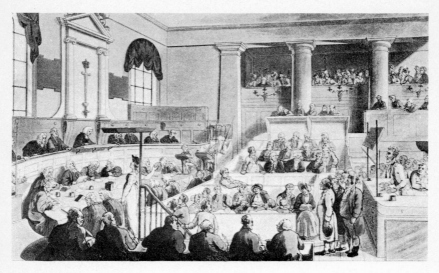

24. Old Bailey in 1800—the scene of the 1794 trials of Thomas Hardy, John Horne Tooke and John Thelwall for high treason.

25. The House of Commons in 1808.

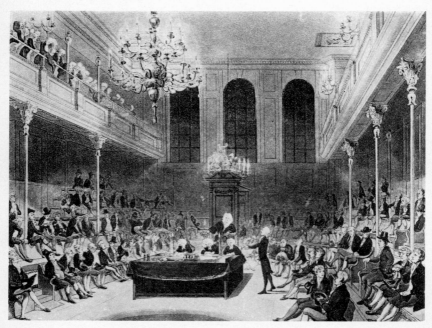

feated; some members thought it too listless, others that it was crude, "too low and contemptible" to go out from London to provincial societies. Hardy doubted whether the address would be ready soon in view of the "silly importance" of some members. Possibly he was referring to Maurice Margarot, a new member. A Marylebone merchant, Margarot had traveled in Europe and was partial to French ways and dress. Small and frail, he was clever, opinionated, courageous—or rash—and possibly not completely honest. Judging from his later performances it is not difficult to imagine him quickly achieving prominence in the LCS. He was chairman before the end of the year 1792. The Society adopted his revision of the address after deciding that it could not wait for Paine to draft one. Paine, who was not a member, was a good friend to Hardy who probably would have preferred him to Margarot as the author of the Society's first address to the public. The business did not end there. Hardy sent the draft to Tooke for criticism. Tooke presented it to the meeting of the SCI which resolved, without permission from Hardy and with lordly condescension, to send out the address for publication. Tooke signed Hardy's name and sent it off to the *Argus*.

Once they saw themselves in print, members of the LCS, none of them literary people, were proud of themselves. The address consisted of eight resolutions, expressing the usual platitudes, or in the minds of the sponsors, great political truths. Every man should have a "share" in the government and then "oppressive taxes, unjust laws, restrictions of liberty, and wasting of the public money," would be ended. The LCS renounced "tumult and violence" as means of obtaining parliamentary reform and pledged itself to employ the weapons of peaceful persuasion, "reason, firmness, and unanimity." Hardy busily circulated reprints to his growing circle of correspondents. The London and Manchester Societies for Constitutional Information acceded to his request for a regular correspondence. Another began in mid-April when Hardy approached the Southwark Friends of the People, just formed "for the Diffusion of Political Knowledge." Initially moderate, the Southwark Society flourished quickly. Its platform, radical in essence but restrained in expression, advocated the sovereignty of the people, the right of all men to "equal, active citizenship," and the need for "adequate representative government."

With the generous help of Horne Tooke, the good wishes of Paine, and the sympathy of the SCI, the LCS grew larger, stronger, and more confident. In May it published another address; it began correspondences with reform societies in Portsmouth and Edinburgh; at the end of July it established its eleventh and twelfth divisions. Six of its members were accepted as associates by the SCI. There is some uncertainty about its total membership. Estimates range from one thousand to ten thousand. Even the smaller figure may be too large if the maximum divisional size of sixty was adhered to. But there is no doubt of its vigor. Members might take it as a measure of their importance that local justices threatened to revoke the license of the Bell Tavern's landlord if he continued to play host to their meetings. So the Society moved into another jurisdiction and met henceforth at the Unicorn in Covent Garden. From there on August 6 it issued another address, even more than the previous ones flamboyant, alluring and naïve. The people of England must be made to understand their stake in parliamentary reform. When it was obtained, "soon then should we see our liberties restored, the press free, the laws simplified, judges unbiased, juries independent, needless places and pensions retrenched, immoderate salaries reduced, the public better served, taxes diminished, and the necessaries of life more within the reach of the poor, youth better educated, prisons less crowded, old age better provided for, and sumptuous feasts at the expense of the starving poor, less frequent." This vision of a great society came straight from Paine —all except the premise. Paine would not agree that a mere reform of the House of Commons would inaugurate Utopia.

The spirit of Paine and the excitement of association were spreading everywhere. In March 1792 the Manchester Constitutional Society sent to the SCI resolutions thanking Paine for his "excellent and practicable plans" for achieving great social improvements. Paine's presence was not needed to encourage the Society's resolution of concurrence in Manchester's sentiments.

At this meeting, the SCI elected to honorary membership the American Joel Barlow, then in London. His *Advice to the Privileged Orders*, as emphatically republican as the *Rights of Man*, took for granted the imminence of an irresistible "general revolution," and so Barlow's pamphlet attempted "to contemplate its probable effects, and to comfort" persons who were alarmed at the prospect of revolution.

From Norwich came cheering news of reformist activity. The Norwich Revolution Society, with seven confederated clubs and "some hundreds" of members, formed the "United Political Societies." In them, somewhat unusually, lower-class and middle-class members associated. The confederation was a kind of library association; books were purchased out of dues and circulated among constituent clubs. Members met twice a month. A committee of correspondence handled book selections and other literary business; a committee of twelve paid regular visits to the confederated clubs. The Norwich Society was ambivalent. They recommended Mackintosh's *Vindiciae Gallicae,* one of the moderate replies to Burke, as the best statement of their principles, although they went beyond Mackintosh's New Whiggism in desiring universal suffrage and annual Parliaments. They did not know quite what to say about Paine and Barlow except that their books had been "read with attention, and circulated with avidity." Norwich desired close relations with the SCI and proposed twelve men for associate membership. They were elected on May 4.

Throughout the first six months of 1792, when new reform societies were springing up, the prestige of the SCI reached heights it had never before attained, at least in the estimation of the working class. In the early 1780's it was the Yorkshire Association and the county movements which were known in the country, while the influence of the SCI was felt mainly in the metropolis, and only by individuals elsewhere. By late 1791 its reputation as the steady champion of reform for over a dozen years made it a kind of Nestor to whom the new societies, lacking in experience and confidence, tended to look for advice. The Society's long campaign of educating England by addresses and pamphlets made it seem the source of ideas about reform, until Paine wrote his *Rights of Man*. The provincial reformers respected individual members of the SCI because they were authors and veterans of reform campaigns. Some of the admiration for Paine rubbed off on the Society because he belonged to it and it had been something of a sponsor to him. Out in the provinces it was natural at first to identify Paine with the SCI whose actions encouraged the error. When the Manchester Constitutional Society sent in resolutions of praise for Paine, the SCI on March 16, 1792, resolved to assure Manchester of their "hearty concurrence." Outsiders were not yet aware of the substantial differences between the SCI and Paine. Though the ideas of other members stopped far short of Paine's, the Society spoke in his support, and so the public was encouraged to identify them. Paine himself mentioned the "honourable patronage" which the Society had given to his *Rights of Man*.

It is not surprising that in June 1794 when the Committee of Secrecy of the House of Commons reported on seditious practices, it emphasized the role of the London SCI. From the documents in its possession, said the Committee, it appeared "that not only the London Corresponding Society, but all the principal societies in the country, have been regulated under the immediate auspices of the Society for Constitutional Information, and have both in their origins and progress, looked up to that society for their guidance and direction in the pursuit of their common object." The evidence hardly justifies the use of so strong a word as "auspices," but it supports the idea that other societies "looked up to" the SCI. The Lords' Committee of Secrecy agreed with its counterpart in the Commons, and for a curious reason. It was incredible that the LCS could flourish without the direction of persons of "superior education, and more cultivated talents" than those possessed by its own members. The Lords refused to believe that the working class could organize agitation and carry on literary correspondence. Lord Grenville was certain that the LCS was "conducted by" higher persons. The Lords' Committee mistakenly concluded that the LCS "appears to have been planned and directed by leading members of the Society for Constitutional Information."

Societies acted on their own initiative in the provinces as well as in London. In April 1792 the Manchester Constitutional Society sent two of its young leaders, the merchant Thomas Cooper and the engineer James Watt, Jr., to Paris, bearing an address to the Jacobin Society. When it learned of this, the London SCI hastened to get in on the act by framing an address to the Jacobins, their "Brothers, and Fellow Citizens of the World." The London Society tried to give the impression that it had not been caught by surprise, and suggested its seniority by saying that the reception given to the delegates of the Manchester Society, "united with our Society, has been communicated to us by the correspondence of those gentlemen." The uncharacteristic flamboyancy of the London Society's address gives the impression of a desperate effort to recover face with the Jacobins. This was an age of "amity" among peoples; the common enemies were governments which had destroyed the "fraternity of the human race," and "a herd of courtiers fattening on the spoil of the public." "Our hearts go with you; and in saying this, we believe we utter the voice of millions." If any society could speak for the English people, it was the London SCI, and the Jacobins were not to think otherwise.

If the parliamentary committees overstated the leadership of the SCI and underestimated the abilities of the provincial and working class leaders, it remains true that in 1792 the SCI was the best known and most highly respected of all those in existence. Its network of correspondence extended more widely than ever before, because now it included many new societies. On June 1, the secretary reported that he had sent out copies of a letter from Paine and the Society's answering resolutions to the following societies and in the following quantities:

1200—Sheffield Constitutional Society
1200—Norwich Constitutional Society
 200—Southwark Constitutional Society
 200—London Corresponding Society
 200—to a person who would send them to Derby
 200—to the Constitutional Whigs
 200—to the Society of Belpar

And he would send:

> 600—to Birmingham
> 200—to the Society of Aldgate
> 1200—to Mr. [Thomas] Walker of Manchester
> 200—to Liverpool via Lord Daer
> 500—to Cambridge via Mr. [John] Rutt
> 200—to Lord Semphill [and Saltoun] for Glasgow

"When bad men combine, the good must associate," Burke had written in 1770. In the spring of 1792 something like that precept influenced the minds of moderate reformers in and out of Parliament. The spreading wildfire of societies infused with the ideas or the spirit of Paine threatened to consume the hopes of less pretentious men who thought that anything so radical even as universal suffrage was not reform but destruction of the constitution. Wyvill feared that the growth of Paine's influence would "operate more, in all probability, against any measures of Reformation, however temperate they may be, than any other circumstance whatever." To counteract radicalism and direct attention to moderate reform, a group of gentlemen organized hastily at the Freemason's Tavern on April 11. They adopted the name "The Friends of the People" and framed a declaration of purpose. They intended to work for "more equal representation of the people" and shorter Parliaments. They appointed a committee of twelve, of whom eight were M. P.'s, and instructed it to bring in on the nineteenth of April an Address to the People. A week later the address was adopted. It argued the case for moderate reform which would "re-instate the constitution upon its true principles and original ground." It ended with a promise to introduce a reform bill in the next session of Parliament. Twenty-three of the signers, or almost one-fourth, were members of the House of Commons, mainly followers of Fox, though he was not a signer. About one-fifth were also members of the SCI. Almost that many were Dissenters, prominent in trade, finance and the pulpit. And all of the members were men who could pay an admission fee of two and one-half guineas, and the same amount as annual dues.

This address was published, and at once the Friends of the People found themselves castigated for timidity. During the day of April 27 some members of the SCI must have been very busy, because when the Society met that evening it approved a long letter and instructed the chairman, Major Cartwright, to sign it and send it to the Friends of the People. This was a nice business. Cartwright had signed the Friends' declaration for moderate reform, and now he signed a very sharp letter criticizing the Friends for their moderation. Not surprisingly, five M. P.'s resigned from the Friends because of Cartwright's behavior.

The letter of the SCI reveals the disunity among reformers. It began politely enough with an expression of satisfaction over the institution of the Friends of the People. Then it hoped that the M. P.'s would not lose their zeal, as formerly some had done. The letter in fact doubted whether a reform would ever come merely from parliamentary initiative. The SCI had never believed that Parliament would reform itself, and that is why it had always insisted upon the necessity of wide public support. The SCI did not doubt that eventually the Friends would "see the wisdom of pursuing a like course." The Friends "may boast of names, of wealth, of talent, and even of principles; but without the fellowship of the people, . . . your association, . . . will most assuredly crumble to dust." This advice the Society offered in order "to warn its new brethren" against the dangers of isolating themselves from the people.

Such unnaturally Painite sentiments expressed with such smug superiority irked the Friends of the People. They responded acidly. "Fully sensible that the Society for Constitutional Information have made no sacrifice to delicacy in their address to us, we on our part shall affect no disguise." The Friends accused the Society of subscribing to Paine's "language of delusion." This letter repudiated the doctrine of the sufficiency of human reason, bending slightly towards the Burkean view of man as a "Creature of habit." It insisted that a moderate reform in harmony with "principles of the constitution" would eliminate the grievances the reformers complained of. The Friends of the People preferred to "decline all future intercourse" with a society whose principles were inimical to the interests of the people.

Notwithstanding this language, the difference between these two societies did not spring from conflicts between universal suffrage and a property based franchise, between representation of people and representation of interests, between confidence in the wisdom of the people and doubt of the ability of the people to vote intelligently.* The SCI was not Painite, though some members, with Cartwright, desired universal suffrage. Others, with Tooke, preferred reforms more like those desired by the Friends than by some of their own colleagues in the SCI. In 1782 and steadily thereafter Tooke rejected Cartwright's contention that every man has a "right to an equal share" in representation, contending instead that a man's share in political power should be proportionate to his "contribution to that power." Men could be free and secure without a voice in government. It was proper to deny the franchise to the dependent and the ignorant. Like most eighteenth century Englishmen, Tooke would connect the franchise with property; specifically he recommended a two-pound ratepaying qualification reinforced with a complicated plural voting arrangement for wealthier persons.

When the SCI thought "the fellowship of the people" necessary for the success of the reformers, it did not mean necessarily that "the people" should receive the vote. It was reminding the Friends that the majority of Parliament opposed reform and would have to be made to yield it by the strength and pressure of extramural opinion. In this the SCI was correct. When it came in 1832, reform was enacted by a Parliament that succumbed to such pressure, yet the bill of 1832 retained the property qualification, making it uniform but without remarkably extending the franchise. The difference between the SCI and the Friends of the People grew out of personal dislikes, the anti-aristocratic bias of some members of the SCI, and the unwillingness of the Friends to recognize any opinions other than their own. The SCI rightly

---

* The Friends nevertheless had moved beyond the position of the old Yorkshire Association. The plan which they envisaged included a ratepayer franchise in the boroughs.

accused the Friends of isolating themselves inside St. Stephen's.

The publication of this disagreement advertised the differences among reformers and caused uneasiness. The Norwich Society for Political Information was puzzled by the variants. Sheffield seemed to desire universal suffrage at one time and then the moderation of the Friends of the People at another. Manchester, by addressing Paine, seemed to show a preference for republicanism. What Norwich really wanted to know was whether the generality of societies favored universal suffrage and annual Parliaments, as they did, or whether "it is their private design to rip up monarchy by the roots, and place democracy in its stead." It was very clear that anyone who showed sympathy for Paine laid himself open to guilt by association.

Except for the Friends of the People, all of the societies by their hyperboles and indiscretions contributed to the uncertainties and misunderstandings. The reticence of the Friends on the other hand encouraged doubts. When on April 30, 1792, Charles Grey, who as Prime Minister would preside over the passage of the Reform Bill of 1832, gave notice of the Friends' intention to move for reform sometime during the next year, he said categorically that they did not yet have a specific plan of reform, though their general views were present in their published declaration and address. The ensuing debate wandered over the ground of reform. Burke dragged in Paine, accusing the societies which recommended his book of being "avowed enemies of the constitution." He refused to admit the possibility of a temperate reform, and therefore could not accept the modest claims of the Friends. To Burke, temperate reform was a contradiction in terms. This parliamentary "conversation" did not clarify anything about the reformers' position. As late as February 1793 the LCS tried to learn what the Friends intended to advocate. The Friends refused to "surrender" their discretion as to the time when they would bring in their plan and the proposals it would contain. The LCS answered with dignity. They merely wanted to know because they had to decide whether to support the Friends' plan; if reformers were to work together in confidence, "there must be no secrets." Their request was in no way an infringement upon the

Friends' discretionary freedom. The "country correspondents" of the LCS had also wanted to know about the Friends' plan, and for the same reason. Moreover, out in the provinces there were suspicions of the Friends' motives. Did they mean to serve the interest of a party, or of the public? The question was blunt, but, with a pun, did not the people always have a right to inquire about "those who call themselves their friends"?

The LCS came close to the mark. It has been customary for historians to admire the courage of the Members of Parliament who advocated reform, mild though it was, and who from their minority positions opposed the government's distaste for public discussion of such questions as war and peace, parliamentary reform, and freedom of opinion. These minority members risked opprobrium and their political careers. But in their privileged positions they never had to risk their physical freedom or their lives as did the working class reformers. The Friends of the People preferred to make their own definitions of the public interest and to work for it in their own way. Their isolation from the people was of their own choosing. They were unable to break with the traditions of the governing class or with inherited assumptions about the nature of the constitution. They recognized the existence of discontent among the lower orders. They proposed a moderate reform, hoping to allay discontent. But they would make the decisions about the means of doing this. The interest of the public was to trust in the wisdom of their governors. The Friends of the People did nothing to bridge the gulf between their class and the lower orders. The emergence of Chartism so quickly after the passage of the Reform Bill of 1832 was anticipated in the separation between the Friends of the People and the working class societies in the 1790's.

The Friends of the People made clear in April 1792 that they had no time for the doctrines of Paine, nor any bond of sympathy with radical reformers, Painite or not. The government, however, opposed even as much reform as the Friends would support, and was even more vehemently hostile to Paine. If his opinions spread, said Pitt, "we should have a bloody revolution." It seemed best, therefore, to suppress him by direct action, and to attempt to stamp out sedition instead of overpowering it by counter argument.

The first step was to proceed against J. S. Jordan, the printer of the second part of the *Rights of Man*. But Jordan pleaded guilty, meaning only that he admitted he was the publisher. It remained to deal with Paine and with the book. On May 21, 1792, the Attorney General filed an information against Paine charging him with seditious libel. Simultaneously there appeared a Royal Proclamation against the "wicked and seditious writings" being spread about the nation. Besides warning the people against such works, the proclamation charged the magistrates to seek out the authors and printers, to inquire into public disorders, and to send the information to the King's ministers, "it being our determination, . . . to carry the laws vigorously into execution against such offenders. . . ." The SCI denounced the Proclamation and circulated six thousand copies of their denunciation among reform societies. The House of Commons, after a furious debate, presented a loyal address testifying their gratitude for the King's solicitude for the "welfare and happiness of his people." Charles Grey expressed the minority argument, one that it would continue to affirm. "There ought to be a perfect liberty for the circulation of all opinions about public affairs." If any publication involved public safety, ministers could prosecute the author and publisher in the courts. This ought to be done openly, not under "a system of espionage" incompatible with the existence of a free people. A clear distinction should be made between advocacy of parliamentary reform and conduct which was destructive of civil society. The debate made clear the growing tendency of government to identify the two, and to sweep all reform efforts into the orbit of Paine. In fact, Dundas admitted as much. The debate also established the position on freedom of speech that the parliamentary minority would hold to during the next years and for which they have received the praise of historians.

Paine took all of this very calmly. Three days before the government initiated action against him he learned of their intentions and thought it all the more important therefore to hasten the production of a cheap edition of the *Rights of Man*. The SCI passed resolutions pledging support to Paine. On June 6 Paine wrote an open letter to Dundas affirming his authorship of the book and his steadfast adherence to its teachings. The SCI circulated twelve thousand copies of the letter. On June 8 the trial was postponed until December, and Paine who had entered a plea of not guilty remained at liberty, but under government surveillance. The LCS undertook a subscription to pay for his defense. Paine attended meetings of the SCI at least twice during the summer although a previous engagement kept him from the Bastille Day dinner. He read proof on new editions of the *Rights of Man*, and wrote a *Letter Addressed to the Addressers on the Late Proclamation*. Its publication in the fall, when Paine was in France, merely re-affirmed what the government already believed about him. He condemned the Friends of the People for insincerity, rejected the idea that Parliament would reform itself, and called for revolution—that is, a convention elected by the people to write a new constitution for Great Britain. Paine had gone to France in September, not stealthily but openly, to attend the National Convention to which he had just been elected. He was accompanied by a Frenchman who had come over to escort him, and by the barrister John Frost, a member both of the SCI and the LCS and a ten-year reform veteran who had once been in Pitt's confidence. Government agents kept the travelers under observation and customs officials searched them before they boarded the packet. This harassment was as much as the government cared to do. No effort was made to prevent his departure; the government was glad to be rid of him. It is not true that Paine left England one jump ahead of the sheriff. England never saw him again.

The Royal Proclamation and the proceedings against Paine not only provoked some momentary second thoughts among radical reformers but encouraged opposition to them. In planning for a Bastille Day dinner, the metropolitan radicals encountered difficulties. The LCS and the Southwark Friends of the People, temporarily intimidated, opposed advance advertising. The SCI could think of no reason for silence and upon their insistence the dinner was publicly announced. Members dutifully assembled at the Shakespeare Tavern where Horne Tooke presided over an apparently uneventful meeting. Tavern keepers were showing increasing reluctance to entertain the societies. The exclusions rather inconvenienced than crippled the reformers. The divisions of the LCS took to meeting in private homes or hired rooms.

The inactivity of ministers disguised their quiet efforts against the reformers. An investigation was made of the state of mind of troops billeted about the country. Government informers and Bow Street runners began to infiltrate the societies; magistrates wrote in about "seditious" activities in their neighborhoods; the files of the Home Secretary and the Treasury Solicitor were filling with disturbing reports. The Marquis of Buckingham asked his brother, Lord Grenville, the Foreign Secretary, for advice about grand jury proceedings. Buckingham was growing impatient with what he thought was governmental laxity in proceedings against those who spread "libellous publications." Dundas, on a visit to Scotland in the autumn, described to Pitt a "very bad" situation there. It would get worse if the Painite "spirit of liberty and equality" continued to spread.

In fact it was, for the reformers increased their activities after the first shock of the Royal Proclamation wore off. At the end of the summer the cheap edition of Paine appeared, and sales, which had been good throughout the summer, increased enormously. The desire to associate continued; new reform societies appeared in Leicester, Coventry, Birmingham, and Edinburgh, where seven or eight were formed. The editor of the Sheffield *Patriot* foresaw Scotland taking the lead. Out in the provinces the spirit of Paine seemed to be stronger than in London. On September 17 the Friends of Universal Peace and of the Rights of Man at Stockport, in a letter to the LCS, seemed to anticipate Paine whose *Letter to the Addressers* described reform as "a worn-out hackneyed subject." Doubting whether reform would come "from the present order of things," Stockport thought that "odious laws" would not be done away with except "by the people assembled in convention."

The word convention was acquiring a deeper meaning than when used by the reformers of the 1780's. These were working class reformers, not the gentlemen, professionals, and affluent businessmen of the preceding decades. When Dr. Jebb or Cart-wright or Price thought of a convention, they envisaged it as composed of and led by their own kind. The people would be followers, merely acquiescing in the actions of their betters. If in both instances a convention was thought of as a body to effect constitutional reforms, the later notions of a convention carried a different content because radicalism by 1792 had changed character.

For this Paine was initially responsible, but events in France also contributed. The latest French example suggested that a convention might also act as a government. After the tumultuous August days and the September massacres in Paris, the French victory over the allied armies at Valmy, and the gathering of the new French assembly under the name of National Convention, it was impossible for defenders of the established order in England to think of a convention except as synonymous with a government of destruction, murder, and terrorism. In fact, the LCS seemed taken aback by Stockport's bold insistence upon a convention. London's views "in as strong terms as prudence will permit" went to "nothing short" of "[but nothing beyond] an honest and annual parliament, . . . chosen by the whole nation."

Prudence was losing ground among the radicals whose societies, strongly stimulated by the exciting news from France, seemed to compete in indiscretions. As the *Annual Register* put it, after some slackening of activity following upon the Royal Proclamation of May, in the autumn of 1792 "sedition broke out again with augmented force." In the same letter in which it avoided even the word "convention," the LCS nevertheless challenged Stockport to associate its name with their own in a rousing address to the French Nation. Under date of September 27, the address of the LCS assured France that five thousand British citizens, and more each day, stepped forth to rescue their country from the disgrace brought upon it by "the supine Conduct of those in Power." The LCS also swore "Inviolable Friendship" with France and with the "Champions of Human Happiness." "Frenchmen you are already free and Britons are preparing to become so!"—especially by throwing off the oppressions imposed by the British aristocracy, as France had freed herself from those of the old regime. This language may not have meant as much as alarmists read into it, but it was liable to various interpretations. The SCI received a copy of the address from the LCS along with a letter explaining its meaning—"should those in power here, dare (in violation of the Nation's pledged faith of Neutrality and in opposition to the well known sentiments of the people at large) to join the German Band of Despots united against Liberty, We disclaim all concurrence therein and will to a Man exert every justifiable means for counteracting their Machinations against the Freedom and the Happiness of Mankind." The SCI voted concurrence with the "intentions" of the LCS and "highly approved" of their spirit. But unlike Manchester and Norwich, the SCI abstained from adopting this address.

Though the LCS had stolen a march, the SCI offered their own address to the National Convention. The Society assured France that only "tyrants and slaves" opposed her; the people were her friends. "Go on, Legislators, in the work of human happiness." And France was assured that the SCI spoke "the sentiments of a great majority of the English nation." It was as though the Society feared losing its prestige in the eyes of the National Convention; as they had done earlier to the Jacobins, they claimed to represent British opinion. Possibly the French wondered who really spoke for England, because the Revolution Society, rousing up on November 4 from its year-long sleep, also claimed this honor in a sympathetic address to France.

There is evidence that these addresses were meant sincerely. Such a substantial person as Thomas Rogers, the Cornhill banker, in letters to his son, expressed sympathy for the French. The Jacobins of France, he said on August 26, had to resort to drastic suppressive actions against domestic enemies of the Revolution to save their country and their lives. Rogers dreaded to open a newspaper for fear it might contain bad news about the war; if Prussian and Austrian armies defeated the French, then "the Liberties of Europe are lost," he wrote on September 13. Rogers was all in favor of aiding France, though he feared that a subscription proposed by Horne Tooke might harm the cause of liberty by creating a reaction in England. Such a proposal "was of a piece with ye rest of Horne Tooke's politics." The man was a fool and his advice was not to be heeded.

These addresses of the societies raised an interesting point. The word "neutrality" sustained different meanings. The official policy of the British government was one of neutrality toward the European war, and this meant not only staying out of the conflict, but also refusing aid to either side. Unwilling to join in a crusade against the revolutionary government in France, Pitt and Grenville distrusted the motives of Prussia and Austria in their war against France. To the English radicals, neutrality was non-participation in the war but sympathy and material aid to the revolutionaries. The addresses of the reform societies were manifestations of moral support. The American, Joel Barlow, and John Frost, both members of the SCI, delivered its address in person to the French National Convention. The Society also gave material support. It took up a subscription and commissioned Thomas Hardy to buy one thousand pairs of shoes to be sent by him to the National Convention. It also appointed a committee for foreign correspondence. These actions hardly evinced neutrality in the strict sense of the word, and they encouraged the French to think that Pitt's government did not speak for the people of England.

In spite of provocations, the government had not been vigorous against the radicals. Before the end of the year 1792 its greatest open act of repression was the trial of Paine in absentia on December 18. This was important symbolically because Paine epitomized all that was susceptible of exaggeration in the radical movement and could be made to appear as revolutionary, republican, levelling, and partisan toward France. The LCS knew this when they addressed reform societies in England just before Paine's trial began. Written by the barrister Felix Vaughan, though signed by Margarot and Hardy, the address denied the accusation that the LCS consisted of levellers and republicans. They desired full civil liberties which they held to be consistent with the principles of the constitution. They asserted the justice of the French Revolution but denied that Britain, with her constitution, however defective, would have to appeal "to the same awful tribunal with our brethren on the continent." The radicals of England, insisted the LCS, advocated parliamentary reform, and that was all.

What the government was prepared to think of such professions of innocence made by friends and admirers of Paine can be deduced from the information filed against him. It charged that Paine, "a wicked, malicious, seditious, and ill-disposed person" did "seditiously and maliciously" intend to "traduce and vilify" the Revolution Settlement and also the government of England by writing and publishing a "seditious libel." The case was tried at the London Guildhall before a special jury, that is with members meeting higher qualifications of social and economic status than the average common jury. The trial consisted mainly of two speeches, the opening by the Attorney General and the speech to the jury by the defense counsel. The only evidence presented established quickly the facts of authorship and publication. The defense offered no evidence; testimony would not avail for the real issues, whether the book was a libel, and whether the prosecution infringed freedom of the press.

The Attorney General, Sir Archibald Macdonald, concentrated upon conjuring up fears in the minds of the jury. He glossed the *Rights of Man* and pictured the chaotic consequences that would follow upon dissemination of the doctrines it espoused. The book was getting into the hands of trusting people who would be swayed by it. Even the little children were exposed to contamination when their sweetmeats were wrapped in pages from it. Besides interpreting the book, the Attorney General presented Paine in the worst possible light. Paine from Paris aided him in this, having written to him a saucy and contemptuous letter which the court permitted the Attorney General to read to the jury. The defense failed to erase the strong impression this letter made upon the jury.

Thomas Erskine argued the case for the defense. He was a member of the SCI and of the House of Commons, possibly the ablest barrister of his time in criminal cases, a keen mind and eloquent orator, a master of histrionics who knew how and when to faint before a jury, and a sincere believer in freedom of expression. He accepted Paine's brief against the arguments of friends who predicted ruin for his career if he did so. According to George Tierney, a Foxite M. P. and a member of the Friends of the People, Erskine worked on his speech for over a month, not expecting that he would be able to save Paine but confident that it would enhance his own reputation. Whether Tierney misrepresented Erskine's motives, he was right about the consequences of the speech.

Meant immediately for the jury, Erskine's oration has found its place in history, along with Milton's *Areopagitica,* as a noble assertion of a fundamental principle of a free society. To Erskine the question before the jury was whether Paine had exceeded the bounds "which the ancient wisdom and liberal policy of the English constitution have allotted to the range of a free press." He tried to persuade the jury against judging this issue by their own anticipations of the possible consequences if people read the book, or within the context of the times. To be a libel, it must be a "criminal publication under any circumstances, at any other time." Therefore the jury must consider the larger question— "the nature and extent of the liberty of the English press." Or, the freedom which every man enjoys, "not intending to mislead," to attempt to enlighten people upon the subject of government.

Erskine, like the Attorney General, glossed the *Rights of Man,* and presented a contrary interpretation. Paine, he said, did not encourage destruction of property rights or disobedience to law. If he criticized the English constitution, it was his right to express his opinions. Paine clearly stated his purpose to enlighten men, to persuade by the force of reason in a public controversy which Burke began. The unpopularity of Paine's opinions was immaterial. The question at issue was the liberty of the press. The jury should be cautious about infringing upon it. The danger of touching the freedom of the press is inability to know when to stop. If Paine's book were condemned, what book, asked Erskine, may be written?

He spoke for four hours in "defense of free opinion." He also fainted once. All, it seemed, in vain. The foreman of the jury dis-

charged the Attorney General from the necessity of speaking
again unless he desired to. When Sir Archibald sat down without
speaking, the foreman announced the verdict, "Guilty." Freedom
of the press and of opinion were not absolutes. They were relative to the times. They were limited by men's opinions of the
possible consequences of books and speeches, of ideas. That, in
effect, was what the special jury said. Yet when Erskine stepped
out of the Guildhall, the crowd in the courtyard cheered him and
bore him away on their shoulders.

CHAPTER VII

CHURCH AND KING

DURING the winter of 1792–1793 the government and the country showed their heightening concern with radical activities. Apart from the prosecution of Paine, who was outlawed, the government was not yet engaging in acts of direct coercion. It was stating its position, expressing its state of mind, and in certain instances laying the groundwork for repression. In the words of a contemporary Tory historian, "it appeared to government that the time was come when further delay would have been a criminal dereliction of their duty to the nation."

Parliament was not in session when on December 1 the King issued a proclamation supplementary to that of May 21. A continuing spirit of tumult and disorder, the efforts of "evil-disposed" persons and of incendiary societies conjoined with one another and in correspondence with foreigners, meaning Frenchmen, persuaded him of the need to prepare for forceful actions. Accordingly His Majesty was embodying the militia in ten counties. Behind the proclamation were overt evidences of discontent in the country corroborating urgent reports that for some months had been coming in to the Home Secretary and the Treasury Solicitor from alarmed magistrates who deplored the inadequacies of the civil power. The emphasis upon domestic troubles did not preclude the possibility of having to use the militia to repel invasion. The worsening of relations with France and the fact that the first calls were made upon the militia of the southeastern counties could not be disregarded. By May 1793 when England had been at war for three months, the call-up was completed.

As required by statute when the militia was embodied, the King directed Parliament to meet in a fortnight. Throughout the kingdom but in London especially arose expressions of gratitude for the royal concern for social order. Just a week earlier a scuffle in Cornhill broke out over the dispersal of a debating society being addressed by John Thelwall, the popular orator and member of the LCS. The London Common Council voted their thanks to the new Lord Mayor, Sir James Saunderson, for his vigorous action in preserving order. Although they were already expressing their loyalty in declarations of the City Companies, on December 5 some 1500 of the City business elite issued from Merchant Taylors Hall a declaration of attachment to the ancient constitution of King, Lords, and Commons. The claims eventually of eight thousand signatures were not exaggerated. Dissenters were among the signers who fretted about levelling threats to the security of property. Three were members of the Newington Green meeting, formerly ministered to by the late Dr. Price and now employing as morning preacher the militantly reformist Reverend Dr. Joseph Towers. He was active in the SCI and as a writer on political subjects.

The London business community should not be considered Birchite prototypes because they declared for social order and the constitution. Criticism of the inequality of representation and demands for reform were expressed at the Merchant Taylors meeting. It is important to remark the existence of reformist sentiments among persons and groups who affirmed allegiance to the constitution because loyalist declarations have been identified with desires for unqualified suppression of reform activities. Thus, the meeting in St. George's parish, Hanover Square, later in December, as well as some of the loyal associations springing up here and there in England and Scotland advocated moderate reform at the same time as they affirmed devotion to King and constitution. Some of the followers of Charles James Fox attended the St. George's meeting. Persons who anathemized reform did not speak for all loyalists. Among the supporters of the constitution who abhorred civil disorder various shades of opinion showed themselves, ranging from approval of moderate reform to detestation of any hint of reform.

A hard core opposition to reform was developing in and out of Parliament, however. When Parliament met on December 13, the speech from the throne called attention to the renewal of "seditious practices" designed to subvert the constitution, and emphasized the concert between the radicals and "persons in foreign countries." Appropriately, Sir James Saunderson moved the address of thanks. The Commons pledged "united vigilance and exertion" to preserve order. The ensuing debate publicized the disagreement between government and the Foxite minority on the state of the public mind, with the minority deploring infringements upon freedom of expression. They mustered only 50 votes against the government's 290. By January 4, 1793, the two houses had passed a bill regulating the entry and activities of aliens. Behind it lay fears of subversive strangers.

This darkening atmosphere of suspicion and fear enveloped Parliament, clouded the correspondence of Dundas, Pitt, Grenville, Burke, Windham, and Lord Fitzwilliam in Yorkshire, and unsettled the minds of substantial people in vestry meetings, quarter sessions, or in the taverns. It thickened not only because of the domestic activities of the reformers but also because of their associations with the French whose undeniable successes against the allied armies were accompanied by ominous movements towards new extremes of revolutionary excesses. The National Convention declared France a republic and in early November 1792 broadcast its readiness to assist other peoples who wished to abolish monarchy. The Convention tried the ex-King of France for crimes against the nation. At the end of the year it remained to decide whether he was guilty, whether the verdict should be ratified by the people, and if guilty, what the sentence should be. A furious struggle for control of the Revolution took place in connection with these questions. The victory went to those who found the King guilty, opposed a referendum and carried the decision for death, absolutely, on January 17 by 11 votes. Four days later Louis XVI was executed.

These events helped blacken the English reformers and strengthen the forces of reaction. The SCI complained of difficulties with the newspapers. Editors seemed fearful of printing its handouts. The SCI considered publishing its own "periodical paper." Attempts to revive the Friends of the Liberty of the Press, which had declined after the passage of Fox's Libel Law, were unsuccessful. The Friends met for this purpose on December 22, and occasionally during the early part of 1793. Their dinner of January 19 was attended by some six hundred people who heard Erskine repeat the arguments he had used in defending Paine. Unfortunately and not for the last time in a public meeting, Horne Tooke made a speech that displeased the audience. George Rous replied to him and then the assemblage broke up in a commotion. At a meeting of March 9 the Friends pledged themselves to a subscription to support the cause of freedom, but the results remain unknown. One of their objects was to oppose the loyal associations then forming in defense of the constitution. The Friends thought these associations dangerous to liberty. But to oppose them at this time was like commanding the tide to cease flowing. It probably made little difference that the Friends of the Liberty of the Press declined, for the members had other means of expressing themselves. In fact they were little more than the Friends of the People under another name and associated with other like-minded people. Many of the members sat in the House of Commons as Fox's minority.

The sentiments of the dominant people in the counties were well represented by the Marquis of Buckingham. He complained regularly to his brother, Lord Grenville, that the government was too inattentive to "libellous publications," that the Attorney General was lax, that the magistrates and the people needed to be invigorated against malign influences, and that the militia was tainted with sedition. Sentiments like these were spreading. Another kind of disaffection was taking hold of many people. Impatient with the ineffectiveness of constituted authority, private persons began to assume responsibility for restraining subversive activities. At Manchester the tavern keepers agreed to keep radical clubs out of their premises; at Cambridge politics were forbidden in the taverns; in many villages people began to regard their neighbors with suspicion and indiscreet individuals found themselves becoming objects of suspicion. John Frost, back from Paris, talked too freely in a public house in Marylebone and was literally kicked out of it. But not before his identity was established. His "crime" was reported to the Middlesex grand jury.

The SCI became so concerned about interferences with the meetings of political societies that it resolved "to consider" the conduct of the offending magistrates. The Society was even more distressed by the progress of the idea that its members were men "of dangerous principles" who favored violent measures. It was still more disturbed by a letter from the editors of the *Morning Post* and the *Morning Chronicle* explaining their refusal to print an address from Manchester. Since the verdict against Paine, they said, newspaper proprietors "tremble at inserting anything except fulsome Panegyrics" of government. Moreover, "the vile associations" then forming were exacerbating the alarms felt by the public and creating pressures which made judges and juries readier to convict. Ironically, the editors of the *Chronicle* printed an old Declaration from Derby four days later, on December 25, and for this were indicted for seditious libel on an information ex officio filed by the Attorney General.*

Anti-radical and anti-French opinions, already coagulating in many localities, were ripe for fuller organization. How much so is demonstrated by the astonishing speed with which scattered, spontaneous loyalist and anti-reform sentiments in the country were gathered together in the last weeks of 1792 and the early part of 1793 into a great force, negative in its repressive instincts, positive in its assertions of loyalty to King, Church and constitution. This kind of opinion was embodied in the "vile associations" mentioned with reprehension by the editors of the *Morning Chronicle*. The headquarters of reaction were at the notably impartial Crown and Anchor where the SCI also met.

At the trial for sedition in December 1793 of Thomas Briellat, a Shoreditch pump maker, Felix Vaughan for the defense described the power of the Association for the Preservation of Lib-

* See Appendix A for the text of the Declaration of the Derby Society for Political Information, July 16, 1792.

erty and Property when it was at the zenith of its influence. Briellat had been indicted on eleven counts, having "with a loud
voice" in the presence of several persons advocated reform in
what the hearers attested were very extreme words. It was
through the Association network that Briellat's statements came
to the attention of the grand jury. The Association, then a year
old, was in fact, said Vaughan, an information society with some
150 branches in London alone. Its ears were everywhere in the
kingdom—"there is not a word spoken by any of you in a
butcher's shop, or any other, but it may be carried" to the headquarters of the Association. From local affiliates organized on the
recommended model, information went from the hearer to the
local or parish committee, thence to the central committee whose
special subcommittee scrutinized the accusations. The serious
ones, particularly if they were not anonymous, were brought to
the attention of the Attorney General or the Treasury Solicitor
and thus prosecutions might be initiated.

No one ever denied this. In fact the *Annual Register* justified
the existence of the Association precisely on the ground that the
arms of the law, meaning the nondescript public police power,
could not effectively deal with secret societies and needed the
kind of help the Association rendered. When in the words of the
Newcastle Reform Society, "none but known friends" were admitted to meetings, ways of penetrating the societies' defences
had to be devised. The government gradually improved its means
of detection; the membership of the Association extended them
privately. Less by its assistance to legal processes than by its intimidating presence and by its propaganda efforts the Association
deepened the public mood of suspicion against reformers and
helped create the distorted impression that a great, monolithic
majority pledged itself to suppressing freedom of expression.

The Association with a capital A was the outstanding organiza-
tional success of this period. Of all the societies in England, whatever object they strove for, the Association most fully and
quickly saw the accomplishment of its stated purpose which was
"to save the Nation" by suppressing the political societies and the
reformers. The times, and the panic which they helped create,

favored its efforts; the government gave it strong support, conniving even at its founding. The well-informed Francis Plowden refused to believe the Association's denials that government had anything to do with its founding. But the energy and abilities of its leaders, and especially of its founder John Reeves ought not be undervalued as explanations of the Association's success. The sketch in the *Dictionary of National Biography* hardly does credit to Reeves' talents. Known best to posterity as the author of a *History of English Law,* his contemporaries knew him as a barrister (Eton, Merton College, Oxford B. A., and the Middle Temple), as a placeman who acquired his first government office at about the age of thirty and his last twenty years later when he became King's Printer in 1800. He was Chief Justice of Newfoundland in 1791–1792, returning to England some months before he formally organized the Association. His contacts with the Home Office and the Treasury Solicitor served well his own ambitions and the Association's, if there was any distinction. In founding the Association, he served the government well. The *Gentleman's Magazine* admitted this. The obituary notice in 1829 said that Reeves' services in organizing the loyal associations "were afterwards liberally rewarded," specifically by the appointment as King's Printer.

The published Papers of the Association tell only part of the story. It was not true that government knew nothing of the Association until its advertisements appeared, and it may be a matter of definition whether the government gave it financial support. It was certainly true, as the preface to the Papers said, that the Association must be understood in relation to the disturbing late months of 1792 and its success evaluated against the sense of crisis within particular segments of the population. It is questionable whether the organization meeting of November 20, 1792 at the Crown and Anchor was a meeting at all. There is reason for thinking that Reeves assigned that date to minutes and resolutions which he prepared and advertised as though a meeting had produced them. In any event the publication in the newspapers aroused enthusiasm, possibly beyond Reeves' most sanguine expectations.

The proceedings state that with Reeves in the chair, the meeting agreed to encourage the formation throughout the kingdom of private societies pledged "to support the Laws, to suppress seditious Publications, and to defend our Persons and Property." Unconnected with any party, these societies, the Association to coordinate them, would counteract the "nefarious designs . . . meditated by the wicked and senseless Reformers" both by discouraging them and by spreading political truth. Four days later, with Reeves again in the chair, another "meeting" expressed its pleasure over the reception accorded to its advertisement. It also described the structure of the Association. The local associations, preferably represented by select committees, would report to the Committee in London. At the top and at the bottom the real control was vested in the committees. There was no need for general meetings oftener than once a month, if that often, for these were not intended as debating societies but to do "real business." The Association units would circulate anti-reform literature sent out as reprints or originally commissioned pieces from Reeves' Committee. The local associations would not act independently against the reformers but rather would serve subordinately to the magistrates and the crown's law officers.

Reeves' Committee was not undistinguished. John Topham and Thomas Plumer were eminent barristers; the latter was Warren Hastings' defense counsel. John Bowles wrote anti-reform pamphlets. George Hobart was the son of an earl and succeeded to the title in 1793 on the death of his older brother who had been a lord-lieutenant of Ireland. Hobart had sat in the House of Commons for almost thirty years before 1780, but was best known as promoter of the opera in the Haymarket. Charles Townshend, a member of a distinguished family, was M. P. for Great Yarmouth. He had suffered in the election of 1784 from Dissenting opposition and only regained his seat in 1790. Charles Yorke, brother of the Earl of Hardwicke, was M. P. for Cambridgeshire and passionately anti-Dissent. William Devaynes had been a chairman of the East India Company. As a group opposing the radicals these men spoke for vested interests—aristocracy, land, rotten boroughs—and they were good Churchmen.

Of the many loyal associations that appeared in England and Scotland during the winter of 1792–1793, not all were affiliated with Reeves' Crown and Anchor Committee and some, as noted earlier, could concede a case for moderate reform. Nor were all of those which made up the national Association dominated locally as Reeves preferred by the tight little groups which were their committees. One authority doubts whether the local or parish associations fully represented the sense of their communities. The problem is misstated by using head-counting democratic terms. In the eighteenth century setting the propertied local people—landed gentlemen, merchants or manufacturers—spoke for their neighborhoods in the traditions of virtual representation and deference of the lower orders towards their social superiors. Ancient social assumptions sanctioned representation of the many by the few, arithmetic to the contrary notwithstanding. And there is evidence that members of the lower orders belonged to local associations, though in what numbers or proportions is not known. Even though there was no monolithic opposition to reform, strong opposition expressed itself in many places and in many ways, and its existence set a tone for the times. In this period the Association for the Preservation of Liberty and Property was the most notorious manifestation of Anti-Jacobinism.

The volume of the Association Papers published in 1793 sets forth the activities of Reeves' Committee and suggests, allowing for differences of circumstances, what local associations did in less ambitious ways. It recommended a boycott of newspapers publishing seditious materials; it advised employers to warn their employees—servants and journeymen—against the devilish principles being disseminated through the country and the hazards of engaging in seditious activities; it compiled court cases and legal decisions relative to the sales of libellous matter; it encouraged public declarations of loyalty by affiliated societies; and not least important, it published numerous penny tracts, pitched at different levels of readers.

Among these tracts, a few left some mark. All emphasized safe points of view on political and social problems. The *Answer to the Declaration of the Friends of the Liberty of the Press* con-

tains an interesting complaint. The Friends ignored societies subversive of the Constitution, "but no sooner are Associations
formed for the maintenance of the Constitution and of the Laws,
then they are full of apprehension and ready with reproof." The
Short Hints upon Levelling took the scriptural view that the poor
will always be with us and must be taught to suffer poverty as
something inherent in "the constitution of society." William
Mainwaring's *Charge to the Grand Jury of Middlesex* pronounced that there is no such thing as equality. William Paley,
archdeacon of Carlisle, suggested many *Reasons for Contentment; addressed to the Labouring Part of the British Public.* The
poor do not know how well off they are. Happiness does not depend on riches. The wealthy are often unhappy, living in ease,
idleness, sensuality and boredom and suffering from bad diges-
tions. The poor, on the other hand, enjoying the "pleasure" of
"frugality," are occupied with their work, comforted by the
sense of serving others by their labors, and blessed with good di-
gestions. Always there is religion to "smooth all inequalities."
Surely Paley made the happy poor shudder with horror at the
thought that by some miracle they might become rich and miserable.

None of these early tracts struck quite the right note. Those
published a little later in 1793 tried hard to avoid condescension
and get down to the level of Paine. The *Dialogue between a
Master-Manufacturer and one of his Workers* almost succeeded.
The workman, having read Paine, intended to take the day off to
attend a liberty meeting. The master straightened out his thinking. "Right, master! and I thank you for explaining all this to me;
and instead of going to the liberty club, I will begin my work;
for, I should not like to see a Frenchman lie with my wife, or
take the bread out of my childrens' mouths."

One of these tracts became a classic. Published anonymously
but written by Hannah More, it was the first of her phenome-
nally successful series called Cheap Repository Tracts which sold
two million copies by the end of 1795. Except for her *Shepherd
of Salisbury Plain* (1794), none of her tracts was so successful as
Village Politics: Addressed to all the Mechanics, Journeymen,

and Labourers in Great Britain. By *Will Chip, a Country Carpenter.* Hannah herself said that it was "as vulgar as heart can wish," meaning that it was of the people. Recommended to him by the Attorney General, Reeves added it to the list of Association tracts. Hannah continued to write tracts until 1798. Her "incomparable statements of political Christianity" comforted the working class with their lot in this world and assured them happiness in the next. They "established her beyond question, and very likely for all time, as the world's leading practitioner in this kind of art."

Village Politics was a dialogue between Jack Anvil and Tom Hod. Jack, the village blacksmith, read his bible, went to church, and looked forward "to a treasure in heaven." Tom, a mason, was a good fellow badly misled. Having read Tom Paine, he had discovered that he did not possess liberty, equality, or happiness. In a dozen pages Jack finally persuaded him that:

A democrat is "one who likes to be governed
    by a thousand tyrants, and yet can't bear a king."
Equality is "for every man to pull down every one
    that is above him."
The rights of man are "battle, murder, and sudden death."
The so-called enlightened people are those who would
    "put out the light of the gospel."
The new patriot is "a man who loves every country
    better than his own, and France best of all."

Needless to say, Tom repented his errors.

If its publication program spread balm of contentment over the country, other activities of the Association aimed at direct repression of radicalism. The numerous local associations brought much of England under loyalist surveillance. Francis Plowden, writing in 1794, saw the greatest danger to England not from the teachings of Paine but from the neo-divine right pretensions of the loyal associations. "The danger became really serious, when we are told, that above two thousand such associations" existed in England. Allowing for exaggeration of the numbers, the state-

ment is still significant. Some associations were inspired by the
justices of peace in quarter sessions, others grew out of formal
county meetings presided over by the High Sheriffs, and still
others arose from the spontaneous coagulation of the fears of citizens which became militant determination to defend the King,
the constitution, and the Church. Thus, in Surrey, the justices in
quarter session on January 15, 1793, followed up the sense of the
county meeting held three weeks earlier by accepting self-
righteous offers of assistance to counteract the evil intentions of
designing men. The justices charged all constables and other peace
officers firmly to suppress disorders, vigilantly to seek out evidences of sedition, and unrelentingly to bring suspects before the
magistrates. Masters of families suspected their servants; inn-
keepers scrutinized their customers with unusual care; and generally people watched out for dangers to good order. At Minehead
in Somerset the Association for preserving Liberty and Property
against Republicans and Levellers expressed its purposes in published resolutions. Lovers of the constitution should publicly de-
clare their loyalty and their intentions to suppress the circulation
of "pernicious doctrines" and to assist the civil authorities in
keeping order. The Committee, any seven of whom could act for
the entire membership, defrayed expenses out of subscriptions.
As in Surrey and Minehead, so in Leicester, Derby, in many
London parishes, and in countless other places throughout the
kingdom, self-appointed trustees for social order encouraged
neighbors to suspect one another and regard strangers with suspicion, conjured up republicans from under every bed, and imag-
ined they saw a tree of liberty on every village green.

Sometimes it was enough to mobilize opinion against radicals,
by its pressure coercing them into silence. The strength of organized local loyalties intimidated persons who, though not radicals,
did not approve of repression but were afraid to speak out against
it. Sometimes it seemed useful to agitate the working class into
demonstrations of loyalty; to cries of "God save the King," Tom
Paine often burned in effigy. How many legal actions, inspired by
local, loyal associations, were dealt with by magistrates and justices of the peace are not known, but they were numerous. Evi-

dence shows local associations behind some legal actions against radicals, notably in the prosecutions of the Reverend Dr. William Winterbotham of Exeter and of William Frend, fellow of Jesus College, Cambridge.

The cases of Winterbotham and Frend are instructive. They illustrate the mood of loyal England in the winter of 1792–1793. Winterbotham was indicted "for Seditious Words" in a sermon preached to the Baptist congregation at Hows-Lane Chapel on November 5, 1792. This was a political sermon, like so many that had been preached on anniversaries of the Revolution of 1688. But in late 1792 conditions were not as they had been in 1789 when Dr. Price delivered his famous *Discourse*. When an Anglican spectator, William Padden, told the mayor of Exeter about the sermon, the processes of justice began. The grand jury indicted; the case came on at Exeter assizes on July 25, 1793, before a special jury. Witnesses were uncertain as to what, precisely, Winterbotham had said, and in consequence contradicted one another. Serjeant Rooke, for the crown, had no doubts. "It has been laid down by divine authority, that there is no power, but what is derived from the Supreme Being—therefore to cry out against the government where there is no occasion, is a crime. And for a man living under mild and equal laws, to preach sedition and discontent, is blasphemy against the majesty of Heaven." The spectators applauded. The defense counsel challenged this view. Winterbotham, he said, spoke in a "fair spirit of discussion," without seditious intent. Summing up, the judge reminded the jury of the disagreements among witnesses, and narrowed the question to two points—whether the accused spoke the words attributed to him, and whether there was intent to excite sedition. On the whole, the judge was fair. The jury, after deliberating two and one-half hours, found Winterbotham guilty.

On the next day, Winterbotham was tried on a separate but similar charge. Two weeks after the first sermon he had preached another alleged to contain seditious language. In this case confusion among the prosecution witnesses irritated the judge. He instructed the jury to disregard the testimony of all but one crown witness, and to remember that he was a youth. In contrast, the defense witnesses, all adults, agreed in their testimony. The judge described the defendant as a man too sensible to repeat the provocation of the earlier sermon. It was clear that the judge did not think the defendant was guilty. After pondering for five and one-half hours, the jury said that he was. Winterbotham received two years' imprisonment on each charge. The times and the place were unfavorable to Winterbotham, especially in view of the influences in Exeter of a strong loyal association.

The evidence for loyalist maneuverings is even clearer in the case of William Frend, May and June 1793. The case became complicated by statutes of Cambridge University, by questions of procedure raised before the Vice-Chancellor's court, and by Frend, who conducted his own defense. He was a clever, conceited, contentious fellow whose shaky knowledge of technical proprieties enabled him to raise all kinds of obfuscating questions. His conduct undoubtedly told against him. Frend's book, *Peace and Union,* was published in early February 1793. Members of the University Senate, not formally in concert, requested censure of Frend. Later they resolved to prosecute him in the Vice-Chancellor's court. Frend, it was charged, had offended against university statutes by impugning not only the church establishment but "all ecclesiastical ranks and dignities." His work contravened the purpose of the University which was to maintain "good and Godly literature, and the virtuous education of youth." Passages from the book were cited in illustration.

Frend thought the proceeding unbecoming to the University, the work of a cabal whose "intriguing disposition" was stimulated by "the contagion of the times," felt even in the University. These men misrepresented Frend. He was not a leveller and had no connections with France. The tendency to indulge in personalities angered Frend. If it came to that, though it was irrelevant, he might say something about the prosecutor Dr. Thomas Kipling. A certain book written by Kipling was a disgrace to scholarship. Throughout his defense Frend stood upon technicalities. He never faced squarely the real issue, freedom of expression, so pertinent to an academic proceeding. He hardly came close when he asked whether a writer could feel safe when exposed to "the limitations of [Kipling's] taste or intellect," or whether he should be charged with a crime from Kipling's "want of comprehension." A good deal of academic politics complicated this trial. In it, personalities were too prominent.

On the seventh day the court found that Frend had violated a particular university statute of the year 1603 by writing and publishing his pamphlet. In an aside, the Vice-Chancellor suggested that if he had "boldly confessed and defended his principles" Frend at least would not have "endangered his reputation as a man of honour and veracity." It is doubtful that frank confrontation of the issue would have won the case for Frend. The Vice-Chancellor conceded the influence of national politics. He asked the junior fellows to think of the present dangers "when several turbulent and democratic spirits still endeavour to persuade the public, that every attempt to punish libellous attacks upon the constitution and government of the kingdom, by enforcing wholesome and established laws, is a species of persecution, and contrary to the *imprescriptible Rights of Man*." The University had an obligation to shield "the unsuspecting minds of youth" from persons who talked "perpetually of candor, of thinking for themselves, of examining things to the bottom. . . ." Frend was sentenced to banishment from the University, and he lost his appeals, the last one in King's Bench.

The precarious status of speech and press was illustrated by other trials held during the early part of 1793. Their success against Paine seemed to encourage the crown's law officers. The evidences of widespread support for their efforts, supplied particularly by Reeves' Association, and numerous testimonials that in many places radical spirits had been dampened, strengthened the determination of ministers to increase the pressure upon the radicals.

In the case of Patrick William Duffin and Thomas Lloyd, it seemed almost that the authorities had lost all sense of humor. Duffin, an Irishman, and Lloyd, an American attorney, were in the Fleet prison for debt. It was alleged that they conspired to escape and posted a notice that "this house" was to let on January 1, 1793, with the beginning of the first year of liberty in Great

Britain. The Attorney General filed an information ex officio charging them with seditious libel. Whether the notice was a seditious libel was never argued in this case. Though the prosecution tried to prove that the defendants had conspired to break out of prison, the judge instructed the jury to return a verdict of guilty if the evidence convinced them only that the prisoners had acted together in posting the notice. This the jury did. There is no doubt that Lloyd was a smart alec who antagonized the jury by his conduct as counsel for the defense. In the end the judge, Lord Kenyon, recovered his equilibrium. He sentenced the convicted prisoners to stand for an hour in the pillory. The punishment hardly fit the crime as charged; it may have been appropriate as chastisement of Lloyd. The trial made no sense. Unfortunately it was the only case for these years recorded in *State Trials* that was not grim and ominous.

At this time the work of suppression was carried on by crown officials in Scotland even more vigorously than in England. Their activity produced in 1793–1794 the series of trials that became notorious in the history of British jurisprudence. The judges breached judicial propriety more flagrantly than their English brethren. Lord Henry Cockburn's *Examination of the Trials for Sedition . . . in Scotland* (1888) indicts the Scottish judges for judicial misconduct. Though Cockburn was "a zealous Whig," he wrote as a learned Scottish judge. He accused his predecessors of giving way to "panic" and "party spirit," of deriving conclusions from unwarranted or unproven assumptions, of usurping functions that belonged properly to juries, and generally of conducting prejudiced, unfair trials.

There was no record of previous trials in Scotland for pure sedition unmixed with leasing-making (libels upon the personal character of the sovereign, his family or his court) or treason. Therefore in 1793 the Scottish judges, without guiding precedents, created the Scottish law of sedition at a time "singularly unfavourable for the calm exercise of judicial reason." Attempts to define sedition are complicated by uncertainties surrounding the political "right" of free expression. Cockburn thought the problem was soluble. It is easy to determine the fact of publication.

It is difficult but not impossible to decide whether the publication produces visible public mischief and whether an evil intention informed it. Sedition cannot consist of mere language separate from these considerations. The jury has to judge in the light
of the evidence, guided by "judicial discretion" but uninfluenced
by political opinions. One who perpetrates clear or "admitted"
sedition cannot plead an existing grievance, that is, "crime cannot
be a legitimate mode of obtaining redress." When "public reason
is unsound" these ideal conditions may not govern sedition trials.

Under the best of circumstances uncertainties obscured the
precise limits of the law of sedition. In England during the eighteenth century the spirit of toleration and the soundness of public
reason usually permitted a latitude of expression denied by the
law. In 1793, especially after France declared war upon England,
a weakened spirit and a disturbed public reason narrowed the
area of free discussion and indiscreet reformers found themselves
crossing unwarily beyond the limits of safety. Judges and juries
had difficulty amid national danger in maintaining the impartial-
ity subsumed in jury trial. Allowing even for this, posterity has
been "nearly unanimous," said Cockburn, in condemning the
Scottish trials of 1793–1794, and particularly the conduct of
the judges. They allowed themselves to think politically, assumed
the truth of the indictments before the trials took place, and in
their zeal became more culpable than the prosecutors or the
juries.*

In early January 1793 John Morton, James Anderson, and Mal-
colm Craig were tried for sedition. In public, according to the indictment, they had toasted "George the third and last, and dam-
nation to all crowned heads." During the preliminary dispute
concerning the relevancy of the indictment, the judges improperly expressed their political opinions. The Lord Justice-Clerk,
Lord Braxfield, whose domineering personality influenced unduly
the other judges, undercut the jury by asserting that the words
spoken by the defendants were seditious. At this stage of the trial

---

* It must be remembered that Scottish law and procedure differed in
important ways from those in England. Thus in Scotland the presiding
judge named the jurors from a panel furnished by the sheriff.

it was not established that the defendants had indeed spoken the words, and it was the business of the jury to determine whether they were seditious. The prosecutor, Robert Dundas, insisted that the jury must take into account the temper of the times. Properly the judges found the indictment relevant, that is, the actions alleged constituted crime under the law. The issue became one of intent when it was quickly established that the words in the indictment had been spoken. The case of the prosecution amounted to an assertion that the words themselves evidenced seditious intent. The jury agreed and the defendants were sentenced to nine months in prison. The trial was conducted properly except for the behavior of the judges. The worst impropriety was the performance of Lord Henderland. He discussed at length whether transportation was a suitable punishment in this case and decided that it was too severe. The other judges agreed with him. In fact no statute prescribed transportation as punishment for sedition. Henderland had no right to raise the question. Because he did it was thereafter accepted that persons found guilty of sedition could be sentenced to transportation.

The case of John Elder, a bookseller, and William Stewart, a merchant, tells something about the state of opinion in this period. According to the indictment they published the French Declaration of Rights, with commentary, and distributed medals with the words "Liberty, Equality and an end to Impress Warrants" on one side, and on the other "Liberty of Conscience, Equal Representation, and Just Taxation." Stewart, failing to appear in court, was adjudged an outlaw. Further action was postponed pending his apprehension, but he was never found. It was not therefore established that they had committed sedition, but it seems clear that Stewart was afraid the jury would find him guilty, and it also seems clear that in the opinion of the prosecutors sedition would be found.

The prosecution of Walter Berry and James Robertson, indicted for printing and publishing a seditious pamphlet, was an example of judicial error. The prosecution talked about the temper of the times; the defense pleaded liberty of the press. The jury found Robertson guilty of printing and publishing, Berry of publishing only. The defense protested this as an improper verdict because neither the seditious nature of the pamphlet nor the criminal intent of the defendants had been proved. The prosecution replied, and the judges agreed that the verdict inferred the decisions on these points. Contrary to Fox's Libel Law, the judges had decided that the material was libellous. The judges may have had some reservations, because they pronounced mild sentences upon Berry and Robertson.

Just what was seditious libel properly depended after 1792 upon the judgment of the jury, and as juries differed, so did judgments. In July 1793 in the case of Daniel Eaton in England, the jury's verdict was "Guilty of publishing [Part II of the *Rights of Man*] but not with a criminal intention." A month later, Eaton was tried for publishing Paine's *Letter Addressed to the Addressers* which was even more provocative than the *Rights of Man*. There was no dispute about the fact of publication, only about criminal intention. The jury's verdict was "Guilty of Publishing the Pamphlet in Question." Because criminal intention was not proved, the case went no further. Yet Daniel Holt, who had also published the *Address*, was found guilty of an identical charge by a special jury at the Nottingham assizes. That men's judgments differed with place and time was further demonstrated in the second trial of Holt. He had published as a pamphlet an article written by Major Cartwright and published originally in a Leeds newspaper in 1783. An argument for parliamentary reform, in 1793 it was adjudged a seditious libel. Holt became a martyr. His premature death was attributed to his imprisonment in Newgate. At Newcastle-upon-Tyne, Alexander Whyte, a baker, was charged with publishing a seditious libel, having read aloud from a reform document in a public house. The prosecution tried to persuade the jury of "the heinousness of the offense, and the necessity of exemplary punishment." Conducting his own defense, Whyte exposed the flimsiness of the evidence. The verdict was Not Guilty.

The last in the series of cases begun by the trial of Paine was that involving John Frost. Just after his return from France where he had delivered the address of the SCI, Frost, at a coffee house in Marylebone, uttered various remarks labeled as seditious by the Westminster grand jury. Frost had defined equality as meaning no king, and he had called the constitution of England "a bad one." Erskine, defending, tried to make the witnesses contradict one another. He also raised the possibility of Frost's intoxication, seeming to think it reasonable that by the time a man had finished dinner he might be, if not drunk, at least not sober. Erskine failed to make the witnesses useful to his client; the greater importance attached to his address to the jury. Erskine tried to persuade them to ignore the times; the history of Europe was not before the court. He expounded upon freedom of expression as he had in defending Paine. The special jury found Frost guilty. He was not forgotten. When after six months he stepped forth from Newgate prison, the crowd drew his carriage. On the way to Frost's home the procession halted, among other places, in front of St. James Palace.

Repeatedly in these trials the prosecution argued the relevance of the times to judgments about freedom of expression. Justice Kenyon, summing up in the case of Frost, told the jury that the times determined the very meaning of words. After February 1, 1793, there was a great difference in the state of public affairs. On that day France declared war on England. Perhaps the French government disdained the feelings of the people of Great Britain who, said the SCI, were averse to a war which gratified only the "confederacy of Foreign Kings." The war gave a new meaning to the relations between English radicals and France. Hitherto friendly with regicides and atheists, the radicals now consorted with England's declared enemies. With patriotism a new ingredient of anti-Jacobin sentiment, the government carried the Traitorous Correspondence Act. The parliamentary minority opposed with arguments that sound naïve to a later age which knows total war. They seemed to place the war of the French Revolution in the gentlemanly eighteenth century tradition which held that for large parts of the population life in wartime could go on normally and intercourse with enemy nationals be continued as though peace prevailed. Restrictions upon economic and personal relationships with Frenchmen under any circumstances were infringements of liberty in Fox's view. But for loyalists the war narrowed the gap between sedition, punishable by fine and imprisonment, and high treason, punishable by death.

The war introduced a new argument into the radicals' array. From the beginning they had hailed the French Revolution as the dawning of an era of peace and brotherhood. Now they opposed the war, called the allies the aggressors, and pictured revolutionary France defending her new won liberties against the tyrants of Europe. French aggressions were acts in defense of liberty; in pushing the war beyond her own boundaries France was aiding the people of Europe to regain their liberties. When they took this position publicly, the radicals heightened the risks they faced, and yet they became increasingly indiscreet. It seemed unnecessarily provocative, for instance, that the LCS should ask its correspondents to report "the state of affairs in your department" or that the Scottish convention in November should move to divide the country into "departments." This word was alien to the English consitutional vocabulary. It was glaringly and flauntingly French. Even more obnoxious to anti-reformers was the word "citizen," now becoming popular among the radicals. Nor did it improve their image when the SCI elected the Girondin leaders, Citizens Barrere and Roland, to honorary membership.

The radicals expanded earlier expressions of sympathy towards France into outspoken opposition to the war. It was easy to interpret such peace-loving sentiments as unpatriotic, pro-French preferences, and the radicals gave reason for doing so when their exuberance betrayed them into indiscretions. Ministers did not welcome gratuitous advice on the conduct and purpose of the war and received even less graciously their demands for instant peace. Because opponents of the war were almost invariably reformers, whether moderate or radical, the cause of reform, now unpatriotic, became doubly dangerous in the view of the King and Church party. Christopher Wyvill exemplified the identity between reform and peace. Only a week after the war began he chastised Pitt in print for apostasy to reform and for warmongering. Wyvill argued for moderate reform as the prudential course and the best means of restoring in the people their waning attachment to the constitution. In England "a tendency to violent

change" was discernible; the "progress of Revolutionary Principles," not yet pronounced in the "middle station of life" and
among the upper class, would continue among the lower orders if
the government "suppressed discussion" and pursued the war.
The "more formidable Enemies of the Constitution" were not
those who desired to reform it but the misguided people who set
themselves up as its defenders. Peace was attainable because
France was conciliatory; reform was in order because the people
wanted it. Lectures from the Wyvills were probably more irritat-
ing to ministers, even if less ominous, than the strident demands
of the working class radicals. The Sheffield Society in April 1793
began its declaration by denouncing war in general as "the curse
and scourge of nations." "No provocatives or manifestoes" of
France justified "an offensive war" against her; rather than fight
her, England should ally with the Republic of France against the
despots of Europe. Such advice was hardly congenial to any
among the governing class but the small parliamentary minority
which was urging peace with Jacobin France.

The societies did not permit their new-found interest in foreign affairs to obscure their original and primary object—parliamentary reform. In January 1793 Sheffield sent out a circu-
lar letter urging all societies to petition Parliament for a reform,
and further to demand the plan of the Friends of the People in
order that other reformers might decide whether they could support it. The LCS, skeptical of the immediate effect of petitions,
conceded that they might be useful in the long run effort to
arouse "the public mind" on the subject. The doubts of the LCS
seemed to be confirmed by the refusal of the Friends to be bad-
gered into premature disclosure of their program. The Friends
would say only that it envisaged "a complete, substantial, and radical reform."

Early in May the petitions came before the House of Commons.
The Sheffield petition of May 2, which was considered individu-
ally, was phrased in respectful, even noble language.

> Your petitioners are lovers of peace, of liberty and
> justice. They are in general tradesmen and artificers,
> unpossessed of freehold land, and consequently have

no voice in choosing members to sit in parliament; but
though they may not be freeholders, they are men,
and do not think themselves fairly used in being excluded the rights of citizens. Their all is at stake
equally with the freeholder's; and whether that all be
much, or little, whilst they pay their full share of
taxes, and are peaceable and loyal members of society,
they see no reason why they should not be consulted
with respect to the common interests of their common
country. They think men are objects of representation, and not the land of a freeholder, or the houses of
a borough-monger.

This was the plain language of the people. It probably represents
as fairly as any reform statement of the period the genuine beliefs
and desires of the members of the popular societies. It was really
snide for Henry Duncombe, who introduced it, to apologize for
its language, the petitioners being "only manufacturers" unfamiliar with the proper terms for addressing the House. The House
rejected it, not for that reason, but because its prayer was too
democratical.

On May 6, some twenty-five other petitions from places in England and Scotland were presented. These represented rather the
opinions of the societies than of the unorganized people. Sheridan
requested withdrawal of the motion for bringing up these petitions because a debate upon it would delay "important business"
that was to come on. Probably Sheridan was right. A protracted
debate and the inevitable defeat for the motion would prejudice
the proposal of the Friends of the People. In Sheridan's remarks
there was a hint of the condescending impatience towards the
lower class characteristic of the Friends of the People.

Charles Grey took charge of the Friends' business, which had
been preparing for a year. During the winter of 1792–1793,
George Tierney, Erskine, Mackintosh and others gathered information about the electoral system and prepared the Friends' proposal. From this work came the famous petition which Grey introduced and whose referral to a committee he moved. The petition said nothing that in a general way Members of Parliament

were not already aware of, both from personal knowledge and from such recent publications as T. H. B. Oldfield's *Representative History of Great Britain and Ireland,* 1792, and Tierney's *State of the Representation,* an abridgement of Oldfield published in February 1793. The information in these could be traced back to the inquiries made in the previous decade by the SCI. The petition showed the gross disproportions between representation and the distribution of population which made it possible for less than 15,000 voters, or $\frac{1}{200}$ of the adult male population, to choose a majority of the House of Commons. Because of the opportunities the system opened to private parliamentary patronage, in fact 144 "powerful individuals" were able to return a majority of the House. The petition prayed for shorter parliaments and uniform franchise requirements.

In his accompanying speech, Grey renounced philosophical analogy with radicalism. He did not argue from natural right but from plain common sense. A Parliament so irregularly chosen could not be adequately representative. Grey, and the Friends, desired only "what was in itself the best system of government, and most conducive to the happiness of the people." Grey brought forward no plan, though the Friends had one. They preferred that a committee recommend to the House a remedy for the grievances the petition complained of. That is, if matters went so far, they hoped that any bill drawn up in a committee would contain the preferences of the Friends. Pitt taunted them. Such a bill would represent only themselves, he said, for outside Parliament the radicals did not think the Friends went far enough while the rest of the nation, the preponderance of it, rejected even the so-called moderation of the Friends. Grey's motion was defeated 282–41.

The Friends survived this defeat and to the extent they did, moderate reform remained alive. They continued to meet at the Freemason's Tavern and even to carry on correspondence with other societies. But in any sense that counted the Friends' ideas were little more than the preferences of the parliamentary minority. The nation at large remained divided as Pitt had described it. Yet the Friends tried once more. In 1797 Grey introduced a specific plan, remarking that in 1793 the House had disapproved of complaints unaccompanied by remedies. The plan proposed to increase the number of county members by twenty-one, to divide the counties into single member districts, to extend the county franchise to copyholders and leaseholders, and to extend the borough franchise to householders. This proposal was beaten 256–91.

The Friends of the People, or the reformers inside Parliament, had never been in touch with the people. They were an interesting, and in the long run significant part of the reform movement, for their survivors were the links between members who tried to pass a reform bill in the 1790's and those who succeeded in 1832. But the Friends were not the English Jacobins. Outside the Parliament to which they had no access the Jacobins continued to struggle for a radical reform, working to educate and arouse the people of England, to make of them such a mighty force that even the unreformed Parliament would have to reform itself. It required courage to attempt that in the England of 1793–1794.

CHAPTER VIII

IN CONVENTION ASSEMBLED

THE House of Commons removed some uncertainties and created others when it crushed the effort of the Friends of the People. The radical societies lost their illusions about Parliament. The LCS had never trusted it to enact reform and the fate of the petitions proved their point. If by some miracle Parliament yielded, the reform would be too limited to satisfy the radicals. What then should the societies do? They could continue their work of public education, but that might go on forever without success. The vote in 1793 showed that the House of Commons was more strongly averse to reform than it had been ten years before. The reform campaign, twenty years old, seemed to have achieved nothing at all. Even the radicals, believers, might weary of paying dues, attending meetings, passing resolutions, and corresponding with one another. Words, words, words!

It was perhaps as much their growing sense of futility as confidence in alternatives that persuaded the English radicals in 1793 to entertain the old idea of a convention. It had been remarkably virile. Radical literature had talked about a convention since the early 1780's. Dr. Price mentioned it; Paine advocated it, never doubting its necessity; America and France had, in certain senses, put it into practice. It had never been quite clear what a convention was supposed to do. James Burgh and later some of the reformers of the 1780's thought of it as a pressure group; Dr. John

Jebb spoke of it as superseding Parliament if need be and acting as a constituent body. Tom Paine, with American experience, conceived of a convention in the sense that America knew its Philadelphia example. Generally Englishmen did not distinguish between constituent and legislative powers; their constitution had not been written by a constituent body but had been formed over centuries, and Parliament, a legislature, had amended it by statute. In the light of this tradition and amid the ambiguities in their talk of a convention, it is necessary to conclude that the pressure group idea predominates in the thinking of English reformers on the problem of convention. Parliament must reform the constitution, but Parliament would have to be coerced into action. Unfortunately, the English Jacobins used strong language. Some of their expressions could be interpreted by opponents to mean that a convention might seize power and act as a constituent body. To the extent that radicals were Painite by association, this was not altogether an unreasonable interpretation to place upon their language, and events in France seemed to give point to the anti-Jacobin construction of the word.

Scotland had set the most recent British example of a convention. The formation of reform societies in Scotland began about six months later than the organization of the English working class societies. Once started the movement developed rapidly out of a background of public discontents and agitations: the rejection in May 1791 of the Scottish General Assembly's petition for repeal of the Test Act as it applied to Scotland; the enactment of a new corn law late in 1791 which aroused protests about high prices in manufacturing centers; the slave trade measure of May 1792 whose inadequacy outraged the Scottish abolitionists; and generally an interest in the French Revolution and the question of parliamentary reform. By the summer of 1792, with Painite sentiments spreading, many Scots began to look upon parliamentary reform as a panacea for all public ills and private grievances. What was new was not discontent or disorder but the infusion of reform ideas with doctrinaire talk about liberty and equality. The spread of these sentiments and the readiness of the governing class to identify them with sedition actually antedated the formation of reform societies.

By the early autumn of 1792 in Edinburgh, Glasgow, Perth, Dundee and many other places, some gentlemen and many weavers, cobblers, tradesmen and shopkeepers were organizing societies which in structure and social composition more nearly resembled the London Corresponding Society than their names, Friends of the People, might suggest. As early as October 1792 delegates from societies in the vicinity of Edinburgh met together and talked over their problems and grievances. In early December, organization and enthusiasm developed so far as to suggest a general convention of Scottish societies. If convention talk had been heard for over a decade in England, it remained for the Scottish reformers to take action.

In this first general reform convention, held in Edinburgh and attended by delegates from some seventy Scottish societies, the reformers showed themselves at their best and their worst. Contentious and disputatious but not ill-humored, sticklers for protocol partly because of their inexperience, convinced of the righteousness of their cause but uncertain how to advance it, looking over their shoulders at the government because they knew it was watching them, the delegates spent three days so fruitlessly as to discourage any but enthusiasts like themselves. When Lord Daer, generally on the side of caution, made some proposals concerning the conduct of business, Thomas Muir, the young vice-president pro tem, "opposed everything that had been proposed." So said the minutes. Muir presented an address from the United Irishmen. Some delegates thought it "contained treason." Muir brashly and meaninglessly offered to assume individual responsibility for the "whole danger" from it. The Convention, after hearing it read, agreed that it contained treason and that in spite of Muir's bravado the Convention would be held responsible for it. Believing that reform rather than destruction of the constitution was their purpose, the Convention prudently rejected the address and then adopted a petition to Parliament urging peaceful reform. After resolving to establish permanent contacts with London societies and agreeing on measures preliminary to another convention, the delegates imprudently rose and as one man took the French oath "to live free or die." Then they adjourned until April 1793.

Within a month after the December Convention adjourned, the authorities moved against Muir. He came from a substantial Glasgow family. His father was a merchant and owned an estate near Glasgow. Thomas Muir used the word "Esquire" after his name. He had been a member of the Faculty of Advocates. His prominence in the Convention and his championship of the Irish address marked him as a dangerous man and drew the Lord Advocate upon his trail collecting evidence to be used against him. Released on bail after his arrest, Muir left for France before his trial was set.

This incident did not frighten the radicals. William Skirving, Secretary to the Convention, kept up a correspondence among the Scottish societies and was instrumental in bringing together the Convention of April 1793. It was smaller than its predecessor and because of the defections of some persons of "a higher situation and rank in life" less respectable in its appearances. Only about a dozen of the 116 delegates from some fifty Scottish societies had attended the December Convention. The April Convention adjourned after four days, having agreed upon a petition supporting the parliamentary efforts of the London Friends of the People. But it also resolved to meet anew on October 29. Skirving meanwhile was to extend his correspondence with English societies. This he did in his continuing capacity of Secretary-General of the Scottish Convention. It appeared that the Convention was conceived of as a continuing body with a secretariat functioning between formal sessions. Skirving carried on regular communication with the LCS, the Friends of the People, and with societies in Sheffield, Leeds, Nottingham and Norwich. Except for the fact of their existence and some individual acts of indiscretion, like Muir's at the December Convention, there was little about the Scottish conventions that need have excited Scottish authorities. They remained observant for portents and false moves, however.

Possibly because of their knowledge of the Scottish Convention of the previous December, or by their awareness of the general idea, the United Societies of Norwich considered a convention even before they were in correspondence with Skirving. On

March 5, 1793, they told the SCI that if Parliament rejected the petitions then being prepared, and if an address to the King was ruled out, then, "as necessity has no law," there might be no alternative to a convention. Norwich thought a convention impracticable at the moment, "yet this is the object we pursue," and "oh! that the period were arrived" when a convention could be held. The SCI agreed, theoretically. A convention of delegates from societies was desirable but not practicable until "the great body of the people shall be courageous and virtuous enough to join us in the attempt." This statement seemed to be more an excuse than an explanation. It anticipated the reluctance of the Society to cooperate in a convention when the time of decision arrived.

After the failure of the petitions and Grey's motion in Parliament, the societies swung more decidedly to the idea of a convention. On May 17 the LCS told Skirving that the united attention of reformers in Great Britain should be turned "to some more effectual means" of obtaining reforms, "provided they are constitutional." Because of their experience with conventions, perhaps the societies in Edinburgh had something to tell the others. Skirving's reply warned of danger ahead. "Arguments of reason" had failed to persuade anyone not already a believer. Nothing more could be expected from an aristocracy impressed with its own self-flattering, comfortable sense of doing good *for* the people. The people must act for themselves. They must be firmly united; "separate meetings in different towns" were not enough. The society for which Skirving spoke was no longer interested in trifling; they had no time for reformers who kept aloof from a strong union. The societies must become "one great and indivisible family."

The idea was spreading and catching. Sheffield, disillusioned by the rejection of the petitions, thought that nothing could suffice but "the powerful interposition of the great body of the people." Leeds was ready to join wholeheartedly with Edinburgh. The LCS, encouraged by its new association with Edinburgh, grew more enthusiastic about a convention. Perhaps it was an opportunity to be seized, for once lost it would not soon be recovered.

Only the Friends of the People were decisively cool. Though they congratulated Skirving for the support to reform given by the April Convention, they thought that a new one, more broadly based, "would be very improper in this country at present." Such a rash step would harm the reform cause.

By the summer of 1793 English radicalism was separating itself into two groups, the doers and the talkers. In the second category fell the Friends of the People and the SCI. The Friends would have nothing to do with a convention besides warning Skirving, as he went ahead with his plans, to avoid violence. The SCI was rapidly losing its traditional prestige. Few looked to it any longer for leadership. Individual members who had formerly seemed heroes were beginning to look like trimmers. Major Cartwright, disillusioned by the French Revolution, was ready to believe that English radicals were also losing their bearings, ignoring the landmarks of the ancient constitution, Magna Carta and the Bill of Rights. He had not attended the SCI since May 1792. Horne Tooke was once again preferring conversations over Sunday teas at Wimbledon. Occasionally he "peeped into public," at meetings of the SCI or dinners where he might offer toasts "breathing all the genuine spirit of the French Revolution." But he was playing no decisive part and seemed to be able to be absent when any compromising matter came up. In any case he had never approved of universal suffrage; his name in the books of the SCI would not, said Erskine on a later occasion, be "evidence in an action for ten pounds." In fact, the SCI, under the new appearance of things, could not be more than a society of gentlemen who "wished well" to the cause of reform.

The leadership was being seized by more extreme persons not so much by usurpation as by default of the older radicals who, as the essayist William Hazlitt said of Tooke, were gentlemen of a former age. Even when these gentlemen advocated universal suffrage it was in a kind of detached manner, more as an abstraction and in calm obedience to doctrinaire precepts than as a matter of heated conviction and deep feeling. The spirit of the SCI was out of the rational past. The new radicalism was vulgar, emotional, of the people, partaking of the life and labor, hardship, sweat, and dirt of the working man. As in a divisional meeting of the LCS with a great variety of occupations represented—watchmakers and weavers, butchers and bricklayers, cabinetmakers and hairdressers, shoemakers and tailors, a musician, a surgeon, and a warehouseman, a bookseller and a glazier among them—and with the divisions choosing delegates, it is easy to believe the report of an informer that a delegate meeting contained men of "tradesmenlike appearance," journeymen, and many of "the very lowest order of society" who were seldom "decent in appearance." Only complete "mastery" over "innate pride" could enable a well-educated man to remain in their company.

But more than physical appearances would repel a gentleman. An educated person able to think and talk in abstractions would be uncomfortable among plain men who grasped a few simple ideas and jumped from them directly to radical conclusions without intellectual qualifications. A man like Horne Tooke, a brilliant conversationalist, a philologist, and a pedant about the meanings of words, might embarrass and defeat his Sunday guests, but he would never be able to move working men from the base of precept upon which their simple conclusions rested. Reform to them was hardly a matter of intellectual vindication; it was a self-evident need requiring no philosophical justification. Direct action rather than reasoned persuasion, and if it required physical embodiment to be effective then a convention of the people, was the means of obtaining reform. By the summer of 1793 the via media of the Friends of the People or the SCI was inadequate, in disrepute. The voice of the people would be heard. As the LCS told Norwich in July, we are "an indignant oppressed people, in whom is not yet entirely extinct the valour of their forefathers." These societies were not saying in so many words that the people were going to rise in arms against their oppressors, but their language carried implications of willingness to do so. Opponents of reform easily persuaded themselves that radical expressions contained such implications. In the eyes of the governing class, not the SCI but the LCS represented the new radicalism, more clearly than ever Painite and not asking for reform but ready to bring about revolution.

Whether reform or revolution, if it was to be brought about by a convention, the radicals recognized the dangers they faced. In August and September 1793 they observed the aftermath of the Edinburgh Conventions played out in the sedition trials of Thomas Muir and the Reverend Thomas Fyshe Palmer. Muir's activity in the December 1792 Convention has been noticed. Palmer, though less prominent, had also been conspicuous. He had urged the Convention to petition Parliament for reform. The indictment of Muir was based only in part upon his conduct at the Convention, and the indictment of Palmer not at all. But Palmer was well known to the authorities. Of an old Bedfordshire family, he was formerly a fellow of Queen's College, Cambridge. Opposition to his religious beliefs drove him from the University. He went to Dundee where he ministered to a Unitarian congregation. By the time of his arrest he was virtually a resident of Edinburgh, spending much time moving among reform societies. It was his missionary activity that made him appear dangerous.

In July Muir returned to Edinburgh by way of Ireland, was arrested, and stood his trial for sedition. He defended his own case when Henry Erskine, brother of Thomas, refused to take it because Muir would not give him a free hand in conducting it. Muir did not always act in his own best interest and seemed to delight in provoking those who disagreed with him. In retrospect, Erskine seemed to think that he might have saved Muir. He wrote that Muir "pleaded his own cause;—and you know the result." The reason why Erskine insisted upon the obedience of his clients was because when they opened their mouths they would "avow principles and views which would supply the crown with the only thing they wanted to make out their case,—THE CRIMINAL INTENTION." Erskine was probably right in thinking that among educated reformers there was a type—a kind of person who in his naïve confidence in the rightness of his cause and in the self-evident persuasiveness of the desirability of reform, could not conceive how men could think otherwise. This confidence was mixed with a bit of arrogant faith in their intellectual superiority, with glibness of expression, and with complete ignorance of the set of mind that could make jurors impervious to the assumed power of a clever, conceited speaker whose self-confidence alienated rather than earned confidence.

The indictment cited examples of the seditious writings Muir had presented to the public, including the address from Ireland and passages from Paine. Muir pleaded not guilty, insisting that he only advocated reform by constitutional means. The selection of the jury was flagrantly irregular and done over Muir's objection that they had prejudged the case. Every member of it was also a member of the loyalist Goldsmiths' Hall Association of Edinburgh which earlier had deleted Muir's name from the list of those who had signed its resolutions. The evidence presented by the Lord Advocate's witnesses was shaky and contradictory. Some of it was irrelevant to the charges and some of it should have told in favor of Muir. The Lords Justices rejected his objections of irrelevancy and generality of the evidence. They held it necessary in sedition cases to go beyond the specific terms of the indictment. The judges admitted as evidence every fact and circumstance that the Lord Advocate thought useful for creating an unfavorable impression of Muir. The testimony of the witnesses confirmed the fact that Muir publicly advocated reform and further that he urged peaceful, constitutional measures for obtaining it. But to the Lord Advocate all of this was "sowing the seeds of discontent and sedition."

Muir's defense presented the usual arguments of reformers when on trial. He desired reform, but by peaceful means, like Pitt or the Duke of Richmond. Exercising the right to freedom of expression he could not be conscious of any guilt. He spoke so eloquently and sincerely that when he finished his address to the jury the spectators applauded. To Lord Henderland, one of the judges, this "indecent applause" proved the existence of "the spirit of sedition." The Lord Justice-Clerk, Braxfield, summed up in a partisan speech. He defined sedition so positively that the jurors could not mistake his opinion. In the circumstances and the times, to advocate reform was sedition. In Great Britain, said Braxfield, expressing crudely the ancient assumptions, government is made up "of the landed interest, which alone has a right to be represented. As for the rabble, who have nothing but personal property, what hold has the nation on them?" The jury brought in a verdict of guilty. The judges announced their approval of it, and then sentenced Muir to transportation to Australia for fourteen years.*

This trial was perhaps the most monstrous of this period. "God help the people who have such judges," said Charles James Fox. As Lord Cockburn said, "History cannot let its injustice alone." Expressions of sympathy and cries of protest arose in England, France and America. Muir's address to the jury became a favorite piece of declamation for New England schoolboys. Muir committed the acts alleged against him, but the evidence did not prove them seditious. The sedition existed in the minds of the judges and the jurors before the trial began; the verdict rested upon an unproved assumption, that it was sedition, *ipso facto,* to advocate reform. The proceedings were full of irregularities. The behavior and speeches of the judges during the trial were grounds for impeachment, said Cockburn. The sentence was outrageous. The jury was aghast; they had expected that Muir would receive a short prison sentence. Many years later, one of the jurors told Cockburn that "we were all mad." The "we" should not have been limited to the jury. Public reason was mad.

Palmer was tried before the Circuit Court of Justiciary at Perth for seditious practices, namely writing or printing and circulating inflammatory matter against the "present happy constitution." The matter in question was an "Address to their Friends and Fellow Citizens" circulated first before a society at Perth and then published. Palmer pleaded not guilty. Lord Alexander Abercromby, the presiding judge, was fair, on the whole. He explained to the jury that under the law a man may publish, but is accountable for what he says, and that the jury should decide whether Palmer was the author and whether the piece was seditious writing. But Abercromby did indicate his own opinion about it before the jury retired to decide upon its verdict. Although the charge asserted Palmer's wicked and felonious inten-

---

* Muir escaped from Botany Bay in 1796 in an American vessel. After many hardships he made his way to France where he died in 1799 at the age of thirty-four.

tions, the proof of this was not in the evidence but rather assumed from the proven fact of publication. The "Address" was on the face of it indiscreet. It blamed the war upon "a wicked ministry and a compliant parliament" who wished to "form chains for a free people, and eventually to rivet them forever" on the people of England. To the judges and the jury this was sedition self-evident, not demanding proof beyond the existence of the publication. The verdict was guilty and Palmer was sentenced to transportation for seven years. He was confined in the hulks of Woolwich until the departure for Botany Bay in April 1794. He died in Guam in 1802 on the way back to England.

The proceedings against Palmer were as shocking as those against Muir. Both were governed and determined by identical states of mind. In each case the prosecution argued the relevancy of the times; the judges identified advocacy of reform with sedition; the juries, seeing dangers in reform, were ready to find sedition in the act of publication without needing proof of intentions and without examining the possibility that reform might not be destruction of the constitution. In the larger sense, these decisions meant that freedom of expression did not extend to discussions which questioned the perfection of the existing constitution.

The convictions of Muir and Palmer only hardened the reformers' determination. In Coventry and Tewkesbury new societies came into existence, affiliating themselves with the LCS. Birmingham guided Coventry; Sheffield and the *Patriot* influenced Tewkesbury. The people in these places were active and alert. In Tewkesbury there was "scarcely an old woman but is talking politics." In Scotland the reformers matured their plans for the Convention though it was not too late to draw back. Deliberately, courageously, and stubbornly they decided to plunge ahead.

The Scottish Convention in its inception owed nothing to the English societies except generalized moral support expressed now and then during the summer. The initiative, the planning, the arrangements were Scottish, and William Skirving was the person mainly responsible for the holding of the Convention. As late as October 5, 1793, just three weeks before the Convention was to open, Hardy had communicated Skirving's letter about a convention only to Maurice Margarot, chairman of the LCS. They approved of a convention and Hardy urged Skirving to extend an official invitation to the LCS to send delegates, without mentioning "that you had written to me privately." Hardy was sure his society would act favorably.

On October 24 in Hackney, a community always disposed favorably to reform and to the repeal of the Test Acts, the LCS held a large open-air meeting, their first one. Some of the crowd of four thousand came under misapprehensions, expecting to see Tom Paine or to learn that the LCS was going to "lower the price of provisions." The meeting, or the persons who guided it, chose Margarot and Joseph Gerrald as delegates to Edinburgh and voted to pay their expenses. Born in the West Indies thirty years before, Gerrald, a man of property, was educated in England. He practiced law in Philadelphia where he learned to admire democracy. Returning to England, he lived comfortably in Bloomsbury Square. In a pamphlet he had already committed himself to a convention as the last hope for reform. He and Margarot were appropriate choices as delegates. They were energetic, able, and enthusiastic. Margarot also held a special commission to represent Norwich at the Convention.

On October 28, in a meeting called hastily upon receipt of a letter from Skirving, the SCI also named delegates and voted expense money. They chose Charles Sinclair of Edinburgh, a combination of indiscreet courage and of good sense, and Henry Yorke of Derby, a brash young man of twenty-one always available for special missions in the interest of reform. Sinclair, who was in London, accepted on the spot. Their instructions were basically the same as Margarot's and Gerrald's—to support any constitutional measure for "general suffrage and annual representation" as well as pay for Members of Parliament. Sheffield received notice too late to find members who could leave their work to go to Edinburgh or to raise money for expenses. Sheffield desired to postpone the Convention until January or February, insisting that unity was essential and that all societies should be represented. Belatedly the Sheffield Society chose one person, who also spoke for Leeds. These were the only English delegates to be chosen, and Yorke withdrew because of illness. The staff work had been poor, especially from the standpoint of the English societies. The call came so late that their delegates missed the opening of the Convention on October 29.

It is tempting to seek economic motivation for the Convention as for the reform agitation in general. A tenuous and ill-formed relationship between economic discontent and the reform movement has been noticed in the minds of some reformers. It was not clear, direct, precisely recognized, or logically worked out. It was more instinctive and emotional than intellectual and dialectical. Before Paine the middle-class reformers complained about economic grievances affecting the propertied classes, as in the early 1780's, but these were more the consequences of war than of unrepresentative government and no necessary connection between parliamentary reform and economic betterment was established. The recovery of lost political rights was a self-sufficient end for the reformers. After February 1793 the working class societies talked of a connection between war and economic troubles. They made of kind of syllogism of this. War brought economic hardships; reform would end wars by making governments popular; therefore reform would eliminate economic grievances. Thus, the Sheffield Society on November 1, 1793, spoke of local unemployment and declining wages caused by the war, and without saying it, implied that reform would solve these problems. The Convention would contribute to an improvement of economic conditions if it could hasten reform and therefore the end of the war. This kind of reasoning, with or without reference to a convention, was more prominent in the societies' statements in 1793 than in the year before. Apart from the war, Paine's *Rights of Man* did something to give an economic and social context to reform ideas. Again, the reasoning was simple and direct. A reformed government would end waste, corruption, and high taxes and by direct monetary contributions would alleviate distress among the lower orders.

Lacking in this was the conception that it was within the power of government by promoting economic growth to improve material conditions in any fundamental way. The old static mercantilist precepts permitted governmental regulation of the commercial system, especially in the area of foreign trade, as well as gestures towards allocation of national resources, especially the labor supply. Men were not yet anticipating the kind of governmental participation in the national productive effort that the twentieth century knows. Parishes might alleviate distress through the poor laws; private charity could aid the unfortunate; statutes might try to direct the flow of commodities under tariff and bounty arrangements. For the most part conditions of the market and private decisions regulated the economy. Adam Smith had already equated self-interest in economic affairs with the public good. The trend of thinking was in this direction rather than towards a dialectic connecting political decisions with economics, and postulating parliamentary reform as the means of determining the nature of the political decisions. The precepts that would insist upon more rather than fewer governmental decisions about the nation's economic life would not win acceptance for another century. Such sophistication could not be expected among working class radicals or for that matter the governing class of the 1790's.

It is better to avoid saying flatly that discontents growing out of economic hardships necessarily produced reform agitation. Statistical analyses and literary sources make possible some conclusions about economic conditions. From 1789 until the autumn of 1792 conditions were good. Production and trade increased, crops were bountiful, incomes rose, jobs were plentiful and labor was scarce. The economic disturbances, the stirrings among the working classes, or strikes and demands for higher wages in 1792 occurred during rising prosperity rather than depression. In the winter of 1792–1793 there was a reversal, caused in part by the European war which in the first place disturbed the money market and the currency. By the spring of 1793 overseas trade was declining and manufacturing dependent on it was suffering. By the summer of 1793 unemployment in certain trades was increasing and wages were declining. To this extent then, the radicals who blamed the war for the hard times were correct; although they understood little about the underlying economic factors in-

volved they were able to connect falling wages and growing unemployment with the war. Yorkshire and Lancashire felt the
effects acutely; the output of wool cloth in the West Riding of
Yorkshire declined by nearly 20 per cent in 1793 and did not rise
again until 1795. The price of bread remained virtually unchanged in 1792, 1793 and 1794, and then in 1795 rose by 75 per
cent because of the poor harvest. There was a marked decline in
tonnage of ships clearing British ports and the monetary value of
exports in the year 1793. Governmental expenditures rose sharply
with the outbreak of the war. The number of bankruptcies doubled in 1793 over 1792 but fell in 1794 and never approached the
peak of 1793 during the remainder of the century.

These dates place the beginnings of the reform agitation and
the founding of the working class radical societies prior to the
war and the economic dislocation which it caused. The intensifi-
cation of reform activities followed England's entrance into the
war and coincided more closely with growing economic distress
in 1793. It is debatable whether increased reform activity was
caused directly by the war, indirectly as the war contributed to
economic discontent, or by economic adversities considered separately. The radical literature often expresses opposition to the
war because war was an evil in itself. A most significant index of
well-being was the price of bread. It did not rise until 1795, and
therefore could not have influenced popular emotions of the two
preceding years.

If economic grievances were present in the thinking of radicals,
beyond the normal grumbling that never ceases, even in the best
of times, the minutes of the Scottish Convention are silent about
them. If connections between economic distress and reform were
in delegates' minds, we know nothing of them from the official
daily proceedings and the resolutions. Taking these at their word,
the delegates appear to have sought reform immediately for its
own sake, as a means of satisfying their pride or of solacing outraged dignity. They sought recognition of their rights as men, of
their ancient rights as Englishmen, and they desired to abolish the
affronts to common sense that were evident in the anomalies and
absurdities of the unreformed representative system.

The General Convention of the Friends of the People opened

in the Mason-lodge Room in Edinburgh on October 29 with about 160 delegates present or expected from thirty-four Scottish societies and fifteen others. Most of the delegates were from the vicinities of Edinburgh and Glasgow. The resolution adopted at the fourth sitting stated the purpose—a more equal representation meant universal suffrage and annual parliaments, and the effort to attain these was justified on the grounds of natural right and expediency. Skirving, the Secretary, a clerk rather than a leader, announced plans for dues, a monthly publication, and continuing close relations with the English societies. These suggested the idea of a permanent organization. With little more to record by way of accomplishment, and amid discouragement, confusion, and a pile of accumulated papers, the Convention, after forming an interim General Committee, adjourned on November 1 to meet again the following April. The reason for the fiasco was the absence of the English delegates; apparently the Convention had given up on them.

But on November 6, Margarot, Sinclair and Gerrald appeared before the General Committee, along with Hamilton Rowan and Simon Butler from the United Irishmen. There was an immediate lift of spirits, stimulated by the hyperbole of Margarot. He said that whole towns in England were reformers; in Sheffield and its neighborhood there were fifty thousand; in Norwich thirty societies acted in unison; and he predicted that a full convention of English and Scottish delegates would represent 600,000 or 700,000 males, a majority of the adults in the kingdom. This exaggerated statement suggested the hopes for the Convention. If it spoke for so many, the "ministry would not dare to refuse us our rights." A convention then was not intended to displace the existing government but to bring the inexorable pressure of numbers to bear against the government. The enthusiasm revived, the Committee decided to recall the Convention, and Skirving sent out letters and advertisements announcing the date as November 19.

It was a different convention when it reassembled. It adopted a new title, the British Convention of the Delegates of the People associated to obtain Universal Suffrage and Annual Parliaments. Sinclair moved the change. The purpose as stated remained the same, but the new name signified national, democratic unity. More important than the name was the change of spirit and leadership. Margarot virtually took charge, and the 180 delegates seemed to approve wholeheartedly. There was no Scottish-English antagonism; the Irish delegates were accorded full privileges of membership. Margarot's motion for a committee to draw up a plan of union carried at once. He, Gerrald, and Sinclair were members of it; Skirving was not. Perhaps he was too busy keeping the paperwork in order. There was a vast amount of busywork, resolutions, addresses, and decisions about procedures. The usage of the title Citizen seemed to become invariable after November 28; Citizen Gerrald gloried in the title and derided the word "gentleman." Beginning on November 29 the minutes are dated, first year of the British Convention.

An important defensive action looked towards the likelihood of government repression. A secret committee was established to summon the Convention into emergency session should the government suspend Habeas Corpus or following Irish precedent, enact a bill making conventions illegal. Margarot added to this on December 4 a motion that if the Convention was dispersed, the secret committee should summon the delegates to a place appointed for an emergency meeting. It might be asked, for what purpose. The minutes do not record one.

On the next day, Skirving, Margarot, Gerrald, Sinclair and three others were arrested. The Convention was broken up only to meet that evening at the appointed place, a carpenter shop in Canongate Lodge. The leaders, out on bail, were present. The Convention met again on December 6. The Sheriff intervened. So ended the last Convention of the century, and along with it, most of the Scottish societies.

The written records do not justify the fears of the authorities in Scotland. Even a sense of novelty is lacking as an explanation for their fears, this being the fourth session of a convention in fourteen months. The activity was mainly speech-making or moving and debating resolutions with great seriousness and attention to procedural detail. Often indiscreet remarks were uttered, as when Citizen Gerrald identified conventions with revolutions and attributed to them all the gains the people had made, or when Citizen Skirving recommended subscription to a solemn league and covenant. These words were ominous but they lacked substance. There seemed to be no real threat to public order. While the Convention expressed its disillusionment with petitions to Parliament, it did not decide on any alternative except to try to persuade the people to support reform. Most important of all, there was no real leadership of a revolutionary character. Skirving was befuddled, Margarot and Gerrald were clever and verbose, but in them and in the Convention there remained a kind of hesitancy behind the brave words, and there was lacking completely the quality of ruthlessness and desperation without which there can be no revolution. A reading of the records of the Convention does not resolve uncertainties. What was it all about? What was it supposed to do? Why did the authorities fear it?

The answers should emerge from the trials (January–March 1794) of the leaders of the Convention, for along with them as individuals, the Convention was on trial. The minutes were submitted as evidence and proved, said the Lord Advocate, that the Convention was "an attempt, . . . to take the first step in that system of anarchy and disorder which they wished for, and which has taken place in a neighbouring country." Perhaps the Lord Advocate saw something in the minutes that escapes a later reader who has to be in the frame of mind of a Lord Braxfield in order to see his full meaning of the Convention. The spirit in which the trials took place, the assumptions upon which the prosecution acted, the judges presided, and the jurors decided were stated by Lord Braxfield when he summed up for the jury in the case of Margarot.

> That therefore taking all these circumstances together, I am afraid that there is nothing but what is irreconcilable with innocence. But gentlemen, in order to constitute the crime of sedition, it is not necessary that the meeting should have had in view to overturn the constitution by mobs and by violence to overturn the king and parliament. For I apprehend, in some sense, the crime of sedition consists in poisoning the minds

of the lieges, which may naturally in the end have a tendency to promote violence against the state; and endeavouring to create a dissatisfaction in the country, which nobody can tell where it will end, it will very naturally end in overt rebellion; and if it has that tendency, though not in the view of the parties at the time, yet if they have been guilty of poisoning the minds of the lieges, I apprehend that that will constitute the crime of sedition to all intents and purposes. Now, gentlemen, take a view of the conduct of this meeting, and attend to the time when all this reform, and all this noise and declamation is made against the constitution. It is at a time when we are at war with a great nation, a cruel ferocious nation, that requires all our strength, and not only our strength, but the strength of all our allies to get the better of them; and the greatest unanimity is necessary. I submit to you whether a man that wishes well to his country would come forward and insist upon a reform, parliamentary or not parliamentary, at such a crisis; which would create discontent in the minds of the people, when every good subject would promote unanimity among the lieges to meet the common enemy. I say in place of that, to bring forward a great reform in parliament is a thing totally inconsistent with the constitution of this country. I say, bringing it forward at that period is a strong proof that they were not wellwishers to the constitution, but enemies to it. I say that no good member of society would have taken those measures. I appeal to you all, that you are living under a happy government in peace and plenty, in perfect security of your lives and property, the happiest nation upon the face of the earth; and when that is the situation of this country, I appeal to you whether I have not given a fair and just description of it; for a set of men in that situation to raise a faction in the minds of the lower order of the people, and create disaffection to the government, and consequently make a division in that country;—I say, these things appear to be from the very conjuncture at which they are brought forward, sedition of a very high nature.

Skirving, whose trial came first, spoke for all of the defendants when he said "I am conscious of no guilt;" and added later, "I know of no law, either of God or man, that I have transgressed in the matter of reform."

No evidence was presented to prove that the purpose of the Convention was anything other than parliamentary reform. But that admitted, the verdict of guilt followed, because the judges and juries equated the advocacy of reform with sedition. It was not considered necessary by the prosecution to do more than establish the participation of the defendants in the activities of the Convention, and to associate them with the utterances of the Convention. The Solicitor-General said the Convention was seditious per se, and the times made it doubly so.

As had happened before, the defendants were enemies to themselves. Skirving and Margarot acted as their own counsel. They made many mistakes, of judgment and of procedure. Perhaps the biggest mistake was to believe so strongly in their own innocence as to think it impossible for a reasonable man to hold them guilty. Thus, Skirving brought in no witnesses of his own because he thought the crown witnesses had proved nothing against him, and in fact had exculpated him "from every suspicion of seditious intention." This was too trusting. The question was not what Skirving thought about this testimony but what the jury might think of it. Both he and Margarot gave long, irrelevant speeches suited for a popular debating society rather than a courtroom. When Margarot was corrected on a technical point, he said "My lords, I do not require the forms of justice, I require the essence of justice." This is the usual layman's attitude about judicial procedure. In fact, the court was rather tolerant of Margarot's mistakes. After the verdict of guilty, Margarot said he did not know Scottish law, but he knew the British Constitution, and he knew that the proceedings had departed from the constitution. All of which meant nothing to the case.

Gerrald came into the court something of a hero because he had returned to Scotland for trial instead of absconding while out on bail in England. Gerrald seemed to have at least one heroic quality, besides courage, and that was the ability to lift people up to him. Thomas Campbell, the poet, attended the trial as a lad of seventeen. Moved by Gerrald's address to the jury, Campbell whispered to a stranger seated next to him that Gerrald was a great man. Not only that, said the stranger, but Gerrald made every one who heard him "feel great."

But not the jury or the judges. With the convictions of Margarot and Skirving, the guilt of Gerrald was a foregone conclusion. He was from the first "a doomed man," said Lord Cockburn. If Gerrald thought he had any chance of acquittal, a comment of Braxfield's should have destroyed it. When Gerrald objected to one juror because he had said he would condemn any member of the British Convention, Braxfield said, "I hope there is not a gentleman of the jury, or any man in this court, who has not expressed the same sentiment." If they had not already, they did in rendering the verdict, guilty. Gerrald, Margarot and Skirving were sentenced to fourteen years transportation. Sinclair became a government spy and the case against him was dropped.

There was a brief aftermath to the dispersal of the Scottish Convention, the conviction of its leaders, and the smashing of the reform movement in Scotland. The secret committee left over from the Convention fell into the control of David Downie, an Edinburgh goldsmith, and Robert Watt, a wine merchant of the same city, neither of whom had been prominent at the Convention. Watt had been an informer since the founding in July 1792 of the first Society of the Friends of the People in Edinburgh. Why he changed his stripes is not clear, but during his trial in September 1794 it was argued that he participated in the latest conspiracy in order to acquire new evidence for the government. Watt and Downie were charged with high treason. Their plot, it was alleged, was to distribute arms, raise insurrection, seize Edinburgh Castle and proclaim a new government. They corresponded with Thomas Hardy of London and encouraged his plans for a convention as part of their own endeavor in the spring of 1794. The measure of their alleged desperation was the evidence found in their rooms—eighteen pikeheads and four battle-axes. It almost seems that in addition to restoring the Anglo-Saxon constitution, they were going to revive Anglo-Saxon battle tactics. They were tried before a special commission in Edinburgh, and fairly. In fact, the arrangements for the trial were made in such a way as to preclude Braxfield from presiding. There was a limit to what even Dundas could stomach. They were found guilty within the meaning of the statute of Edward III by the reasoning that to rise against the government was to compass and imagine the King's death. On the jury's recommendation, Downie was pardoned on condition that he serve a one-year prison sentence and then go into exile from Great Britain for the rest of his life. The day before the execution of Watt, he confessed to the plan to seize Edinburgh Castle, to make attempts in London, Dublin, and in other towns, and to form a new government. He was hanged and beheaded.

Excluding Downie and Watt, the reformers who met in the Edinburgh Conventions and the leaders who suffered prosecution and deaths in exile were sincere and courageous men. In them was a fierce indignation, a sense of wrong being done to the people, a passionate desire to honor the right of the common man to have a voice in public affairs, that is, a vote for Members of Parliament. They had a naïve confidence in the efficacy of parliamentary reform as the panacea for all the ills that the people suffered. They met their fate with courage and single faith in the future; their minds were at ease in the consciousness of rectitude. Just before he sailed for Australia, Thomas Muir wrote to the SCI, "The Man, who has acted in obedience to the law of his own conscience, has simply discharged his duty." Soon after arriving in Australia, Joseph Gerrald died. His last words were "I die in the best of causes, and, as you witness, without repining." He was buried in the garden of his cottage outside Sydney. Three days later, on March 19, 1796, Skirving also died, having contracted dysentery while working the small farm he had purchased. Scotland supplied the martyrs of reform.

CHAPTER IX

WE ARE NOT INTIMIDATED

THE results of the Scottish trials encouraged the government to proceed by judicial action against the leaders of English radicalism. But not until they took false steps that seemed to ministers to provide the evidence needed to make conviction certain. In the meantime there were some lesser persons to deal with.

The record of prosecutions in the English courts in 1793 and early 1794 was spotty. Some little fish were caught in the net and some bigger ones got away. Thomas Briellat, the Shoreditch pump-maker, was indicted for some Painite expressions made in public and tried in December 1793 for seditious libel before the Clerkenwell sessions. The jury found that his words were intended to excite discontent in his hearers, but recommended mercy. Briellat spent twelve months in prison. Dr. William Hudson (or Hodgson), physician, writer on various subjects, and a noted radical, spoke indiscreetly at the London Coffeehouse in Ludgate Hill. The proprietor of the house sent for the constable. Hodgson was charged with uttering seditious words, bound over, and appeared for trial at Old Bailey on December 9. He did not deny having said, "The French Republic; and may it triumph over all the governments in Europe!" But he meant only the success of the French people in their war against continental powers, not against England. As for the expression "George Guelph, a German hog-butcher, a dealer in human flesh by the carcass" who sold his subjects for military service to Britain at thirty pounds per head—that, insisted Hodgson, was a statement of fact. Acting as his own counsel, Hodgson failed to explain away these utterances and received two years in Newgate.

In two more important cases the government failed. Before a special jury in King's Bench, Thomas Erskine defended the three printers and proprietors of the *Morning Chronicle* against the charge of publishing a seditious libel.* The Declaration at issue was described in the Attorney General's information as a "false, wicked, scandalous and seditious libel." Erskine won the first procedural point, insisting that the original jury impaneled in the previous term of court hear the case rather than a new jury impaneled in the new court term. Both prosecution and defense agreed that freedom of the press was at issue, and that the case had unusual significance because it was the first to be tried "completely" upon the principles of Fox's Libel Law of 1792. Under the law there could be no previous restraints upon publication. But once published, the matter was subject to the determination of a jury. There being no dispute about the fact of publication, the "gist of the case," said Erskine, was intent. The jury must believe "in your consciences that they are guilty of malicious and wicked designs" before conviction can be made. There was nothing new in the Declaration; the defendants published it with the intention of doing good. The state of the times was irrelevant. The Attorney General argued, as it had been done in Scotland, that the fact of publication was evidence of evil intention. In summing up, Lord Kenyon ignored the Attorney General's opinion, but went on to say that the state of the times was relevant, and in that light expressed his belief that the defendants published with a malicious intent. After deliberating five hours, the jury handed in the verdict "Guilty of publishing, but with no malicious intent." Lord Kenyon rejected this verdict, the jury withdrew, and after deliberating all night, at 5 A.M. decided that the defendants were "Not Guilty."

In February 1794 the government proceeded for the third time against Daniel Eaton. He was indicted by the grand jury for publishing a seditious libel, "Politics for the People, or Hog Wash,"

* Appendix A.

and tried at the Old Bailey before the Recorder of London. There were no new issues in this trial. The fact of publication was established without dispute. It was for the jury to decide whether the material was seditious and whether Eaton's motives were criminal. The jury needed only one hour to decide that Eaton was "Not Guilty."

One of the most disgraceful trials in its inception and satisfying in its outcome was that of Thomas Walker. Indicted for conspiracy, along with a paper-stainer, a chapman, a surgeon, and four laborers, one of whom had fled to America before the trial, Walker was tried in April 1794 at the Lancaster assizes. In fact, he had urged the trial as the only means of clearing away rumors about him. Walker was the founder and all of the accused were members of the Manchester Constitutional Society. The chief witness for the crown was one Thomas Dunn, a weaver, who a year before had sworn out a warrant for high treason against Walker. No indictment had then been returned. Dunn testified that the Society had as its object the overthrow of the constitution, not help for the poor as he had thought when he joined it. Walker was specified as having said "Damn the King." Dunn also said that members were practicing military exercises. Thomas Erskine, defending, went after Dunn with a vengeance, exposed him as an illiterate drunkard, destroyed the credibility of his testimony, and forced him to admit perjury. The crown lawyers gave up the case and the jury pronounced Walker not guilty. At the autumn assizes Dunn was convicted of perjury and sentenced to two years imprisonment. A magistrate who had put Dunn up to his misdeeds was not punished. There were two other interesting facets to the trial. The case had been taken to Pitt, Grenville, and Loughborough, the Lord Chancellor, before it was brought to trial, and Loughborough had expressed doubts about Dunn's reliability. Why the crown proceeded with the case is not known. The other interesting part was the admission of the judge that a petition to Parliament for reform, the avowed object of Walker, "can be no offence."

England, it seemed, was different from Scotland. Juries were not as easily swayed by emotion or panic, and some judges could be judicial. When someone as able as Erskine or John Gurney, who had defended Eaton, acted for the defense, the crown seemed to have little chance of success. The contrast between England and Scotland was obvious and notorious, and became the subject of debates in the spring of 1794 in both the Lords and the Commons. Much of the discussion was technical, relating to substance and procedures of Scottish law. The Foxite minority remained a small minority on the various motions relating to the trials of Muir and Palmer, and the problems of Scottish law in general. The successful motion of Lord Chancellor Loughborough that there was no ground for interfering in the practice of the courts represented the judgment of the majority in both houses, even admitting that in the cases in question there might have been some irregularities.

Encouraged by the government's failures in the courts of England, angered by Parliament's rejection of attempts to gain reconsideration of the cases of Muir and Palmer, and hardened to a determination to press the reform issue by the suppression of the Scottish Convention, the English societies in the spring of 1794 gathered themselves for another effort. They agreed with Skirving who wrote from on board the *Surprise* at Spithead that the martyrdom he and his friends suffered would not be in vain. But the English radicals were not willing to admit with Skirving that the revolution in human affairs was yet distant. The SCI became more indecorous than at any time in its history. If not by specific adoption, then by unspoken consensus the members called one another "Citizen." They approved the conduct of the British Convention at Edinburgh. They asserted that the law "ceases to be an object of obedience whenever it becomes an instrument of oppression." And they resolved to "oppose tyranny by the same means by which it is exercised" as a means of preserving British liberties. If these were not idle words, they meant that the reformers were ready to take matters into their own hands.

As to the means of doing that, the LCS supplied the answer. On January 20 they agreed to call another convention, conditional upon certain provocations by government.* As the idea of a convention was discussed it took firmer hold of their minds and

* See Appendix B for the text of the Declaration of January 20, 1794.

became their object unconditionally. The LCS took the lead in the correspondence of March and April looking towards this end. Assurances of support and promises of delegations came from various societies, including Norwich, Bristol, and Sheffield. "We are not in the least intimidated," wrote Sheffield. On April 7 a great open-air meeting at Sheffield, attended by four thousand persons, approved of an address to the King on behalf of the Scottish martyrs and renewed its support for parliamentary reform and the abolition of Negro slavery. Two weeks later another such meeting at Halifax, attended also by reformers from Leeds, Wakefield, Huddersfield and Bradford approved of a convention and agreed to hold a meeting at Bristol to prepare themselves for it.

In the meantime, the LCS and the SCI were coordinating their efforts. On March 27 the LCS challenged the SCI to commit itself. The next day the SCI resolved unanimously that "there ought to be immediately a convention of the people" and that "every legal method" of achieving reform be pursued. On the suggestion of the SCI a joint committee was appointed to consider preliminaries. The committee reported on April 11 in favor of a general convention and each society appointed five members to form a standing committee of cooperation. Its activities are not mentioned in existing records. Nor, in the resolutions of the SCI relative to the report received on April 11, is the word "convention" used, though the first resolution spoke of the desirability of "a general meeting of the friends of liberty." When testifying before the Privy Council, Thomas Thompson, M. P., thought he remembered that the SCI opposed a convention at meetings on April 4 and April 11.

At this point the records are confusing. It is not finally clear whether the Society opposed or favored a convention, or whether it abandoned the idea. The opinion of the LCS was equivocal. In several documents in which it would have been pertinent to mention a convention, Hardy did not refer to it. The famous Chalk Farm meeting of the LCS on April 14 did not act on the subject, per se, but the word convention appeared in two letters read at the meeting, and the idea was implied in at least two of the resolutions passed at Chalk Farm. But there was no resolution on the subject of a convention as such. The meeting was held on the trap-ball green near the Hampstead Road, with about two thousand persons present. The proceedings were printed; in fact the meeting resolved to publish two hundred thousand copies of them. Under the chairmanship of a hairdresser, John Lovett, the assemblage was orderly, and why not, thought Francis Place, for these were "*thinking* and *reasoning* men." Two letters were read to the crowd, one from the LCS to the Friends of the People soliciting their cooperation in assembling as speedily as possible a convention for the purpose of obtaining reform. Just how a convention would achieve this, the letter did not say, although it expressed confidence that "there is no power which can finally withstand the just and steady demands of a people resolved to be free." The other letter was the Friends' reply, giving assurance of support for "every peaceable and constitutional measure" which might advance the cause of reform. But the Friends did not think a convention was such a measure and declined to send delegates.

If this was the opinion of the Friends, it is not difficult to realize what was the opinion of government about the dangers of a convention—or of the language used in the ten resolutions passed by the Chalk Farm meeting and in its address to the "martyr," Joseph Gerrald. The resolutions condemned the repressive actions of the government, lamented the "advances of despotism," applauded the Scottish Convention, abhorred the recent trials in Scotland, and promised to redress the wrongs suffered by Gerrald and Margarot. They warned the government that violations of the "yet remaining laws" intended to protect Englishmen against tyranny would "be considered as dissolving entirely the social compact between the English nation and their governors," and would force the people to appeal to that "maxim of eternal justice" which makes "the safety of the people . . . in cases of necessity, the only law." The resolutions ended on a note of confidence—"Steady perseverance in the same bold and energetic sentiments which have lately been avowed by the friends of freedom" would make their cause "invincible and omnipotent." The letter to Gerrald completed a thought left incomplete in the second resolution which had mentioned Charles the First. The letter described the sentence upon Gerrald as one of the most abominable "since the days of that most infamous and ever-to-be-detested court of star-chamber, the enormous tyranny of which cost the first Charles his head."

Such language, reminiscent of Patrick Henry, might stimulate febrile imaginations. When the Secret Committee of the House of Commons on June 6 reported on radical activities, it asserted that of late the societies had given up the idea of obtaining a reform by application to Parliament. Instead, there were two alternatives. The milder one was so to arouse the people that Parliament would be unable to resist their "collective sense." The other and more recent one said the committee was to assemble a convention which would seek the reform not from Parliament but "from themselves, and from their own strength and valour, from their own laws." Obtained by such means, a reform would be nothing "short of an entire destruction of the constitution." For the convention would create a new representative body, based on universal suffrage and claiming to possess "the whole legislative authority of the nation." If the Committee really believed this, it is easy to understand why the government feared a convention, why it had moved against the Scottish Convention, and why it proceeded against those who were thought to be the ringleaders of the movement for an English convention. The radicals had not helped their own cause when they failed to make clear what a convention was supposed to do—whether to petition Parliament, act as a pressure group, or more directly to supersede Parliament and either act themselves as a government or create a new one. It was not impossible to derive the last idea from some of the reform literature, and especially from the writings of Tom Paine to whom a convention was, in the American style, a constituent body representing directly and embodying the authority of the sovereign people.

Though at Chalk Farm the radicals had not resolved to hold a convention, the assemblage contained the frightening threat of a force which might grow to assume constituent authority. Then came the famous meeting of the SCI on May 2. Some three hundred persons gathered at the Crown and Anchor to celebrate the Society's fourteenth anniversary and as it turned out, its swan song. During the excellent dinner and between toasts, the band played patriotic numbers—"Ça Ira," "Carmagnole," "The Marseillaise," "The Democrat," and a new song, "The Free Constitution." The meeting seems to have been a bibulous affair. Horne Tooke, who gave a speech that was violent even for him, introduced it by announcing vehemently that he was not intoxicated. He was especially virulent against Pitt. When later the Privy Council examined one who had been present, it was unusually interested in the toasts. They were:

The Rights of Man

A Free Constitution

The Swine of England, the Rabble of Scotland,
and the Wretches of Ireland *

Equal Laws and Liberty

May Despotism be trodden under the Hoofs
of the Swinish Multitude

The Armies Contending for Liberty

Wisdom, Firmness, and Unanimity to all the Patriotic Societies
in Great Britain

To the Reign of Peace and Liberty

May all Governments be those of the Laws,
and all the Laws those of the People

Except for the one to the French armies, these hackneyed toasts suggested little more than indiscretion and possibly the influence of wine, but the Privy Council found dark meanings in them.

Putting things together, the Sheffield and Halifax open-air

* The toast had been drunk at Belfast on November 14, 1793, at a dinner in honor of Hamilton Rowan of the United Irishmen. The swine referred to Burke's phrase, "swinish multitude"; the word "rabble" was used often to describe the Scots; and the Lord Advocate at Muir's trial spoke of the United Irishmen as "wretches."

meetings, the Chalk Farm assemblage, the raucous dinner of the SCI, and numerous reports from magistrates, agents and informers, the government decided that a major radical effort was maturing. Or, in the words of a contemporary Tory historian, "Informed of these facts, both by public notoriety and private communications, government took the necessary measures to avert danger and punish crime." The government descended upon selected individuals with the object not only of arresting them but of seizing records and papers in the search for incriminating evidence. As early as May 10 the cabinet began interrogating the Hackney coal merchant, William Stone, suspected of implication in an invasion scheme. Among those called in to give evidence were Sheridan, the Earl of Lauderdale, and the bankers Samuel Rogers and his brother-in-law John Towgood. There was surprise and bewilderment about the calling of these witnesses; they knew Stone but even the *Times* took pains to say that it was unthinkable to connect these gentlemen with any plot.*

Two days later the government moved again. Hardy, the Secretary of the LCS and Daniel Adams, a law clerk who for ten years had been Secretary of the SCI, were prime targets. Bearing warrants, agents entered their homes in Piccadilly and Covent Garden early in the morning of May 12, arrested them, rummaged through their rooms and carried off their papers. Mrs. Hardy, far advanced in pregnancy, watched from her bed while her husband was led away. Hardy remained in the custody of the King's Messenger for a fortnight and was interrogated by the Privy Council before being transferred to the Tower of London. Also on May 12 Thelwall and the Reverend Jeremiah Joyce were taken up. Joyce, a Unitarian, lived in Lord Stanhope's home and was tutor to his son. Others, including Horne Tooke, were arrested during the next three days. The round up continued through the next weeks. It extended into the provinces. On May 26 King's Messengers arrived in London from Sheffield, having in

* Stone was committed to Newgate on a charge of High Treason but did not stand trial until January 1796. Erskine defended him and won acquittal. Rogers, who had met Charles Fox in Stone's house, testified at the trial. His evidence helped Stone's cause.

custody the chairman and the secretary of the Sheffield Constitutional Society as well as a man named Moody who was alleged to have been making seven-foot-long pikes. A radical leader from Norwich, named Saint, was also brought to London. During this time the Privy Council met regularly to interrogate the suspects.

Parliament was still in session when the first arrests were made. On May 12 Dundas, the Home Secretary, read a message from the King to the House of Commons announcing the actions that had been taken, justifying them, laying before the House for its consideration the confiscated papers, and recommending that appropriate measures be taken to prevent the fulfillment of the "dangerous designs" then afoot. Within a week each House had chosen by ballot a Secret Committee to examine the papers and by June 7 each Committee had produced two reports to its parent body. The reports were what might be expected when Pitt, Dundas, Windham, the Attorney-General, the Solicitor-General, the Lord Advocate of Scotland, Sir Henry Hoghton who had been foreman of the grand jury which indicted Thomas Walker, Robert Jenkinson the future Lord Liverpool, Charles Townshend of Reeves' Association, and Edmund Burke were among the twenty-one members of the Commons Committee, and when Loughborough, the Duke of Portland, the Earl of Hardwick and Pitt's older brother were four of the nine members of the Lords' Committee.

The reports, especially the long second report of the Commons' Committee, reproduced in part or in full many of the seized documents and drew strong conclusions from them. The main ones were that "a traitorous conspiracy hath been formed" by the radical societies; that the intended convention was to be "itself the means of obtaining" reform; that the reform contemplated would be a "total subversion of the constitution"; that the English societies and the French revoluntionary government were closely connected; and finally, that of late trusted, select members of certain societies in Sheffield, Scotland and London were gathering firelocks and pikes, and that though the number of weapons so far discovered seemed "inconsiderable," it was the intention to use them to resist any attempts to disperse the conven-

tion. The Commons' Committee also suggested a further intention "to have recourse to arms" if reform could not be secured in
any other way.

Simultaneously the government resorted to a very extreme
measure. Pitt introduced it in a panicky speech.

> Who was there that knew what Jacobins and Jacobin
> principles were, but must see, in the pretenses of re-
> form in parliament held out by these societies, the ar-
> rogant claims of the same class of men as those who
> lorded it in France. . . ; the dark designs of a few,
> making use of the people to govern all; a plan founded
> in the arrogance of wretches, the outcasts of society,
> tending to enrich themselves, by depriving of prop-
> erty, and of life, all those who were distinguished ei-
> ther for personal worth, or for opulence?

On the principle that emergencies justified "the temporary sacrifice of the law" to preserve the constitution, Pitt moved for leave
to bring in a bill suspending Habeas Corpus until February 1,
1795. To Fox and a few others this was worse than the mischief it
was intended to prevent. Most of the speakers in the debate were
members of the minority; supporters of the government merely
sat, their minds made up, until impatience forced the end of the
debate. The bill was rushed through the Commons in two sit-
tings; the minority never numbered more than 39 on any motion
along the way. The Lords passed it on May 22, the vote on the
third reading being 92–7.

The supporters of Church and King began to breathe more easily. With warrants out for radical leaders and some already in
prison, and with removal of Habeas Corpus as a barrier to their
indefinite detention, with incriminating evidence accumulating
against the prisoners, with the Secret Committees' reports vindi-
cating its conduct, and having struck blows against radical leadership in Sheffield and Scotland, the government could expect with
some confidence that after the trials of the prisoners metropolitan
radicalism would be effectively suppressed. Early in June came
news of a "glorious" naval victory over the French off the coast

of Brittany. Both houses of Parliament voted thanks to Lord
Howe. Far from "reconquering" Habeas Corpus, as Fox hoped
the victory might also have done, it rather intensified an upsurge
of loyalty to King and constitution. The illuminations in celebration of the "glorious first of June" were also occasions for demonstrating hostility towards pro-French radicalism. Lord Stanhope's house suffered many broken windows. A mob attacked the
unilluminated home in Piccadilly where Mrs. Hardy, her husband
in the Tower of London, awaited the birth of a child. Frightened,
she escaped through a window, and in struggling through the
small opening injured herself. Members of the LCS including
some Irish "armed with good shillelahs" defended the house until
cavalry arrived to restore peace. A young Irish plumber who had
just come to England, John Binns, remembered with relish that
he "never was in so long-continued and well-conducted a fight"
as that one.*

The determination of the government to suppress radicalism
was strengthened by the improvement of Pitt's political position
in July. The Duke of Portland, Lord Fitzwilliam, Windham and
others at last did what Burke had been urging them to do. They
broke with Fox and formed a coalition with Pitt. The remnant of
the old opposition party, the Foxites, many of them Friends of
the People, had been at odds both with Pitt and the Portland
wing over the French Revolution, the war, and reform. Now that
the breach within the Opposition was complete, and now that radicalism was on the run, there seemed neither within nor outside
of Parliament to be any prospect of successfully opposing either
the domestic or foreign and military policy of the government.
On the same day that Portland became Home Secretary and Fitzwilliam became Lord President of the Council, the King ended
the session of Parliament with assurances to his Lords and Gentlemen that supported by the "loyalty and public spirit" of his
subjects he had no doubt "of speedily and effectually repressing
every attempt to disturb the public peace, and of defeating the
wicked designs which have been in agitation."

* Binns wrote his *Recollections* a half-century later, when in America.
He places this event in 1795–1796, but all other details make it certain that
it was connected with the celebration of mid-June 1794.

One of the means of doing this, though ostensibly it was to strengthen home defense against a French invasion, was to augment the militia. Counting upon the same spirit that had supported the loyal associations in 1793, the government encouraged the counties to raise subscriptions to pay for volunteer forces, both infantry and cavalry, to be used for local services. No one tried to hide the fact that the volunteers would be used to suppress riots. Led by the Marquis of Buckingham, Grenville's brother, the gentlemen of his neighborhood raised £5851 to support "The Armed Yeomanry" of Buckinghamshire; Lord Cornwallis was chairman of the committee that took subscriptions for £3012 in the Tower Hamlets of London. In other parts of England the local responses were comparably generous, and under the arrangements about eleven thousand cavalry and militiamen joined up. These forces, like the embodied militia, were never put to the test of resisting an invasion but they served a useful purpose in demonstrating both the popularity and the physical strength of the government.

Yet it was not a quiet summer. Anti-Jacobin outbursts here and there throughout the kingdom, though disturbances of the peace, were not of the kind the King had referred to. In some places the local authorities condoned them. The riots in London in August, in Holborn, Charing Cross and Southwark, resulted in destruction of some houses used by recruiting officers. The rioters were suspected of having insidious connections with Jacobinism. Because in many places the societies which had not dissolved had gone underground, suspicion and rumor were actually excited. Before magistrates and at assizes many actions against suspected dangers took place. Yet there were instances of reactions against the government practice of relying upon informers. Juries, instinctively hostile to spies, sometimes seemed to acquit for that reason only. In the view of one anti-Jacobin writer, the government experienced "unimportant successes and mortifying failures" in its prosecutions during the middle six months of the year 1794.

In London, the Corresponding Society continued to function, though less openly and on a diminished scale. Just before the May arrests the Society had been increasing in strength and influence in the east end of London and along the docks and had begun to present a somewhat different character than formerly. The May arrests were not a permanent check. John Baxter, who had succeeded Margarot as chairman, remained active until the warrant sworn out against him in May was served at the end of June. A journeyman silversmith, his physical appearance encouraged the observer to think of him as a dark designer. As much as any of the LCS members whose individuality emerges from the records, he was a proponent of physical force and was ready to resort to arms. After his arrest, others carried on in the secret executive committee. One of them, also ready to use arms and a persuasive speaker like Baxter, was Richard Hodgson, a Westminster hatter. He managed to evade the Bow Street Runners who had a warrant for him. Even allowing for exaggeration, the reports of the spy, "Citizen Groves," bring these men, some of their associates, and their activities during the summer of 1794 as close to ominousness as the English Jacobins came in this decade. But it is easy to exaggerate the danger. Even the evidence for the spread of Painite doctrines during the two preceding years does not refute the judgment that English Jacobinism lacked members, leadership, organization, and money in the amounts and quality necessary for success in their endeavors. No one in England at this time appeared as a potential Mirabeau, Danton or Robespierre. English Jacobinism had so little revolutionary substance that considering the nature of society in the 1790's it is difficult to persuade oneself that England faced either political or social revolution.

This is not to say that contemporaries who feared revolution were fools or that people who professed fears were hypocrites. It was easy and natural to magnify the evidence and the dangers. It would have been unusual for readers or listeners always to be discerning critics who could analyze calmly and discount hyperbole when they met with the overenthusiastic statements of the radicals. If radicals used exaggerated language, then they had no one but themselves to blame if the statements were received as meaning more than the authors intended.

It must also be remembered that the phenomenon of working class political agitation, on a national scale and seemingly moving toward institutional form in a great body intended to be repre-

sentative of many local societies, was new in English experience.
Approximate precedents such as the Yorkshire Movement or the
idea of a convention advanced in the early 1780's by members of
the SCI were different in important respects from the Scottish
Convention or the projections of the LCS. There was no Paine in
the 1780's to infuse the idea of convention with constituent qualities; there was no example of the French Revolution to arouse
fears; and a sans culotte appearance was lacking in the county associations like Yorkshire's or in the SCI. As much as anything
else, the newness of the LCS and its provincial counterparts, in
organization, in social composition, in proletarian appearances,
and in the extremity of programs created fears. The governing
class in 1794 faced something England had not known before—
they feared the unknown and their alarm was greater than it need
have been.

These sentiments were not masks to disguise political ambitions. It has been said that Pitt deliberately took advantage of
public uneasiness and encouraged panic to split his political opponents by separating the followers of the Duke of Portland
from their former Foxite friends. In this reading of events,
Burke unwittingly gave Pitt the cue by first calling up the dangers from the French Revolution and the reform societies. Pitt
then played the game cynically and expertly, achieving his political ends with the formation of the July 1794 coalition. Evidence of government earnestness in its anti-Jacobin efforts and
in the private correspondence of ministers qualifies this view.
The details of the political negotiations leading to the coalition
also throw doubts upon it. The Regency debacle frustrated the
Portland Whigs. The election of 1790 secured Pitt's parliamentary position. The parliamentary Opposition thereafter was not a
real threat to him. The government enjoyed strong support
from the Portland followers in its anti-Jacobin policy for two
years prior to the coalition and would have continued to enjoy it
had there been no coalition. It has been said that the desire to
gain support for the government's war effort was also an aspect
of this alleged political maneuver. Again, the Portland camp was
already demanding vigorous military action. If anything it was

less willing than Pitt himself to make peace with the revolutionary government in France. Pitt and Grenville saw the war as
necessary to protect certain traditional national interests. They
did not, like some of the Portland followers, think that it should
be a crusade against the French Jacobin regime. William Windham, the Burkite Secretary at War in the coalition government,
was "in practice the minister for co-operation with the émi-
grés." The invasion of Brittany in June 1795 to cooperate
with the uprisings against the French government was largely
Windham's scheme, endorsed by Burke. In spite of its failure,
Windham bitterly opposed peace overtures to the revolutionary
government in Paris. It was Pitt who sponsored the negotiations
of 1795–1797, encouraged by his friend Wilberforce and his political opponent Fox.

To what extent Pitt really feared the English radical societies
in 1794 is difficult to say. He desired to suppress them for the
sake of political and social order and in the interest of getting on
with the war. His desire to do these things was not so insincere
as to justify the assertion that the political coalition was exclusively a political tactic. To throw up at him his support of reform in 1785 does not make of him a turncoat. That reform was
not intended to depart from the traditional concepts about the
nature of the representative system and its dependence upon
property. The radicals of 1794 were in his eyes not reformers
but Painites—democrats who would make men rather than interests and property the bases of representation, and who talked as
if in order to do so they would go over the heads of Parliament
to the people.

It was not their advocacy of a parliamentary reform, but suspicions (or conviction) of their darker and ulterior designs that
brought against the radicals the extreme actions of 1794. These
suspicions were revealed in the charge to the Middlesex grand
jury which on October 6 returned indictments against twelve
men. All of them were members of the LCS or the SCI. William
Godwin said, in his published attack upon the charge, "it was
behind this avowed and innocent intention [parliamentary re-
form] that hidden and treasonable acts were to be discovered

and punished." It was in his charge to the grand jury rather than in his conduct while presiding at the ensuing trials that Lord Chief Justice Eyre was vulnerable to criticism. He began impartially enough by explaining the nature of treason as defined by the statute dating from Edward III, namely levying war or compassing or imagining the death of the King. But then he went far beyond. It was the duty of the grand jury to decide whether parliamentary reform was a mere pretext "to cover deeper designs" which would be treasonable. An association for promoting reform "can work itself up to the crime of high treason." A convention organized to exert pressure upon the legislature must be distinguished from one designed to usurp the powers of the legislature and overthrow the constitution. In the second instance there would be a conspiracy against the government preliminary to an overt act tantamount to compassing the death of the King; in the first instance treason was more doubtful. In order to settle doubts, true bills should be returned so that the case "should be put into a judicial course of inquiry." When laid open by Godwin's indignant analysis this charge had implications not foreseen by Justice Eyre or by the ministers. Readers of Godwin's pamphlet *Cursory Strictures* saw that ministers did not have "clear and undoubted grounds" for establishing treason. They could now hope that with a new and heavier burden of proof upon the prosecution, the defendants had a chance for acquittal particularly with Erskine defending. For it was necessary to prove, under the indictment, that "being moved and seduced by the instigation of the devil," and under the guise of seeking parliamentary reform, the defendants had conspired to break the tranquillity of the realm, to raise "rebellion and war" against the King, to subvert the government, and to put the King to death. Guilt would be punishable by death—hanging, disembowelling before death, and quartering.

Except that he was named first in the indictment, there is no apparent reason why Hardy was tried first. Perhaps this was a mistake by the prosecution. Though he had founded and remained Secretary of the LCS, there was much in his background to evoke respect and sympathy. He had a simple intuitive dignity; he was brave and calm; his sincerity was obvious; his integrity was well-known. In fact, as the *Annual Register* admitted, "the goodness of his character" perhaps as much as the arguments of Erskine, refuted the insinuations of the prosecution. And a recent event, genuinely pathetic, created much feeling for Hardy. His wife had died two months earlier after the stillbirth of their child. Of the twelve, Hardy was the figure who most completely represented the virtues of the common people, and they felt for him as they could not feel towards the other defendants. Perhaps the hugeness of the crowds outside the Old Bailey and the national interest in the trial were not altogether explained by realization of the importance of the cause at issue. Hardy was the likeliest martyr of the twelve.

The trial began on October 28 at eight in the morning and before that day ended, after midnight, no one doubted that it would be a test of physical endurance among other things. Erskine and the crown lawyers went through eighty-six names before a jury was agreed upon. The Attorney General, Sir John Scott, opened for the crown and talked for nine hours. When he heard of this, Lord Thurlow, the former Lord Chancellor, exclaimed, "Nine hours. Then there is no treason, by God!" Scott's address explained the law of treason and attempted to show how the alleged acts of the radicals would depose the King from his royal majesty. He then reviewed the history of the SCI and the LCS with the preparations for a convention the climax of his account. When the prosecution began to call its witnesses, Erskine interrupted. There were two practical questions. Erskine would need an opportunity to examine the mass of papers before he addressed the jury. And it would be physically impossible to complete the evidence in one sitting. The court agreed and broke the ancient rule that a felony case must be disposed of in one day. The jury was locked up and the resumption of the trial was set for 8 A.M. There would be little sleep that night for any of the participants, and the trial had hardly begun.

During the next three days, with the court in session on each of them from 8 A.M. until after midnight, the prosecution read through the papers seized on May 12, thus repeating or reinforcing much of Scott's presentation, and presented its witnesses. In cross examination Erskine, who was capable of handling witnesses roughly, scored some points along the way, but when the prosecution closed its case at 2 P.M. on November 1, the fifth day of the trial, a great weight of suggestive evidence telling against Hardy had been laid before the jury. But the very thoroughness and diligence of the prosecution gave to Erskine an advantage that he seized. On the preceding day Erskine had asked that the court not assemble until noon of November 1 in order that he might have four more hours to prepare the opening for the defense. This had been granted, and so on the first, after the prosecution had used an hour to close its case, the initiative was Erskine's. November 1 was a Saturday. Erskine would have the last word to the jury before the Sunday respite and would fill their heads with the thoughts he wanted them to carry uppermost until Monday.

Erskine spoke for seven hours, but the echoes of the speech have not died. If possible, it was a more magnificent effort than the speech in defense of Paine. Erskine called the jury back to the plain meaning of words. Construction and interpretations of evidence could not obscure the necessity of construing literally the treason statute. If there was a conspiracy, it must be against the life of the King, not his regal character or his government. The jury had been presented with opinions that the radicals had further intentions, but these had not been proved. Much of the prosecution's case was irrelevant because it did not relate to treason as defined in the statute. The "grammatical sense" of the evidence presented by the prosecution and reviewed now by Erskine went only to establish that Hardy and his colleagues sought reform of Parliament.

Erskine's clarity, precision of thought, and eloquence had given his cause a momentum, and the Attorney General could not check it. The defense continued throughout the Saturday night, eliciting from its witnesses testimony upholding Erskine's argument that Hardy sought no more than reform of Parliament. And on into Sunday morning, concluding at noon. On Monday, Erskine questioned the Duke of Richmond, Sheridan,

Sir Philip Francis, the colleague of Burke in the Hastings impeachment and a member of the Friends of the People, and the Earl of Lauderdale, an opponent of Pitt's government, all to the same effect concerning Hardy's intentions. The rest of Monday, until midnight, and the sixteen hour session on Tuesday were occupied with closing addresses to the jury by the assistants to the defense and the prosecution, and the summing up by the Lord Chief Justice Eyre. This was eminently fair. Justice Eyre cautioned the jury against laying too much stress "on particular expressions. God forbid that men's lives should depend on nice interpretations and construction of words." The verdict must "proceed on clear grounds of fact."

On Wednesday, November 5, the eighth day of the trial, the jury retired at 12:30 P.M. and returned three hours later with its verdict, "Not Guilty." For the first time during the trial, Hardy spoke. With the eloquence of simplicity he said to the jury, "My fellow countrymen, I return you my thanks." And after eight days of waiting, the crowds in the streets around the Old Bailey cheered at the vindication of their liberties, as had their ancestors a hundred years before when the seven bishops went free. Hardy did not return that night under guard to Newgate. In a coach drawn by the people whose cause he had represented he was taken on a triumphant circuit, down the Strand, past Westminster Palace, along Pall Mall, around St. James's. The coach stopped for a few minutes, amidst silence, before the empty house at No. 9 Piccadilly. Hardy could not bear to try to live there again, and he spent the next fortnight with his brother-in-law in Lancaster Court, Strand.

Severe as was the ordeal of the initial trial, it was better for Hardy and better for the other defendants that he was tried first. The acquittal of the Secretary of the LCS which was identified so completely by the prosecution with the plans for a convention was bound to weaken the remaining government cases. It is at least possible that if Horne Tooke had been tried and acquitted first, the influence of this victory would not have helped the other defendants, especially Hardy, as much as Hardy's acquittal helped them. This was partly because of the line of defense that prevailed in Tooke's case. Descriptions of Tooke's trial usually emphasize his own role in it, and his conduct, as Hazlitt said, as "a masterpiece of acuteness, dexterity, modest assurance, and legal effect." Though Erskine was the counsel, he left for Tooke an active part after the court permitted him to sit near his counsel rather than take his place in the prisoner's dock —ostensibly because of ill health. Tooke was clever and conceited, a showman, skilled in repartee, and now had the chance to be the master cross-examiner which had been denied him years before when he had been refused admission to the bar. Thus, when cross-examining Daniel Adams, Secretary of the SCI, Tooke established that the income of the Society was about £60 a year and its expenses £50 a year. Tooke commented, the Society then had £10 a year "left to overturn the government with." Erskine may have been taking a chance, but as things turned out he knew what he was doing in giving sufficient latitude for the display of Tooke's negativism—his ability to dissect the arguments of others without advancing the argument himself. He was as much a success in the courtroom as later he was a failure in the House of Commons. In his trial he was on the defensive. He did not have to establish a case of his own, he had only to expose the inadequacies of the case against him.

But the admiration for Tooke's display of his talents has obscured the revelation of his worst side. Hazlitt's sketch of Tooke has him dead to rights, and the trial is the outstanding example. Not only did Tooke attack the evidence and the witnesses against him, but he attempted completely to dissociate himself from the people with whom he had been consorting politically for twenty years. The consequence of this was to ease the pressure and lighten the stain on his own reputation, but it tended to darken the appearance of those with whom he contrasted himself. It was clever and effective to bring Pitt himself to the witness stand in order to show that on questions of reform Tooke had always been closer to Pitt's earlier position than to his associates in the SCI. But in doing this he made them look worse. If his trial had preceded Hardy's, Tooke's defense might have frustrated the efforts to make Hardy appear only as a parliamentary reformer. Thus, Major Cartwright was called as a witness. The tendency of the examination was to emphasize that Cartwright was more radical than Tooke, and that Tooke had always differed from him as to the length to which reform should be carried. Tooke emphasized that he was the one who got out of the reform coach at Hounslow, while other passengers, members of the SCI and the LCS, and Paine, stayed on for the more distant journey. Of course, Tooke was on trial for his life, and Hardy had already been acquitted. Without diminishing the feeling of relief over Tooke's acquittal, the record of the trial makes a reader quite willing to let him enjoy himself henceforth at Wimbledon and unwilling to attend there on Sunday afternoons to hear him embarrass his guests who in spite of it all had to admire his wit and knowledge.

There is no record showing Erskine dissatisfied by all of this. It was his duty to win acquittal for his client. He was not so completely left out of it as the preceding remarks might suggest. His speeches reviewed the activities of the SCI and revealed it as a society much more modest in its ambitions than the LCS. It was in fact a society of gentlemen who "wished well" to the cause of constitutional reform. As for conspiratorial activities, when the SCI committee met on April 28, 1794, allegedly to concert with the committee from the LCS concerning a convention, all they did was to "co-operate in taking snuff out of one another's boxes" and adjourn. If some of Tooke's spirit seemed to rub off on him, it remained true that Erskine planned the overall strategy, delivered the speeches and summed up. Tooke was a tactician, not the commander-in-chief. If the acquittal of Hardy upheld the argument that advocacy of reform was not treasonable, then the conduct of the defense was already dictated. Tooke was revealed as a reformer, but a moderate one, and the jury needed only ten minutes to decide that he was not guilty.

Of the remaining ten who were indicted, three had never been seized and the four who were members of the SCI received a directed verdict of not guilty on the grounds that the evidence against them was the same as the evidence in the case of Tooke.

But John Thelwall's was a different kind of case and there was new evidence to present. The crown persisted and Erskine faced a difficult problem. Thelwall, thirty years old, was self-educated, sharp tongued, with a natural gift for speaking to crowds and likely in his forensic enthusiasm to use extravagant language. His activities had furnished government spies with a good deal of compromising information. Knowing this, Erskine refused to Thelwall the liberties he had permitted Tooke. Of the three cases, perhaps in this one Erskine's speech to the jury told heaviest, because he had to explain away a good deal more than in the others. Even with two acquittals and four dismissals in the immediate background, the jury needed nearly two hours to decide that Thelwall was not guilty. And with that the two remaining prisoners went free because no evidence was brought in against them. This was on December 15. The trials had lasted, off and on, for nearly two months.

CHAPTER X

AFTER THE TRIALS

THE State Trials of 1794 were much more victories for the government and much more decisive defeats for the reform cause than the verdicts of not guilty might indicate. The trials clarified if they did not enlarge the limits of legal freedom of expression. Public discussion and the reform agitation continued, not with less risk of prosecution but with less likelihood of indictment for high treason so long as real acts of rebellion were avoided. The idea of parliamentary reform remained permanently lodged in the minds of the working classes, but after 1794 they were pretty much on their own. The temporary alliance of working and middle-class reformers was broken. Only the reconstituted LCS spoke for organized metropolitan radicalism. It maintained tenuous contacts with the remnants of provincial societies and some members established an association with the United Irishmen, thereby giving greater substance than existed in 1794 to fears that certain radicals engaged in treasonable activities. English Jacobinism after 1794 had its open manifestations but along with these it had a subterranean element. In both characters it wore an aspect of surliness more forbidding than the appearance it presented before the trials.

There were other trials after the twelve went free, but the government initiated them with greater precision. When Henry (Redhead) Yorke was brought into court in 1795 for his activities in Sheffield in April 1794, he was found guilty of conspiracy only. When two new leaders of the LCS were taken up in Birmingham in 1796 and tried the next year, they were charged with sedition. John Gale Jones, a surgeon, was found guilty and imprisoned; John Binns was acquitted. But in 1798 Binns was charged with high treason for consorting with representatives of the United Irishmen. There were grounds for suspicion, certainly, but Binns was acquitted of the charge. While it is true that jurors could not clear their minds entirely of prejudices against reformers, even when admonished by the judges to do so, it was also true after the 1794 trials that it was only when reformers went beyond advocacy of reform that they exposed themselves to the dangers of the extreme penalty. Admitting the grievances of the Irish people, the United Irishmen were engaging in rebellion and conniving at a French invasion. Anyone who involved himself in these enterprises knew very well the dangers he was courting.

It was perhaps a measure of the changed character of the reform agitation and its sense of desperateness that some post-1794 reformers engaged in these activities. The earlier agitation had the semblance of a movement, internally divided on details of the reforms desired, but clear in its focus upon the broadly stated object, parliamentary reform. After 1794 parliamentary reform remained an object, and because of middle-class defections even more decidedly involving universal suffrage and annual elections. But the focus was blurred because of the secret activities of some reformers, and because of their willingness to become implicated in enterprises that were clearly something beyond reform and patently illegal. Some of these were related to combinations or trade unions, some to continued intercourse with kindred souls in Paris, some to the naval mutinies of 1797 which were inspired by grievances over conditions of physical existence but also were tinged with Painite egalitarianism in the way that trade union activities had been since 1792. To the extent that mutineers, in war time, had contacts with the LCS, the cause of parliamentary reform was bound to be compromised, just as in 1798 the rebellion of the United Irishmen and their dealings with France made traitors not only of such as their

leader Wolfe Tone, who cheated the executioner by commit-
ting suicide, but of English Jacobins who were connected with
them.

One of the most striking changes after the 1794 trials was the
falling away from the movement of the middle-class element
which had started it in the first place and remained prominent in
1792-1794 even while working class participation was spreading.
The importance of this separation is the more easily apparent
when viewed in reverse from the middle of the nineteenth century. Chartism failed in the short run because it had no strong
middle-class support or membership. The great Reform Bill of
1832, moderate to be sure, passed because there was strong lower-
and middle-class support for the leadership supplied by Members
of Parliament. This union of 1831–1832 had never existed previ-
ously and did not occur again until Chartism as a movement was
gone. The leadership for the second installment of reform in the
1860's was once again supplied by Members of Parliament. Nineteenth century experience reaffirmed what the decade of the
1790's had taught, that reform would not be achieved unless
lower- and middle-class reformers were joined with reformist
M. P.'s in a united effort on a particular program or bill.

In the 1790's such union had not existed. The Friends of the
People kept themselves separate, personally, socially, emotionally
and intellectually, from the working class societies. The specific
proposals of the Friends were rejected by the popular societies
as being too modest. There was not a defection of the Friends
from the popular movement after 1794 because they had never
been a part of it. Perhaps the greatest role of the Friends was
played in their capacity as Members of Parliament in opposition
to Pitt's government. They kept alive and handed on the principle
of opposition which in the 1790's was still young in parliamentary
history and not then accepted universally among politicians as
something quite respectable. The parliamentary Opposition also
contributed much to the preservation of the right of dissent.

The middle-class defection after 1794 was of the non-parlia-
mentary types who composed the SCI and were found in other
reform societies, as in Norwich. The Society never met after

May 1794; it seems not to have been formally dissolved but rather evaporated and disappeared. Some of its members reappeared as reformers and participated in the revived movement after the Napoleonic Wars, for example Major Cartwright or Sir James Mackintosh. The Society as such did not revive. With it the old Commonwealthman doctrinairism vanished from the reform arguments. The movement that culminated in the Reform Bill of 1832 was based not upon the eighteenth century philosophy of the rights of man or upon the primitivism of Anglo-Saxon democracy and the Norman Yoke, but upon the pragmatic, utilitarian premises that the Friends of the People had asserted and that the nineteenth century Whigs and Benthamites argued from. The end of the SCI was the end of a phase in English thought that had begun with the Levellers, carried through the disputes of the Restoration period, and found its last expressions in the millennialism of Dr. Price, in Major Cartwright's "vague and absurd" misreadings of English history, and in the enlightenment philosophy of the right of revolution.

Though the last leaves of the eighteenth century tree of liberty were falling to the ground, and the gentlemen who had sought its shelter were departing, the seed of a new tree of liberty was growing upward. Perhaps Tom Paine had planted it, and his spirit nourished it. The quasi-philosophical apparatus that he had constructed was less important to the new politically conscious working man than the emotional appeal of Painite egalitarianism and suggestions for social reforms. It was a very simple proposition, expressed appealingly by Robert Burns in "Is There for Honest Poverty?" and without any pretense of sophistication:

> What though on hamely fare we dine,
>   Wear hodden-gray and a' that;
> Gie fools their silks, and knaves their wine,
>   A man's a man for a' that.
> For a' that, and a' that,
>   Their tinsel show, an' a' that;
> The honest man, though e'er sae poor,
>   Is king o' man for a' that.

All that the poor, honest man needed was an opportunity, and freedom. "The Tree of Liberty" would provide it.

> Upo' this tree there grows sic fruit,
> Its virtues a' can tell, man:
> It raises man aboon the brute,
> It mak's him ken himsel', man!
> Gif ance the peasant taste a bit,
> He's greater than a lord, man,
> And wi' the beggar shares a mite
> O' a' he can afford, man.

Here was expressed the spirit embodied by nineteenth century unphilosophical radicals like the reformist orator Henry Hunt, the writer William Cobbett who conducted the *Political Register* aimed at lower-class readers, thousands of nameless Chartists, and eventually Keir Hardie, a Scottish miner who, about a century after the trial of the shoemaker Thomas Hardy, led in the founding of the modern Labour Party—all of them simple, unsophisticated, indignant but ultimately confident of the goodness and worth of the individual working man.

Here was the great contribution of the English Jacobins. They challenged, though unsuccessfully, the ancient social assumptions that public affairs were the concerns of gentlemen only, of men who were identified with property, especially land, that orders, or later, interests, were the proper objects of representation in Parliament, and that a man for being only a man counted for nothing. The Jacobins denied these assumptions, asserting instead that men were important because they were men, not because they were property holders or members of interests. It would be nearly a century before Parliament was ready to translate this idea into statutory reality. Not even the Reform Bill of 1867 gave full expression to it. But the idea was abroad after the 1790's and a certain spirit of the new times kept it alive.

Thomas Hardy the shoemaker, founder of the LCS, of all the reformers of the 1790's anticipated best and most completely this spirit, even though he did not belong to the age of industrialization and urbanization. He was a new man in England; his char-

acter and career suggested the nineteenth century type celebrated in Mark Rutherford's *The Revolution in Tanner's Lane*.
But Hardy was worn out after the trial of 1794 and retired from
public activity, discouraged but not pessimistic, hoping that
others might continue the work he had begun. He enjoyed the
celebration at the Crown and Anchor given in his honor shortly
after his acquittal. More than a thousand persons attended. Lord
Stanhope presided and Sheridan spoke. After his day of glory,
Hardy moved his shop to Covent Garden and there renewed his
trade. But not in obscurity. His name and fame drew many customers. After a while the novelty wore off, his trade declined to
a steady level, and he moved to a less commodious shop in Fleet
Street. There, and as a Freeman of the Cordwainers Company he
conducted his business until his retirement in 1815. Hardy lived
on in the hagiology of reform. Each November 5 the reformers
met in commemoration not of the landing of William III in
1688, for the Glorious Revolution had lost much of its inspiring
force, but of the acquittal of Thomas Hardy in 1794. When he
could, Hardy attended. In his old age he would send a rambling
letter, heard respectfully, repeating his oft-told tales of the people and events he had known in the days when the working men
were just awakening to a sense of their political grievances.
Hardy helped usher in the nineteenth century.

The LCS not only survived but thrived for a short time after
1794. Like all of the societies it had been hurt financially by the
expenses contingent upon the trials. During the winter of 1794-
1795 there were internal dissensions and some secessions, as well
as the separation of two splinter societies. By the spring of 1795
the Society was smaller but what remained was a hard core
which grew rapidly during the remainder of the year. In part
the growth was the result of discontents exacerbated by hard
times; the first six months of 1795 were probably the worst of
the decade. A poor harvest in 1794 sent up the price of wheat
and bread. A quarten loaf in London had cost seven and a half
pence in 1794 and was twelve and a quarter pence the next year.
The price fell in 1796 but remained above earlier levels. Even in
the building trades, slower to react to a slump, there was pro-

nounced depression in 1795. It is not surprising, therefore, that among reformers there was somewhat less talk of parliamentary reform and considerably more discussion of social grievances and economic hardships. John Thelwall, who had resumed his public lectures, had much to say about these. The ideas of Paine on social questions, already well-known, were reinforced by those of Thomas Spence. His *The Real Rights of Man*, published first in 1773, was reprinted in 1793 and 1796, and became widely read. Spence was contemptuous of those who thought a mere reform of Parliament would remove basic social and economic grievances. The *real* rights of men were rights to the use of land which he would vest in the people organized in parish cooperatives. Even Parliament in 1795 had to consider the problems of want, and though the Commons decided that government should not interfere with "the unassisted operation of principles," members had to admit that the times were urgent. One response was that of the justices of the peace in Berkshire. In May 1795 as a matter of humanity and social peace, they decided to supplement wages by allowances out of the poor rates in order to provide a minimum level of subsistence for the poor.

Aided by these discontents, and supported by specific resolutions of the revived LCS, the new leaders John Binns and John Gale Jones called for great public display of the strength and feelings of the reformers. Against a background of food riots and attacks upon recruiting stations and crimping houses in various parts of the country, the LCS held on June 29 in St. George's Fields what was probably the largest reform meeting up to that time. Perhaps men remembered that here, fifteen years before, Lord George Gordon's anti-Catholic meeting took place, preliminary to the great riots of 1780 which destroyed a large part of the City of London. It is easy to overestimate the size of a crowd. If there were a hundred thousand assembled to try to hear the violent language of Jones, then certainly London was lucky that the meeting did not get out of hand. Some precautions were taken by the authorities; possibly many of the curious who attended could not hear the wild speech of Jones. In so far as it was intended to present a point of view, the meeting adopted an address to the nation demanding universal suffrage. Generally the spirit of the occasion, partly political, partly economic, was expressed in such slogans as "Freedom and plenty" or "Unanimity, firmness, and spirit." The meeting also condemned the war as unnecessary and as the cause of hardships.

During the summer the LCS grew. By autumn it had possibly seventy divisions and about two thousand subscribing members, according to the Chairman of the General Committee, the tailor Francis Place. John Binns, writing years later when living in America, thought there must have been nearly twenty thousand members. They were nearly all "shopkeepers, artisans, mechanics, and laborers"; very few "professional or wealthy" men were among them.

Encouraged by this growth, and in anticipation of the opening of Parliament, the Society planned another great demonstration. It was held on October 26 in the fields adjoining Copenhagen House, an Islington tavern. This time, it was said, 150,000 persons attended. "A man named John Binns" presided, being called to the chair on recommendation of a "committee" headed by Jones. The contemporary historian who spoke of Binns as that "man" was a bit condescending. Although he was only twenty-two and had been over from Ireland only a year, John Binns was much more than a name to thousands of Londoners. He presided over a meeting which for all of its size was not only orderly but unenthusiastic. No one answered the invitation from the platform to any one who desired to make a speech. And so the men who manipulated the election of Binns also gave the speeches, among them Jones, Thelwall and Hodgson. Then the meeting, or a part of it, passed some resolutions, addressed the nation and remonstrated to the King. The remonstrance claimed to speak for two hundred thousand persons who in turn spoke for the "wearied and afflicted" people "whose grievances are so various that they distract, so enormous that they terrify." The voice of the people demanded parliamentary reform, the removal of the present ministry, and peace, in place of starvation, want and misery.

This meeting, held in good order however ominous its expressions, was greatly in contrast with the conduct of the crowds gathered along the King's route to open Parliament on October 29. From the throngs came cries of "Bread," "Peace," "No Pitt," "Down with George." A pebble or a missile penetrated a window of the royal coach. The return journey to St. James's Palace was equally disturbed, and the ride in a carriage from the palace to Buckingham House even more so. After the King descended from the carriage, part of the crowd followed it into the royal mews and destroyed it. If there was meaning in the events of this day, they bore little relationship to parliamentary reform. But neither did they give the appearance of an organized attempt to overthrow the government.

Ministers did not underestimate the possibility, however, that such mobs, assembled in the first place to voice grievances, might get out of hand. A royal proclamation enjoined the magistrates to "discourage and suppress" seditious and unlawful assemblies and to apprehend their ringleaders. This, like the next proposals of the government, was furiously opposed by the Foxite minority. In December 1795 came the passage of the so-called Two Acts, to be in force for three years. Their preambles show that the attitude of government towards the purposes of reform meetings and societies had not been altered by the failure of the trials the year before. The first was entitled "An Act for the safety and preservation of his Majesty's person and government against treasonable seditious practices and attempts," and the preamble scourged recent reform activity as "attempting to the overthrow of the laws, government, and happy constitution of these realms." Any who compassed, devised, etc. death to the King or his heirs, who levied war against England or intimidated Parliament, or who invited invasion of the realm, and who expressed such intent in writing, speech, or overt act, should upon trial and conviction suffer death for high treason. Any who merely stirred up discontent should be punished for misdemeanor, and be transported for seven years upon the second offense. This bill in effect introduced a new law of treason so extended as virtually to forbid discussion of constitutional and public grievances.

The second entitled "An Act for the more effectually preventing seditious meetings and assemblies" stated that recent
meetings, obstinately to formulate petitions and grievances "have
of late been made use of to serve the ends of factious and seditious persons." The size of meetings (with exceptions) was limited to fifty persons and strict regulations were imposed as to
publicity, conduct, and the hiring of halls, and the authority of
magistrates in connection with such assemblies was clarified. If a
meeting tended to stir up the people or advocated alteration of
the constitution by methods other than through Parliament assembled, and being ordered to disperse, twelve or more members
remained after an hour had passed, they could be punished by
death. The same punishment applied to any who obstructed the
peace officers.

These measures were a terrible threat. Francis Place attested
years later that they were highly popular, but contemporary
evidence contradicts this judgment. Lord Thurlow, to the surprise of many, opposed them as unwise and unnecessary restrictions upon constitutional liberties. While they were passing
through Parliament there was great public debate about them,
and generally about the problem of domestic peace. They caused
uneasiness among people who would have been shocked to be
considered reformers. On December 2 was issued a "Declaration
of the Merchants, Bankers, Traders and Other Inhabitants of
London," bearing 5,850 signatures. The signers regretted the
temporary need to restrict some liberties, but this was done in
the interest of preserving the whole body of Englishmen's rights.
The signers resolved their discomfort by expressing confidence
that Parliament would go only as far in its restraints as the
exigencies of the times required. This hopeful caution expressed
the attitudes of many persons who admitted that the acts were
inimical to the principles of the constitution but thought them
justified by the necessities of the moment. Some persons had
no reservations. John Reeves and his kind supported the Acts
wholeheartedly, Reeves so extravagantly that he was prosecuted
for a libel on the House of Commons by his excessive emphasis
upon the prerogative power. He was acquitted on the grounds

that no libellous intention was proved. According to the *Annual Register*, the "far superior majority" of people would accept the acts straightforwardly, "on no pretence whatever" of public necessity.

This judgment seems extravagant in view of the widespread opposition to the Acts. The LCS organized two huge protest meetings, one on November 12 at Copenhagen Fields and the other on December 9 in the fields near the Jew's-harp Tavern in Marylebone. On both occasions the throngs were greater than ever before. The Foxite Whig Club approved of these meetings. The ubiquitous Jones and Thelwall spoke. At the Marylebone meeting there also appeared as out of the past the Cambridge University dissident, William Frend, who was then at the Middle Temple. Besides these better known ones, other meetings, some to support but most to protest the bills, were held throughout the country. Wyvill succeeded in arousing much opposition in Yorkshire, and Erskine's brother, Henry, organized great protests in Edinburgh. Neither of these men sympathized with Jacobinism but both were alarmed at the measures proposed for suppressing it. Generally the line of opposition was directed against the tendency of the bills to restrict freedom of speech and assemblage. And in this persons of the type who belonged to the Friends of the People were at one with the working class radicals. In fact, during the month when the two bills were before Parliament the peak of public agitations and demonstrations in the 1790's was reached. But the opposition was too generalized to impress the government. It was estimated that ninety-four petitions bearing 131,284 signatures were produced against the bills, and for them sixty-five bearing 29,922 names. These signatures seemed to bear out the broader contention of the *Annual Register*, contradicting itself, that no statute was ever received by the nation "with such evident and general marks of ill will and disapprobation" as these two. More clearly in this instance than in any of its suppressive actions did Parliament seem to defy public opinion and ignore responsible opposition. The public was aroused because the Acts swept much too widely. Though ostensibly directed against radicals they infringed so generally upon freedom of expression as to threaten the basic constitutional rights of all people, whether radicals or not.

The Acts served their purposes, more by their intimidating and hampering effects upon the radicals than because they supported a wave of prosecutions in the courts. The existing societies, instructed by missionaries from London like Binns, Jones, and Thelwall who explained the examples of the LCS, tried to transform their organizations in order to comply with the Seditious Meetings Act. They met harassment, and Binns and Jones were arrested. Some debating societies evaded the law by avoiding political subjects in favor of religious topics. As one complainant wrote to the Duke of Portland, these societies, "pests of good order," were aiming to eradicate religious sentiments, and the dreadful consequences of their discussions could only be rapine, anarchy and murder. Thelwall was one of those who disguised his politics, but he was only partly successful. After a year of difficulties, in 1797 he retired into private life. But as long as "single-minded" and "simple" people like Thomas Spence were around, the agitation for change would continue. "At enmity with the world" as he knew it, said Francis Place, Spence still loved mankind and hoped the time would come when all men would be comfortable and happy. If his panacea, abolition of private property in land, were adopted, then the world would be a heavenly city. From his book shop at the Holborn end of Chancery Lane, and by 1797 at No. 9 Oxford Street, he dispensed materials on the theme of the Rights of Man, including his own tract of that name, his periodical *Pig's Meat*, and even a ballad called "The Rights of Man." Spence hired boys to hawk his tracts. Charles Connally, age eleven, who lived with his mother at Spence's house in Oxford Street, told the authorities in May 1797 that he earned four pence out of each shilling's worth of the "Rights of Man" that he sold, and on some days earned as much as four shillings. This was a fantastic commission. But then, Place had said that Spence "was unpracticed in the ways of the world." Perhaps he really believed that the laborer was worthy of his hire. And somehow he managed to stay out of prison until 1801. Possibly he gave the impression of being a crackpot and the government thought him a walking advertisement for the notion that extreme radicalism bordered on lunacy.

After the passage of the Two Acts the membership of the LCS dropped off rapidly; no new members were taken in, and within a year the Society was virtually defunct. Its financial resources were depleted, in part by the expenses incurred in an unsuccessful effort to publish the *Moral and Political Magazine*. Francis Place, who had never liked public agitation, preferring the gradualism of education, yielded up his offices in the Society by stages, and in June 1797 resigned altogether. Place at this time was trying to establish himself as a tailor, and the demands of his struggling business absorbed much of his attention.

The LCS made one last public effort. In July 1797 it held a meeting near St. Pancras Church, only to encounter the magistrates who arrested the persons on the platform. The remnant, which thought of itself still as the LCS, continued to meet and conspire. There were contemporary suspicions, shared by some modern scholars, of radical infiltration, perhaps by members of the LCS, among the sailors who mutinied in 1797. The main causes of the mutinies were material, but they were exacerbated, said the *Annual Register*, by "the contagion of a general spirit of inquiry into rights, natural and conventional," and by the presence on the ships of persons who were rather professional agitators than sailors. In 1798 certain members of the LCS made the fatal mistake of treating with delegates from the United Irishmen with a view to aiding its efforts by forming a companion society to be called the United Englishmen. The government seized the leaders, and then arrested the Committee of the Society. Habeas Corpus being still suspended, they were kept in prison for three years. John Binns was acquitted of high treason for his dealings with the United Irishmen but later was picked up on another charge and kept in Gloucester jail until 1801. Released, he migrated to America where some good Jacobins had already taken refuge—Dr. Priestley, John Gale and Thomas Cooper in 1794, and others along the way. It seemed almost anti-

climactic that the Combination Acts of 1799-1800 which banned
secret societies and trade unions should name among those
"hereby utterly suppressed and prohibited" the London Corresponding Society.

Since its inception in the 1770's, the movement for parliamentary reform had broadened out beyond the limited imaginations
of the doctrinaires like Jebb, Cartwright and Price. It had
reached down into the working classes whose needs and wants
could not be satisfied merely with possession of the franchise.
The vote was to be used for some purpose. It was in fact uncertainty about this purpose that so disturbed the governing classes.
They thought that the awakening of the lower classes was in
itself dangerous; the social composition of the popular societies
was sufficient as proof of their subversive tendencies. When the
lower classes became organized and militant, connected by a
network of correspondence, and permeated with the Painite
spirit, it seemed to many of the upper classes that the agitation
for reform prepared the way for "any attempt that might be
made to overturn the government of the country." Even if the
vote was used peacefully there was fear of the consequences.
Constitutional processes would be a struggle of the orders and
numbers would give the victory to the lower orders. The literary controversy between Burke and Paine symbolized all of this,
for it was fought out between spokesmen for the patricians and
the plebs. In the House of Lords, Lord Lansdowne made little
impression with his argument that the English Jacobins of the
1790's could not be dangerous because they and their societies
were indigenous, the offspring of the reform movements of the
1780's, not of the French Revolutionaries. Lansdowne was right
in part, but his hearers thought the differences between the two
decades were fundamental and the similarities were superficial.
They were also right in part. For the story of the English Jacobins of the 1790's is part of the history of the last decade of the
eighteenth century at the same time that it is the beginning of
the reform movement of the nineteenth and twentieth centuries.
More broadly it was the beginning of the rise of the English

working class when the old rural, landed order was giving way to the new urban, industrial order, and when ancient assumptions about the nature of society and politics were being challenged by new contentions that all men as individuals counted in life and in public affairs.

DECLARATION OF

THE DERBY SOCIETY

FOR POLITICAL INFORMATION,

JULY 16, 1792

PRINTED IN THE *MORNING CHRONICLE*

DECEMBER 25, 1792.

1. "THAT all true government is instituted for the general good, is legalized by the general will, and all its actions are, or ought to be, directed for the general happiness and prosperity of all honest citizens.

2. "THAT we feel too much not to believe, that deep and alarming abuses exist in the British government; yet we are at the same time fully sensible, that our situation is comfortable, compared with that of the people of many European kingdoms; and that as the times are in some degree moderate, they ought to be free from riot and confusion.

3. "YET we think there is sufficient cause to inquire into the necessity of the payment of seventeen millions of annual taxes, exclusive of poor-rates, county rates, expences of collection, &c.

by seven millions of people; we think that these expenses may be reduced, without lessening the true dignity of the nation or the government: and therefore wish for satisfaction in this important matter.

4. "WE view with concern the frequency of wars. We are persuaded that the interests of the poor can never be promoted by accession of territory, when bought at the expense of their labour and blood, and we must say, in the language of a celebrated author, 'We who are only the people but who pay for wars with our substance and our blood, will not cease to tell kings, or governments, that to them alone wars are profitable: that the true and just conquests are those which each makes at home, by comforting the peasantry, by promoting agriculture and manufactories, by multiplying men, and the other productions of nature; that then it is that kings may call themselves the image of God, whose will is perpetually directed to the creation of new beings. If they continue to make us fight and kill one another in uniform, we will continue to write and speak, until nations shall be cured of this folly.' We are certain our present heavy burthens are owing, in a great measure, to cruel and impolitic wars, and therefore we will do all on our part, as peaceable citizens, who have the good of the community at heart, to enlighten each other, and protest against them.

5. "THE present state of the representation of the people calls for the particular attention of every man, who has humanity sufficient to feel for the honour and happiness of his country; to the defects and corruptions of which we are inclined to attribute unnecessary wars, &c. &c. We think it a deplorable case when the poor must support a corruption which is calculated to oppress them when the labourer must give his money to afford the means of preventing him having a voice in its disposal; when the lower classes may say, 'We give you our money, for which we have toiled and sweat, and which would save our families from cold and hunger; but we think it more hard that there is nobody whom we have delegated, to see that it is not improperly spent; we have none to watch over our interests; the rich only are represented. The form of government since the revolution, is in

some respects changed for the worse; by the triennial and septennial acts we lost annual parliaments: besides which, the wholesome provisions for obliging privy counsellors to subscribe their advice with their names, and against placemen and pensioners, sitting in parliament have been repealed.' It is said, that the voice of the people is the constitutional control of parliament; but what is this but saying, that the representatives are naturally inclined to support wrong measures, and that the people must be constantly assembling to oblige them to do their duty? An equal and uncorrupt representation would, we are persuaded, save us from heavy expenses, and deliver us from many oppressions; we will therefore do our duty to procure this reform, which appears to us of the utmost importance.

6. "IN short, we see with the most lively concern an army of placemen, pensioners, &c. fighting in the cause of corruption and prejudice, and spreading the contagion far and wide; a large and highly expensive military establishment, though we have a well regulated militia; the increase of all kinds of robberies, riots, executions, &c. though the nation pays taxes equal to the whole land rental of the kingdom, in order to have his property protected and secured; and is also obliged to enter into separate associations against felonious depredations. A criminal code of laws, sanguine and inefficacious; a civil code so voluminous and mysterious as to puzzle the best understandings; by which means, justice is denied to the poor on account of the expense attending the obtaining it; corporations, under ministerial or party influence, swallowing up the importance, and acting under the voice of the people; penalties inflicted on those who accept of offices without conforming to the violation of their consciences and their rights; the voice of free inquiry drowned in prosecutions, and the clamours of the pensioned and interested; and we view, with the most poignant sorrow, a part of the people deluded by a cry of the constitution and church in danger, fighting with the weapons of savages, under the banners of prejudice, against those who have their true interest at heart; we see with equal sensibility the present outcry against reforms, and a proclamation (tending to cramp the liberty of the press, and

discredit the true friends of the people) receiving the support of numbers of our countrymen; we see the continuation of oppressive game laws and destructive monopolies; we see the education and comfort of the poor neglected, notwithstanding the enormous weight of the poor-rates; we see burthens multiplied, the lower classes sinking into poverty, disgrace, and excesses, and the means of these shocking abuses increased for the purposes of revenue; for the same end, excise laws, those badges and sources of oppression kept up and multiplied. And when we cast our eyes on a people just formed in a free community, without having had time to grow rich, under a government by which justice is duly administered, the poor taught and comforted, property protected, taxes few and easy, and that at an expense as small as our pension list, we ask ourselves, 'Are we in England? Have our forefathers fought and bled, and conquered for liberty? And did they not think that the fruits of their patriotism would be more abundant in peace, plenty, and happiness? Are we always to stand still or go backwards? Are our burthens to be as heavy as the most enslaved people? Is the condition of the poor never to be improved?' Great Britain must have arrived at the highest degree of national happiness and prosperity, and our situation must be too good to be mended, or the present outcry against reforms and improvements is inhuman and criminal. But we hope our condition will be speedily improved, and to obtain so desirable a good is the object of our present association; a union founded on principles of benevolence and humanity; disclaiming all connection with riots and disorder, but firm in our purpose, and warm in our affections for liberty.

7. "LASTLY, we invite the friends of freedom throughout Great Britain to form similar societies, and to act with unanimity and firmness, till the people be too wise to be imposed upon, and their influence in the government be commensurate with their dignity and importance.

"THEN SHALL WE BE FREE AND HAPPY.

"By order of the Society,

"S. Eyre, Chairman."

AT A GENERAL MEETING

OF THE

LONDON CORRESPONDING SOCIETY,

HELD AT THE GLOBE TAVERN, STRAND,

ON MONDAY THE 20TH DAY OF JANUARY, 1794.

CITIZEN JOHN MARTIN, IN THE CHAIR.

"The following ADDRESS to the PEOPLE of Great Britain and Ireland was read and agreed to.

"CITIZENS;—We find the nation involved in a war, by which, in the course of ONE Campaign, immense numbers of our countrymen have been slaughtered; a vast expense has been incurred, our Trade, Commerce, and Manufactories, are almost destroyed, and many of our Manufacturers and Artists [sic] are ruined, and their families starving.

"To add to our affliction, we have reason to expect, that other taxes will soon be added to the intolerable load of imposts and impositions with which we are already overwhelmed; for the purpose of defraying the expenses which have been incurred, in a fruitless crusade, to re-establish the odious despotism of France.

"When we contemplate the principles of this war, we confess ourselves to be unable to approve of it, as a measure, either of justice or discretion;—and if we are to form our calculation of the result, from what has already passed, we can only look forward to defeat and the eternal disgrace of the British name.

"While we are thus engaged in an expensive and ruinous and foreign war; our state at home is not less deplorable.

"We are every day told, by those persons who are interested in supporting the *Corruption* List, and an innumerable Host of *Sinecure* Placemen, that the Constitution of England is the perfection of human wisdom; that our laws (we should rather say, Their laws) are the perfection of justice; and that *their* Administration of those laws is so impartial and so ready, as to afford an equal remedy, both to the rich and to the poor; by means of which, we are said to be placed in a state of absolute freedom, and that our Rights and Liberties are so well secured to us as to render all invasion of them impossible.

"When we ask, how we enjoy these transcendant privileges; we are referred to MAGNA CHARTA, and the BILL OF RIGHTS; and the glorious REVOLUTION in the year 1688, is held out to us, as the bulwark of British liberty.

"CITIZENS;—We have referred to *Magna Charta*, to the *Bill of Rights*, and to the *Revolution* and we certainly do find that our ancestors did establish wise and wholesome laws; but we as certainly find, that, of the venerable Constitution of our ancestors, hardly a vestige remains.

"The only Chapters of the Great Charter, which are now in legal existence, are the 14th and 29th.

"The important provision of the 14th Chapter, runs thus:

" 'A Freeman shall not be amerced for a small fault, but after the manner of the fault; and for a great fault after the greatness thereof, saving to him his contenement; and a Merchant likewise, saving to him his merchandize; and any other's villain than ours shall be likewise amerced, saving to him his wainage; and none of the said amerciaments shall be assessed, but by the oath of honest and lawful men of the Vicinage.'

"But by the usurped power of the judges, in assessing Fines (and what Fines!) in the cases of Misdemeanor; this glorious Right of the Subject, of having these fines assessed by the Jury (the only possible protection from slavery and the vilest oppression), is unjustly and infamously ravished from us.

"The provision of the 29th chapter runs thus:

" 'No Freeman shall be taken or imprisoned, or be disseised of his freehold, or liberties, or free customs, or be outlawed or exiled, or any otherwise destroyed, nor we will not pass upon him, nor condemn him, but by the lawful judgment of his peers, or by the law of the land. We will sell to no man, we will not deny, or defer to any man, either justice or right.'

"The various methods now in constant practice by which the benefits of this provision are totally defeated and destroyed, might induce us to suppose, that the GREAT CHARTER has been repealed; if we did not assuredly know, that it is the fundamental basis of our constitution; which even the REAL representatives of the people (much less the miserable nominees of HELSTONE and OLD SARUM) have not the right, nor (as we trust it will be found by experience) the POWER to repeal. Yet what do we find in practice? Unconstitutional and illegal INFORMATIONS EX OFFICIO, that is, the arbitrary will of the king's Attorney General, usurping the office of the ACCUSING Jury; and the interested oath of a vile common informer, with the judgment of as vile a common trading or pensioned justice, substituted in the room of our birthright, an impartial trial *by our country*.

"Add to this, that the exorbitant expense of judicial proceedings, the novel practice of arbitrarily and repeatedly annulling the verdicts of juries, and the dilatory practice of the courts, most openly and shamefully contradict the clause which forbids the denial, the delay, and the sale of justice.

"A man accused of Felony (for which by the common law of England, his life and goods are forfeited) may be bailed on finding two sureties for forty pounds each; but upon a charge of MISDEMEANOUR by *words* only, bail to the amount of ONE THOUSAND POUNDS has been demanded.

"Upon conviction also, for such misdemeanour, enormous

fines, long and cruel imprisonments unknown to our ancient laws, and unsanctioned by any new statutes, have of late (and but of late) been too frequently and too oppressively inflicted. And all this, although by this bill of rights it is declared, that 'excessive bail shall not be demanded, nor cruel and unusual punishments inflicted.'

"If we look to IRELAND we find that acknowledged privilege of the people, to meet for the support and protection of their rights and liberties, is attempted, by terror, to be taken away by a late infamous act of parliament: Whilst titles of honour! No, but of dishonour, are lavished; and new sources of corruption opened, to gratify the greedy prostitution of those, who are the instruments of this oppression.

"IN SCOTLAND, the Wicked Hand of Power has been impudently exerted, without even the wretched formality of an act of Parliament, Magistrates have forcibly intruded into the peaceful and lawful meetings of Freemen; and, by force (not only without law, but against law), have, under colour of magisterial office, interrupted their deliberations, and prevented their association.

"The wisdom and good conduct of the BRITISH CONVENTION at Edinburgh, has been such as to defy their bitterest enemies to name the law which they have broken; notwithstanding which, their papers have been seized, and made use of as evidence against them, and many virtuous and meritorious individuals, have been, as cruelly as unjustly for their virtuous actions disgraced and destroyed by infamous and illegal sentences of transportation. And these unjust and wicked judgments have been executed with a rancour and malignity, never before known in this land; our respectable and beloved Fellow-citizens have been cast *FETTERED* into Dungeons amongst felons in the Hulks, to which they were not sentenced.

"CITIZENS:—We all approve the sentiments, and are daily repeating the words for which these our respectable and valuable brethern are thus unjustly and inhumanly suffering. We too, associate in order to obtain a fair, free, and full representation of the people in a house of real national representatives. Are we

also willing to be treated as *FELONS*, for claiming this our inherent right, which we are determined never to forego but with
our lives, and which none but thieves and traitors can wish to
withhold from us? Consider, it is one and the same corrupt and
corrupting influence which at this time domineers in Ireland,
Scotland, and England. Can you believe that those who send virtuous Irishmen, and Scotchmen fettered with felons to Botany
Bay, do not meditate and will not attempt to seize the first moment to send us after them? Or, if we had not just cause to apprehend the same inhuman treatment; if instead of the most im-
minent danger, we were in perfect safety from it; should we not
disdain to enjoy any liberty or privilege whatever, in which our
honest Irish and Scotch brethren did not equally and as fully
participate with us? Their cause then and ours is the same. And
it is both our duty and our interest to stand or fall together. The
Irish parliament and the Scotch judges, actuated by the same
English influence, have brought us directly to the point. There is
no farther step beyond that which they have taken. We are at
issue. We must now choose at once either liberty or slavery for
ourselves and our posterity. Will you wait till BARRACKS are
erected in every village, and till *subsidized* Hessians and Hano-
verians are upon us?

"You may ask perhaps, by what means shall we seek redress?

"We answer, that men in a state of civilized society are bound
to seek redress of the grievances from the laws; as long as any
redress can be obtained by the laws. But our common Master
whom we serve (whose law is a law of liberty, and whose service is perfect freedom) has taught us not to expect to gather
grapes from thorns, nor figs from thistles. We must have redress
from our own laws and not from the laws of our plunderers,
enemies, and oppressors.

"THERE IS NO REDRESS FOR A NATION CIRCUM-
STANCED AS WE ARE, BUT IN A FAIR, FREE, AND
FULL REPRESENTATION OF THE PEOPLE.

"RESOLVED, that during the ensuing session of parliament,
the general committee of this society do meet daily for the
purpose of watching the proceedings of the parliament and of

the administration of the government of this country. And that upon the first introduction of any bill, or motion inimical to the liberties of the people, such as, for LANDING FOREIGN MEETING IN SOCIETIES for CONSTITUTIONAL IN-TROOPS IN GREAT BRITAIN or IRELAND, for suspending the HABEAS CORPUS ACT, for proclaiming MARTIAL LAW, OR FOR PREVENTING THE PEOPLE FROM FORMATION, or any OTHER INNOVATION of a similar nature, that, on any of these emergencies, the general committee shall issue summonses to the delegates of each division, and also to the secretaries of the different societies affiliated and corresponding with this society, forthwith to call a GENERAL CONVENTION of the PEOPLE, to be held at such place and in such a manner as shall be specified in the summons for the purpose of taking such measures into their consideration.

"Resolved, that the preceding Address and Resolution be signed by the chairman, and printed and published.

"J. MARTIN, Chairman.

"T. Hardy, Secretary."

WHETHER influenced by Fabianism, by the intrusion of the Labour Movement into politics, by the so-called "New History," or by all as they reacted upon one another, historians just before World War I seemed to show unusual interest in the history of the movement for parliamentary reform and the stirrings of political self-consciousness among the lower orders in Britain. The first of a group of books on these subjects was Henry Jephson's *The Platform* (1892). In 1906 appeared two books by Charles Cestre, a biography, *John Thelwall,* and then *La Révolution Française et Les Poetes Anglais.* W. T. Laprade's *England in the French Revolution* (1909), H. W. Meikle's *Scotland and the French Revolution* (1912), W. P. Hall's *British Radicalism 1791–1797* (1912), and G. S. Veitch's *The Genesis of Parliamentary Reform* (1913), are other works of pre-war vintage which discuss some of the matters with which my book is concerned. In 1918 came one of the best studies in this area, Philip Anthony Brown's *The French Revolution in English History,* perhaps the one most generally used for the story of radicalism in the 1790's. Graham Wallas' *Life of Francis Place* was published in 1898 and again in 1919.

Now, nearly two generations later, historians are restudying these movements and this period, using many of the materials used by earlier students but using new materials as well, and asking deeper and different questions of them. They are also taking the radical movement backwards rather than beginning with the French Revolution. In 1947 came Herbert Butterfield's provocative "The Yorkshire Association and the Crisis of 1779–1780," *Transactions of the Royal Historical Society*, Fourth Series, XXIX, 69–92. More recently we have had Lucy Sutherland, "The City of London in Eighteenth Century Politics," *Essays Presented to Sir Lewis Namier* (1956) and *The City and the Opposition to Government, 1768–1774* (1959), Caroline Robbins, *The Eighteenth Century Commonwealthman* (1959), George Rudé, *Wilkes and Liberty* (1962), I. R. Christie, *Wilkes, Wyvill and Reform* (1962), Eugene Black, *The Association 1769–1793* (1963), E. P. Thompson, *The Making of the English Working Class* (1963), especially Part One, and J. R. Pole, *Political Representation in England and the Origins of the American Republic* (1966).

Some recent useful articles are: Donald E. Ginter, "The Loyalist Association Movement of 1792–93 and British Public Opinion," *The Historical Journal*, IX (1966), 179–90; E. J. Hobsbawm, "Methodism and the Threat of Revolution in Britain," *History Today* (February, 1957), 115–24; Austin Mitchell, "The Association Movement of 1792–3," *The Historical Journal*, IV (1961), 56–77; and R. B. Rose, "The Priestley Riots of 1791," *Past and Present*, No. 18 (November, 1960), 68–88.

The last third of the eighteenth century was an important period in the history of pamphleteering, and many pamphlets bear upon the subjects of reform and Jacobinism. In the Appendix to his important *The Language of Politics* (1963), James T. Boulton presents a chronological list of pamphlets stimulated by Burke's *Reflections on the Revolution in France* (November, 1790). Newspapers and periodicals are also important sources for the political controversies of the time. *The London Times* (between January 1, 1785, and December 31, 1788, called *The Daily Universal Register*) among newspapers, and the *Annual Register*, the *Gentleman's Magazine*, *The European Magazine*, and the *Monthly Review* of the periodicals are perhaps the most readily available to modern students.

Of primary printed sources, the appropriate volumes of T. B.

Howell, ed., *A Complete Collection of State Trials* (1809–1826) and William Cobbett, ed., *The Parliamentary History of England* (1806–1820) are essential. The reports of the Committees of Secrecy of the House of Commons and of the House of Lords (1794) are printed in volume 31 of Cobbett. The printed volume of Papers of The Society for Preserving Liberty and Property appeared in 1793. The list of biographies, memoirs, and diaries is a long one. Special mention should be made of Thomas Hardy, *Memoir of Thomas Hardy* (1832).

The manuscript sources most useful to me were: the Burke Papers and the Fitzwilliam Papers in the Sheffield Central Library; the Treasury Solicitor's Papers in the Public Record Office, especially TS 11/1133, 11/961 and 11/962 which are the Minute Books of the Society for Constitutional Information; and the Place Papers in the British Museum which among other things contain the Books of the London Corresponding Society.

Finally in a category by itself should be mentioned T. H. B. Oldfield, *The Representative History of Great Britain and Ireland* (6 vols., 1816) which drew upon information compiled by the Society for Constitutional Information.

Generally suggestive though they are concerned mainly with the seventeenth century are C. B. Macpherson, *The Political Theory of Possessive Individualism* (1962) and Peter Laslett, *The World We Have Lost* (1965).

INDEX